P9-DHL-125

For Charles and Juliana

MEDIEVAL SCIENCE AND TECHNOLOGY

MEDIEVAL SCIENCE AND TECHNOLOGY

Elspeth Whitney

THE BRYANT LIBRARY
2 PAPER MILL ROAD
ROSLYN, N.Y. 11576-2198

Greenwood Guides to Historic Events of the Medieval World
Jane Chance, Series Editor

GREENWOOD PRESS
Westport, Connecticut • London

Library of Congress Cataloging-in-Publication Data

Whitney, Elspeth.
    Medieval science and technology / Elspeth Whitney.
        p.   cm.—(Greenwood guides to historic events of the medieval world)
    Includes bibliographical references and index.
    ISBN 0–313–32519–7 (alk. paper)
    1. Science, Medieval.   2. Technology—History—To 1500.   I. Title.
    II. Series.
    Q124.97.W45   2004
    509'.02—dc22   2004042498

British Library Cataloguing in Publication Data is available.

Copyright © 2004 by Elspeth Whitney

All rights reserved. No portion of this book may be
reproduced, by any process or technique, without the
express written consent of the publisher.

Library of Congress Catalog Card Number: 2004042498
ISBN: 0–313–32519–7

First published in 2004

Greenwood Press, 88 Post Road West, Westport, CT 06881
An imprint of Greenwood Publishing Group, Inc.
www.greenwood.com

Printed in the United States of America

The paper used in this book complies with the
Permanent Paper Standard issued by the National
Information Standards Organization (Z39.48–1984).

10 9 8 7 6 5 4 3 2 1

Copyright Acknowledgment

Every reasonable effort has been made to trace the owners of copyright materials in
this book, but in some instances this has proven impossible. The author and publisher
will be glad to receive information leading to more complete acknowlegments in
subsequent printings of the book and in the meantime extend their apologies for any
omissions.

CONTENTS

Primary Documents   **173**

ILLUSTRATIONS

SERIES FOREWORD

The Middle Ages are no longer considered the "Dark Ages" (as Petrarch termed them), sandwiched between the two enlightened periods of classical antiquity and the Renaissance. Often defined as a historical period lasting, roughly, from 500 to 1500 c.e., the Middle Ages span an enormous amount of time (if we consider the way other time periods have been constructed by historians) as well as an astonishing range of countries and regions very different from one another. That is, we call the "Middle" Ages the period beginning with the fall of the Roman Empire as a result of raids by northern European tribes of "barbarians" in the late antiquity of the fifth and sixth centuries and continuing until the advent of the so-called Italian and English renaissances, or rebirths of classical learning, in the fifteenth and sixteenth centuries. How this age could be termed either "Middle" or "Dark" is a mystery to those who study it. Certainly it is no longer understood as embracing merely the classical inheritance in the west or excluding eastern Europe, the Middle East, Asia, or even, as I would argue, North and Central America.

Whatever the arbitrary, archaic, and hegemonic limitations of these temporal parameters—the old-fashioned approach to them was that they were mainly not classical antiquity, and therefore not important—the Middle Ages represent a time when certain events occurred that have continued to affect modern cultures and that also, inevitably, catalyzed other medieval events. Among other important events, the Middle Ages saw the birth of Muhammad (c. 570–632) and his foundation of Islam in the seventh century as a rejection of Christianity which led to the imperial conflict between East and West in the eleventh and twelfth centuries. In western Europe in the Middle Ages the foundations for modern nationalism and modern law were laid and the concept of romantic love arose in the Middle Ages, this latter event partly one of the indirect consequences of the Crusades. With the shaping of national identity came the need to defend boundaries against invasion; so the castle emerged as a military outpost—whether in northern Africa, during the Crusades, or in Wales, in the eleventh century, to defend William of Normandy's newly acquired provinces—to satisfy that need. From Asia the invasions of Genghis Khan changed the literal and cultural shape of eastern and southern Europe.

In addition to triggering the development of the concept of chivalry and the knight, the Crusades influenced the European concepts of the lyric, music, and musical instruments; introduced to Europe an appetite for spices like cinnamon, coriander, and saffron and for dried fruits like prunes and figs as well as a desire for fabrics such as silk; and brought Aristotle to the European university through Arabic and then Latin translations. As a result of study of the "new" Aristotle, science and philosophy dramatically changed direction—and their emphasis on this material world helped to undermine the power of the Catholic Church as a monolithic institution in the thirteenth century.

By the twelfth century, with the centralization of the one (Catholic) Church, came a new architecture for the cathedral—the Gothic—to replace the older Romanesque architecture and thereby to manifest the Church's role in the community in a material way as well as in spiritual and political ways. Also from the cathedral as an institution and its need to dramatize the symbolic events of the liturgy came medieval drama— the mystery and the morality play, from which modern drama derives in large part. Out of the cathedral and its schools to train new priests (formerly handled by monasteries) emerged the medieval institution of the university. Around the same time, the community known as a town rose up in eastern and western Europe as a consequence of trade and the necessity for a new economic center to accompany the development of a bourgeoisie, or middle class. Because of the town's existence, the need for an itinerant mendicancy that could preach the teachings of the Church and beg for alms in urban centers sprang up.

Elsewhere in the world, in North America the eleventh-century settlement of Chaco Canyon by the Pueblo peoples created a social model like no other, one centered on ritual and ceremony in which the "priests" were key, but one that lasted barely two hundred years before it collapsed and its central structures were abandoned.

In addition to their influence on the development of central features of modern culture, the Middle Ages have long fascinated the modern age because of parallels that exist between the two periods. In both, terrible wars devastated whole nations and peoples; in both, incurable diseases plagued cities and killed large percentages of the world's population. In both periods, dramatic social and cultural changes took place as a result of these events: marginalized and overtaxed groups in societies rebelled against imperious governments; trade and a burgeoning middle class came to the fore; outside the privacy of the family, women began to have a greater role in Western societies and their cultures.

How different cultures of that age grappled with such historical change is the subject of the Greenwood Guides to Historic Events of the Medieval World. This series features individual volumes that illuminate key events in medieval world history. In some cases, an "event" occurred during a relatively limited time period. The troubadour lyric as a phenomenon, for example, flowered and died in the courts of Aquitaine in the twelfth century, as did the courtly romance in northern Europe a few decades later. The Hundred Years War between France and England generally took place during a precise time period, from the fourteenth to mid-fifteenth centuries.

In other cases, the event may have lasted for centuries before it played itself out: the medieval Gothic cathedral, for example, may have been first built in the twelfth century at Saint-Denis in Paris (c. 1140), but cathedrals, often of a slightly different style of Gothic architecture, were still being built in the fifteenth century all over Europe and, again, as the symbolic representation of a bishop's seat, or chair, are still being built today. And the medieval city, whatever its incarnation in the early Middle Ages, basically blossomed between the eleventh and thirteenth centuries as a result of social, economic, and cultural changes. Events— beyond a single dramatic historically limited happening—took longer to affect societies in the Middle Ages because of the lack of political and social centralization, the primarily agricultural and rural nature of most countries, difficulties in communication, and the distances between important cultural centers.

Each volume includes necessary tools for understanding such key events in the Middle Ages. Because of the postmodern critique of authority that modern societies underwent at the end of the twentieth century, students and scholars as well as general readers have come to mistrust the commentary and expertise of any one individual scholar or commentator and to identify the text as an arbiter of "history." For this reason, each book in the series can be described as a "library in a book." The intent of the series is to provide a quick, in-depth examination and current perspectives on the event to stimulate critical thinking as well as ready-reference materials, including primary documents and biographies of key individuals, for additional research.

Specifically, in addition to a narrative historical overview that places the specific event within the larger context of a contemporary perspective, five to seven developmental chapters explore related focused aspects of the event. In addition, each volume begins with a brief chronology and ends with a conclusion that discusses the consequences and impact of the event. There are also brief biographies of twelve to twenty key individuals (or places or buildings, in the book on the cathedral); primary documents from the period (for example, letters, chronicles, memoirs, diaries, and other writings) that illustrate states of mind or the turn of events at the time, whether historical, literary, scientific, or philosophical; illustrations (maps, diagrams, manuscript illuminations, portraits); a glossary of terms; and an annotated bibliography of important books, articles, films, and CD-ROMs available for additional research. An index concludes each volume.

No particular theoretical approach or historical perspective characterizes the series; authors developed their topics as they chose, generally taking into account the latest thinking on any particular event. The editors selected final topics from a list provided by an advisory board of high school teachers and public and school librarians. On the basis of nominations of scholars made by distinguished writers, the series editor also tapped internationally known scholars, both those with lifelong expertise and others with fresh new perspectives on a topic, to author the twelve books in the series. Finally, the series editor selected distinguished medievalists, art historians, and archaeologists to complete an advisory board: Gwinn Vivian, retired professor of archaeology at the University of Arizona Museum; Sharon Kinoshita, associate professor of French literature, world literature, and cultural studies at the University of California–Santa Cruz; Nancy Wu, associate museum educator at the Metropolitan Museum of Art, The Cloisters, New York City; and Christopher A. Snyder, chair of the Department of History and Politics at Marymount University.

In addition to examining the event and its effects on the specific cultures involved through an array of documents and an overview, each volume provides a new approach to understanding these twelve events. Treated in the series are: the Black Death; the Crusades; Eleanor of Aquitaine, courtly love, and the troubadours; Genghis Khan and Mongol rule; Joan of Arc and the Hundred Years War; Magna Carta; the medieval castle, from the eleventh to the sixteenth centuries; the medieval cathedral; the medieval city, especially in the thirteenth century; medieval science and technology; Muhammad and the rise of Islam; and the Puebloan society of Chaco Canyon.

The Black Death, by Joseph Byrne, isolates the event of the epidemic of bubonic plague in 1347–52 as having had a signal impact on medieval Europe. It was, however, only the first of many related such episodes involving variations of pneumonic and septicemic plague that recurred over 350 years. Taking a twofold approach to the Black Death, Byrne investigates both the modern research on bubonic plague, its origins and spread, and also medieval documentation and illustration in diaries, artistic works, and scientific and religious accounts. The demographic, economic, and political effects of the Black Death are traced in one chapter, the social and psychological patterns of life in another, and cultural expressions in art and ritual in a third. Finally, Byrne investigates why bubonic plague disappeared and why we continue to be fascinated by it. Documents included provide a variety of medieval accounts—Byzantine, Arabic, French, German, English, and Italian—several of which are translated for the first time.

The Crusades, by Helen Nicholson, presents a balanced account of various crusades, or military campaigns, invented by Catholic or "Latin" Christians during the Middle Ages against those they perceived as threats to their faith. Such expeditions included the Crusades to the Holy Land between 1095 and 1291, expeditions to the Iberian Peninsula, the "crusade" to northeastern Europe, the Albigensian Crusades and the Hussite crusades—both against the heretics—and the crusades against the Ottoman Turks (in the Balkans). Although Muslim rulers included the concept of jihâd (a conflict fought for God against evil or his enemies) in their wars in the early centuries of Islam, it had become less important in the late tenth century. It was not until the middle decades of the twelfth century that jihâd was revived in the wars with the Latin Christian Crusaders. Most of the Crusades did not result in victory for the Latin Christians, although Nicholson concedes they slowed the advance of Islam. After Jerusalem was destroyed in 1291, Muslim rulers did permit Christian pilgrims to travel to holy sites. In the Iberian Peninsula, Christian rulers replaced Muslim rulers, but Muslims, Jews, and dissident Christians were compelled to convert to Catholicism. In northeastern Europe, the Teutonic Order's campaigns allowed German colonization that later encouraged twentieth-century German claims to land and led to two world wars. The Albigensian Crusade wiped out thirteenth-century aristocratic families in southern France who held to the Cathar heresy, but the Hussite crusades in the 1420s failed to eliminate the Hussite heresy. As a result of the wars, however, many positive changes occurred: Arab learning founded on Greek scholarship entered western Europe through the acquisition of an extensive library in Toledo, Spain, in 1085; works of western European literature were inspired by the holy wars; trade was encouraged and with it the demand for certain products; and a more favorable image of Muslim men and women was fostered by the crusaders' contact with the Middle East. Nicholson also notes that America may have been discovered because Christopher Columbus avoided a route that had been closed by Muslim conquests and that the Reformation may have been advanced because Martin Luther protested against the crusader indulgence in his Ninety-five Theses (1517).

Eleanor of Aquitaine, Courtly Love, and the Troubadours, by ffiona Swabey, singles out the twelfth century as the age of the individual, in which a queen like Eleanor of Aquitaine could influence the development of a new social and artistic culture. The wife of King Louis VII of France and later the wife of his enemy Henry of Anjou, who became king of England, she patronized some of the troubadours, whose vernacular lyrics celebrated the personal expression of emotion and a passionate declaration of service to women. Love, marriage, and the pursuit of women were also the subject of the new romance literature, which flourished in northern Europe and was the inspiration behind concepts of courtly love. However, as Swabey points out, historians in the past have misjudged Eleanor, whose independent spirit fueled their misogynist attitudes. Similarly, Eleanor's divorce and subsequent stormy marriage have colored ideas about medieval "love courts" and courtly love, interpretations of which have now been challenged by scholars. The twelfth century is set in context, with commentaries on feudalism, the tenets of Christianity, and the position of women, as well as summaries of the cultural and philosophical background, the cathedral schools and universities, the influence of Islam, the revival of classical learning, vernacular literature, and Gothic architecture. Swabey provides two biographical chapters on Eleanor and two on the emergence of the troubadours and the origin of courtly love through verse romances. Within this latter subject Swabey also details the story of Abelard and Heloise, the treatise of Andreas Capellanus (André the Chaplain) on courtly love, and Arthurian legend as a subject of courtly love.

Genghis Khan and Mongol Rule, by George Lane, identifies the rise to power of Genghis Khan and his unification of the Mongol tribes in the thirteenth century as a kind of globalization with political, cultural, economic, mercantile, and spiritual effects akin to those of modern globalization. Normally viewed as synonymous with barbarian destruction, the rise to power of Genghis Khan and the Mongol hordes is here understood as a more positive event that initiated two centuries of regeneration and creativity. Lane discusses the nature of the society of the Eurasian steppes in the twelfth and thirteenth centuries into which Genghis Khan was born; his success at reshaping the relationship between the northern pastoral and nomadic society with the southern urban, agriculturalist society; and his unification of all the Turco-Mongol tribes in 1206 before his move to conquer Tanquit Xixia, the Chin of northern China, and the lands of Islam. Conquered thereafter were the Caucasus, the Ukraine, the Crimea, Russia, Siberia, Central Asia, Afghanistan, Pakistan, and Kashmir. After his death his sons and grandsons continued, conquering Korea, Persia, Armenia, Mesopotamia, Azerbaijan, and eastern Europe—chiefly Kiev, Poland, Moravia, Silesia, and Hungary—until 1259, the end of the Mongol Empire as a unified whole. Mongol rule created a golden age in the succeeding split of the Empire into two, the Yuan dynasty of greater China and the Il-Khanate dynasty of greater Iran. Lane adds biographies of important political figures, famous names such as Marco Polo, and artists and scientists. Documents derive from universal histories, chronicles, local histories and travel accounts, official government documents, and poetry, in French, Armenian, Georgian, Chinese, Persian, Arabic, Chaghatai Turkish, Russian, and Latin.

Joan of Arc and the Hundred Years War, by Deborah Fraioli, presents the Hundred Years War between France and England in the fourteenth and fifteenth centuries within contexts whose importance has sometimes been blurred or ignored in past studies. An episode of apparently only moderate significance, a feudal lord's seizure of his vassal's land for harboring his mortal enemy, sparked the Hundred Years War, yet on the face of it the event should not have led inevitably to war. But the lord was the king of France and the vassal the king of England, who resented losing his claim to the French throne to his Valois cousin. The land in dispute, extending roughly from Bordeaux to the Pyrenees mountains, was crucial coastline for the economic interests of both kingdoms. The series of skirmishes, pitched battles, truces, stalemates, and diplomatic wrangling that resulted from the confiscation of English Aquitaine by the French form the narrative of this Anglo-French conflict, which was in fact not given the name Hundred Years War until the nineteenth century.

Fraioli emphasizes how dismissing women's inheritance and succession rights came at the high price of unleashing discontent in their male heirs, including Edward III, Robert of Artois, and Charles of Navarre. Fraioli also demonstrates the centrality of side issues, such as Flemish involvement in the war, the peasants' revolts that resulted from the costs of the war, and Joan of Arc's unusually clear understanding of French "sacred kingship." Among the primary sources provided are letters from key players such as Edward III, Etienne Marcel, and Joan of Arc; a supply list for towns about to be besieged; and a contemporary poem by the celebrated scholar and court poet Christine de Pizan in praise of Joan of Arc.

Magna Carta, by Katherine Drew, is a detailed study of the importance of the Magna Carta in comprehending England's legal and constitutional history. Providing a model for the rights of citizens found in the United States Declaration of Independence and Constitution's first ten amendments, the Magna Carta has had a role in the legal and parliamentary history of all modern states bearing some colonial or government connection with the British Empire. Constructed at a time when modern nations began to appear, in the early thirteenth century, the Magna Carta (signed in 1215) presented a formula for balancing the liberties of the people with the power of modern governmental institutions. This unique English document influenced the growth of a form of law (the English common law) and provided a vehicle for the evolution of representative (parliamentary) government. Drew demonstrates how the Magna Carta came to be—the roles of the Church, the English towns, barons, common law, and the parliament in its making—as well as how myths concerning its provisions were established. Also provided are biographies of Thomas Becket, Charlemagne, Frederick II, Henry II and his sons, Innocent III, and many other key figures, and primary documents—among them, the Magna Cartas of 1215 and 1225, and the Coronation Oath of Henry I.

Medieval Castles, by Marilyn Stokstad, traces the historical, political, and social function of the castle from the late eleventh century to the sixteenth by means of a typology of castles. This typology ranges from the early "motte and bailey"—military fortification, and government and economic center—to the palace as an expression of the castle owners' needs and purposes. An introduction defines the various contexts—military, political, economic, and social—in which the castle appeared in the Middle Ages. A concluding interpretive essay suggests the impact of the castle and its symbolic role as an idealized construct lasting until the modern day.

Medieval Cathedrals, by William Clark, examines one of the chief contributions of the Middle Ages, at least from an elitist perspective—that is, the religious architecture found in the cathedral ("chair" of the bishop) or great church, studied in terms of its architecture, sculpture, and stained glass. Clark begins with a brief contextual history of the concept of the bishop and his role within the church hierarchy, the growth of the church in the early Christian era and its affiliation with the bishop (deriving from that of the bishop of Rome), and the social history of cathedrals. Because of economic and political conflicts among the three authorities who held power in medieval towns—the king, the bishop, and the cathedral clergy—cathedral construction and maintenance always remained a vexed issue, even though the owners—the cathedral clergy—usually held the civic responsibility for the cathedral. In an interpretive essay, Clark then focuses on Reims Cathedral in France, because both it and the bishop's palace survive, as well as on contemporary information about surrounding buildings. Clark also supplies a historical overview on the social, political, and religious history of the cathedral in the Middle Ages: an essay on patrons, builders, and artists; aspects of cathedral construction (which was not always successful); and then a chapter on Romanesque and Gothic cathedrals and a "gazetteer" of twenty-five important examples.

The Medieval City, by Norman J. G. Pounds, documents the origin of the medieval city in the flight from the dangers or difficulties found in the country, whether economic, physically threatening, or cultural. Identifying the attraction of the city in its *urbanitas*, its "urbanity," or the way of living in a city, Pounds discusses first its origins in prehistoric and classical Greek urban revolutions. During the Middle Ages, the city grew primarily between the eleventh and thirteenth centuries, remaining essentially the same until the Industrial Revolution. Pounds provides chapters on the medieval city's planning, in terms of streets and structures; life in the medieval city; the roles of the Church and the city government in its operation; the development of crafts and trade in the city; and the issues of urban health, wealth, and welfare. Concluding with the role of the city in history, Pounds suggests that the value of the city depended upon its balance of social classes, its need for trade and profit to satisfy personal desires through the accumulation of wealth and its consequent economic power, its political power as a representative body within the kingdom, and its social role in the rise of literacy and education and in nationalism. Indeed, the concept of a middle class, a bourgeoisie, derives from the city—from the *bourg*, or "borough." According to Pounds, the rise of modern civilization would not have taken place without the growth of the city in the Middle Ages and its concomitant artistic and cultural contribution.

Medieval Science and Technology, by Elspeth Whitney, examines science and technology from the early Middle Ages to 1500 within the context of the classical learning that so influenced it. She looks at institutional history, both early and late, and what was taught in the medieval schools and, later, the universities (both of which were overseen by the Catholic Church). Her discussion of Aristotelian natural philosophy illustrates its impact on the medieval scientific worldview. She presents chapters on the exact sciences, meaning mathematics, astronomy, cosmology, astrology, statics, kinematics, dynamics, and optics; the biological and earth sciences, meaning chemistry and alchemy, medicine, zoology, botany, geology and meteorology, and geography; and technology. In an interpretive conclusion, Whitney demonstrates the impact of medieval science on the preconditions and structure that permitted the emergence of the modern world. Most especially, technology transformed an agricultural society into a more commercial and engine-driven society: waterpower and inventions like the blast furnace and horizontal loom turned iron working and cloth making into manufacturing operations. The invention of the mechanical clock helped to organize human activities through timetables rather than through experiential perception and thus facilitated the advent of modern life. Also influential in the establishment of a middle class were the inventions of the musket and pistol and the printing press. Technology, according to Whitney, helped advance the habits of mechanization and precise methodology. Her biographies introduce major medieval Latin and Arabic and classical natural philosophers and scientists. Extracts from various kinds of scientific treatises allow a window into the medieval concept of knowledge.

The Puebloan Society of Chaco Canyon, by Paul Reed, is unlike other volumes in this series, whose historic events boast a long-established historical record. Reed's study offers instead an original reconstruction of the Puebloan Indian society of Chaco, in what is now New Mexico, but originally extending into Colorado, Utah, and Arizona. He is primarily interested in its leaders, ritual and craft specialists, and commoners during the time of its chief flourishing, in the eleventh and twelfth centuries, as understood from archaeological data alone. To this new material he adds biographies of key Euro-American archaeologists and other individuals from the nineteenth and twentieth centuries who have made important discoveries about Chaco Canyon. Also provided are documents of archaeological description and narrative from early explorers' journals and archaeological reports, narratives, and monographs. In his overview chapters, Reed discusses the cultural and environmental setting of Chaco Canyon; its history (in terms of exploration and research); the Puebloan society and how it emerged chronologically; the Chaco society and how it appeared in 1100 c.e.; the "Outliers," or outlying communities of Chaco; Chaco as a ritual center of the eleventh-century Pueblo world; and, finally, what is and is not known about Chaco society. Reed concludes that ritual and ceremony played an important role in Chacoan society and that ritual specialists, or priests, conducted ceremonies, maintained ritual artifacts, and charted the ritual calendar. Its social organization matches no known social pattern or type: it was complicated, multiethnic, centered around ritual and ceremony, and without any overtly hierarchical political system. The Chacoans were ancestors to the later Pueblo people, part of a society that rose, fell, and evolved within a very short time period.

The Rise of Islam, by Matthew Gordon, introduces the early history of the Islamic world, beginning in the late sixth century with the career of the Prophet Muhammad (c. 570–c. 632) on the Arabian Peninsula. From Muhammad's birth in an environment of religious plurality—Christianity, Judaism, and Zoroastrianism, along with paganism, were joined by Islam—to the collapse of the Islamic empire in the early tenth century, Gordon traces the history of the Islamic community. The book covers topics that include the life of the Prophet and divine revelation (the Qur'an) to the formation of the Islamic state, urbanization in the Islamic Near East, and the extraordinary culture of Islamic letters and scholarship. In addition to a historical overview, Gordon examines the Caliphate and early Islamic Empire, urban society and economy, and the emergence, under the Abbasid Caliphs, of a "world religious tradition" up to the year 925 C.E.

As editor of this series I am grateful to have had the help of Benjamin Burford, an undergraduate Century Scholar at Rice University assigned to me in 2002–2004 for this project; Gina Weaver, a third-year graduate student in English; and Cynthia Duffy, a second-year graduate student in English, who assisted me in target-reading select chapters from some of these books in an attempt to define an audience. For this purpose I would also like to thank Gale Stokes, former dean of humanities at Rice University, for the 2003 summer research grant and portions of the 2003–2004 annual research grant from Rice University that served that end.

This series, in its mixture of traditional and new approaches to medieval history and cultures, will ensure opportunities for dialogue in the classroom in its offerings of twelve different "libraries in books." It should also propel discussion among graduate students and scholars by means of the gentle insistence throughout on the text as primal. Most especially, it invites response and further study. Given its mixture of East and West, North and South, the series symbolizes the necessity for global understanding, both of the Middle Ages and in the postmodern age.

Jane Chance, Series Editor
Houston, Texas
February 19, 2004

Advisory Board

Sharon Kinoshita
Associate Professor of Literature
(French Literature, World Literature, and Cultural Studies)
University of California–Santa Cruz

Christopher A. Snyder
Chair, History and Politics
Marymount University

Gwinn Vivian
Archaeologist
University of Arizona Museum

Nancy Wu
Associate Museum Educator

PREFACE

The attempt to understand and control the natural world is part of what makes us human. As such, the articulation of some kind of mythic or scientific explanation of natural phenomena and the practice of technology have been part of every human culture. For the emergence of the modern science and technology in Europe after 1500, however, the Middle Ages have special significance.

Although, as we will see, medieval scientific methods were significantly different from those of modern science, many of the characteristics associated with science as it came to be practiced during the Scientific Revolution and in the modern world appeared in at least partial or rudimentary form between 1100 and 1500. During the Middle Ages, also, new and improved technologies helped transform Europe from a subsistence, almost entirely agricultural society in the early Middle Ages to an increasingly commercial and mechanized one by 1500. All and all, we can say that it was in the Middle Ages that the institutional, technological, and intellectual frameworks responsible for the later success of western science first developed.

This book presents a historical overview of medieval science and technology from the early Middle Ages to 1500. Chapters 1 and 2 provide the historical and institutional context for the practice of science. Chapter 3 explains the basic premises and concepts of premodern science as developed by the great Greek philosopher Aristotle and adopted by medieval scientists. Chapter 4 examines the exact sciences (mathematics, astronomy and cosmology, astrology, statics, kinematics and dynamics, optics) and Chapter 5 the biological and earth sciences. Medieval achievements in technology are surveyed in Chapter 6, along with an assessment of how historians have explained medieval enthusiasm for new and improved techniques. Chapter 7 summarizes the impact of medieval science and technology on the modern world.

A Chronology gives a sense of the chronological relationships of important events over the 2,000-year span relevant to this subject. A selection of primary documents provides an opportunity for the reader to get a taste of how medieval people themselves wrote about scientific ideas and technological achievements. A set of biographical sketches provides a brief introduction to the lives and work of key figures. Twelve illustrations help elucidate the text. A glossary provides a handy reference list of terms. Finally, an annotated bibliography serves as a guide to further reading and investigation.

Some aspects of medieval science and technology will seem familiar to readers; many other aspects probably will not. Throughout this book, I have tried to bridge the gap between modern and medieval expectations of what science is and how science and technology should be practiced. Modern practice, for example, assumes that science and technology are closely related enterprises. During much of the Middle Ages, on the other hand, despite significant exceptions, science was usually conceptualized as a purely theoretical enterprise while technological innovation typically took place with little reference to scientific knowledge or information.

These differences are reflected in the language used by medieval writers to talk about science and technology. Medieval writers, for example, used the terms *natural philosophy* or *physics* to refer to the subjects we today would call "natural science." *Science*, which meant simply "knowledge," was divided into three theoretical branches: moral philosophy, metaphysics, and natural philosophy. *Physics*, on the other hand, was derived from a Greek word meaning "nature"; it lacked the specialized meaning it has today and meant simply the study of the natural world. The word *technology* or its equivalent similarly did not exist in the Middle Ages; instead medieval writers coined the term *mechanical arts* to refer to crafts and arts with a physical aspect, including not only architecture, agriculture, weaponry, and the like, but also commerce and theater. When we talk about science or technology in the Middle Ages, therefore, we must be careful not to import modern notions about the nature of these enterprises into our discussion. We must take similar care with such terms as *physician*, *architect*, and *engineer*, professions which in the Middle Ages were shaped by very different social and intellectual circumstances than exist today.

In writing this book I have tried to remain faithful to medieval conceptions while at the same time avoiding an overly pedantic use of medieval terminology. For example, I have generally referred to medieval "natural philosophers" rather than medieval "scientists," although at times I have used the term *scientist*. I have retained the words *physician*, *architect*, and *engineer*, while trying to remind the reader that these terms denoted different senses of professional identity in the Middle Ages than they do today. Throughout, I have tried to mediate between medieval and modern notions of science and technology, enabling the reader to appreciate both what is different and what is familiar in the past.

When I tell people that I study medieval science and technology, the response is often "Oh, I didn't know there was any." I hope this book helps to rectify this false impression and convince its readers that science and technology in the Middle Ages were vital, innovative enterprises which helped create the modern world.

A book such as this owes an enormous debt to the many historians whose original research has illuminated the depth and breadth of medieval scientific thought and technological achievement. I refer the reader to the notes and bibliography for the names and works of the scholars, too many to name here, who continue to extend the boundaries of our understanding of medieval science and technology. I would like also to thank Jane Chance, series editor of the Greenwood Guides to Historic Events of the Medieval World, for her encouragement, support, and sharp critical sense throughout this project. In addition, I thank the editorial assistants Ben Burford and Gina Weaver and the anonymous reader who provided thoughtful suggestions. Nancy Cleveland of the University of Nevada, Las Vegas Office of Publications was generous with her time and technical expertise in processing documents and illustrations. Finally, I would like to thank Irving Kelter, who provided a most helpful reading of the manuscript and saved me from several missteps. All errors, of course, remain my own.

CHRONOLOGY

388 B.C.E.	Plato founds the Academy in Athens.
335 B.C.E.	Aristotle founds the Lyceum in Athens.
323 B.C.E.	Death of Alexander the Great; beginning of the Hellenistic period.
c. 307 B.C.E.	Founding of the Museum and Library in Alexandria; Alexandria becomes the leading center for scientific research in the Hellenistic world.
c. 300 B.C.E.	Zeno founds a school for Stoic philosophy in Athens.
c. 300 B.C.E.	Euclid writes the *Elements*, the standard textbook in geometry in the West into the modern period.
44 B.C.E.	Death of Julius Caesar; Rome controls the Mediterranean.
c. 67 C.E.	Death of Paul.
79 C.E.	Death of Pliny the Elder, Roman author of the *Natural History*, a major source of information about the natural world during the Middle Ages.
c. 150	Claudius Ptolemy, author of the *Syntaxis* (later known in the Latin West as the *Almagest*), the

	fundamental astronomical text until the sixteenth century, working in Alexandria.
c. 155	Birth of Tertullian, Church Father who warns against pagan philosophy.
c. 200	Death of Galen, the foremost authority in medicine until the seventeenth century.
313	The Edict of Milan makes Christianity a legal religion in the Roman Empire.
394	Paganism made illegal in the Roman Empire.
430	Death of Augustine, one of the most influential theologians of the Middle Ages.
476	Last Roman emperor in the West deposed.
500	Watermills well known in Italy.
c. 520	Benedictine monasticism founded in the West.
524	Death of Boethius; Boethius unable to carry out his plan to translate all of Plato and Aristotle into Latin.
600	Isidore of Seville becomes archbishop of Seville.
632	Death of Muhammad.
711	Muslims conquer Spain.
760	Arabs adopt Indian numerals.
762	Founding of Baghdad by al-Mansur.
c. 775–c. 850	Charlemagne and his successors promote an intellectual and artistic revival, often called by historians the "Carolingian Renaissance," at the royal court.
793	Alcuin, a learned cleric, arrives in Charlemagne's court from York in England.

830	The "House of Wisdom," a scientific research institute and translation center, founded in Baghdad.
871–99	King Alfred the Great encourages learning in England.
929	Death of al-Battani; improved the accuracy of the Ptolemaic system.
960s	Gerbert of Aurillac goes to Spain to study Arabic mathematics.
961–76	Rule of the caliph al-Hakam II of Spain; al-Hakam II ordered scientific and philosophical books for the library in Cordoba, making it one of the major libraries of the Islamic world, said to contain over 400,000 books.
990	Fulbert, a disciple of Gerbert of Aurillac, opens a cathedral school at Chartres.
999	Gerbert of Aurillac becomes Pope Sylvester II.
c. 1000	Almost all of Greek medicine, natural philosophy, and mathematics translated into Arabic and known to Arabic scholars.
c. 1000	Population in Europe begins to increase; Europe begins to become more urbanized.
1037	Death of Avicenna.
c. 1040	Death of Alhazen.
1085	Toledo reconquered from the Muslims by Christian forces.
1086	The Domesday Book records 5,624 watermills in England.
1095–99	First Crusade.
1126	Adelard of Bath translates the astronomical tables of al-Khwarizmi.

1130s or 1140s	Gerard of Cremona arrives in Spain looking for copy of Ptolemy's *Almagest*.
1140s	Beginning of Gothic style of architecture.
1140s–1200	Revival of intellectual activity in Europe, often referred to by historians as the Renaissance of the Twelfth Century.
1179	Death of Hildegard of Bingen.
1180s	First references to windmills in Europe.
1187	Death of Gerard of Cremona; translated Greek and Arabic scientific texts from Arabic into Latin.
1190s	Paris constructs a public water system.
1200s	Horizontal loom used in Europe.
c. 1200	Introduction of Arabic numerals into Europe.
1209–15	University of Paris formally recognized and incorporated.
1210	Franciscan order founded.
1210	Earliest decree restricting teaching of Aristotle's natural philosophy at the University of Paris.
1214	Papacy establishes privileges and immunities for professors and students at Oxford University.
1216	Dominican order founded; in the thirteenth century most university professors are either Franciscans or Dominicans.
1220s	Robert Grosseteste writes commentary on Aristotle's *Posterior Analytics* on scientific method.
1225	Beginning of construction of Beauvais Cathedral, one of the highest in Europe.
1229	Foundation of the University of Toulouse.

1230s	Averroës, called "the Commentator," supplants Avicenna as the main guide to Aristotle.
1231	Renewal of 1210 ban on Aristotle until "purged of error."
1235	Cordoba captured by Christian king of Castile.
1237–50	London begins work on the Great Conduit public water system.
c. 1244–48	Frederick II completes a draft of his work on the art of hunting with birds.
1253	Death of Robert Grosseteste.
1255	The faculty of arts at the University of Paris makes lectures on all known works of Aristotle mandatory.
1257	Thomas Aquinas begins teaching at Paris; synthesizes Aristotelian philosophy and Christian theology.
1260	William of Moerbeke translates Aristotle's *Parts of Animals* into Latin from Greek for the first time.
1269	William of Moerbeke translates seven works of Archimedes into Latin from Greek.
1269	Petrus Peregrinus writes his *Letter on the Magnet*.
1274	Death of Thomas Aquinas.
c. 1275	Alfonsine tables composed at court of Alfonso X "the Wise" at Castile in Spain.
1277	The Condemnations of 1277 issued by the bishop of Paris condemns and forbids the teaching at the University of Paris of 219 propositions taken from Aristotelian and Arabic natural philosophy.
1280s	Invention of eyeglasses in Italy.
1280	Death of Albertus Magnus.

1284	Collapse of the choir vault at Beauvais Cathedral.
1286	Death of William of Moerbeke; translated ancient scientific texts from the original Greek.
1286	The bulk of translations from the Greek completed.
1291	Genoese ship attempts to reach India by sailing around Africa but does not return.
1292	Death of Roger Bacon.
c. 1298	Marco Polo writes his description of his travels to the Far and Middle East.
c. 1310	Death of Theodoric of Freiberg.
1325	The Condemnations of 1277 partially annulled.
c. 1325–70s	Oxford Calculators develop innovative mathematical techniques.
1326	City government of Florence requests that bronze cannons and iron shot be made for the defense of the city; one of earliest references to cannon.
1327	Richard of Wallingford begins to build his planetary clock, the most complex mechanism in Europe to date, in St. Albans, England.
1330s	Probable date for the invention of the mechanical clock with verge-and-foliot escapement.
1330s–40s	Natural philosophy of Aristotle read at Paris; by 1341 the natural books of Aristotle and his commentators were required reading at the University of Paris.
1348–52	Black Death devastates Europe for the first time, killing about one-third of the population.
1348–64	Giovanni Dondi produces his astrarium (planetary clock).

c. 1358	Death of John Buridan.
1363	Guy de Chauliac, one of the most important physicians and surgeons of the fourteenth century, completes his *Chirugia* (Surgery).
1377	First recorded reference to a portable clock.
1377	Nicole Oresme translates Aristotle's *De caelo* into French at the request of Charles V.
1382	Death of Nicole Oresme.
c. 1400	Modern timekeeping with public clocks striking equal hours becoming increasingly common.
1420–62	Construction of the dome of the Cathedral of Florence, under the direction of Filippo Brunelleschi, until his death in 1446.
1424	First known representation of the crankshaft.
1450s	Translation of the full corpus of Plato's works.
1452–56	Production and publication of Gutenberg's Bible, the first book printed using movable type.
1453	Ottoman Turks take Constantinople using massive cannon; end of Byzantine Empire.
1462	Inventory of the city of Nuremberg includes 2,230 firearms.
1462–70	Printing presses established throughout Europe.
1480s–90s	Invention and diffusion of the blast furnace.
1492	Columbus on his voyage west across the Atlantic.
c. 1500	Invention of the wheel-lock pistol.

CHAPTER 1

OVERVIEW AND HISTORY:
THE CLASSICAL TRADITION AND THE EARLY MIDDLE AGES

Medieval science, like modern science, was shaped by contemporary conceptions of the nature and purpose of science and the conditions under which it was taught and practiced. "Natural philosophy," as science was called in the Middle Ages, was part of a broader intellectual tradition going back to ancient Greece which considered what human beings could know about the physical world and how this knowledge was best attained. This chapter therefore begins with a brief survey of Greek and Roman science and shows how ideas inherited from the ancient world influenced science in the Middle Ages. We also look at how broad historical changes affected how and where science was taught. Finally, we see how science was part of a wide-ranging debate over the proper relationship of "reason" and "faith." Overall, the pursuit of scientific knowledge was an integral part of medieval thought and culture, a tradition the Middle Ages bequeathed to the modern world.

THE HERITAGE FROM THE ANCIENT WORLD

The Greeks of the ancient world laid the foundations of western science. Scientific speculation was initiated by a group of thinkers known to historians as the "Pre-Socratics" because they flourished in Greek city-states on mainland Greece and Ionia in the sixth to fourth centuries B.C.E., before the time of the famous Athenian philosopher Socrates. The Pre-Socratics speculated about the nature of physical reality and were the first known thinkers in the West to clearly state that questions about the physical universe could be answered without reference to the gods or religious belief. The earliest of these thinkers, Thales, suggested that all things were made out of water. Later Pre-Socratics speculated that the primal substance or substances were the four elements of earth, water, air, and fire, or small, massy, indivisible particles called atoms, or a featureless, indefinite material called the "Boundless." One Pre-Socratic, Pythagoras, argued that numbers and numerical relationships were the basis of physical reality. At the same time that the Pre-Socratics flourished, a group of medical writings known collectively as the "Hippocratic corpus" asserted that diseases had natural causes and that those who attributed them to supernatural causes were simply covering up for their own ignorance.

By the time of Socrates (469–399 B.C.E.), the city-state of Athens had become the cultural center of the Greek world. Socrates' student, Plato (c. 429–347 B.C.E.), and Plato's student, Aristotle (384–22 B.C.E.), articulated the first comprehensive systems of philosophy to come down to us. These philosophies incorporated scientific ideas within a broader outlook in which metaphysical principles largely determined the approach to the study of the natural world.

The influence of both Plato and Aristotle on the Middle Ages was immense. Plato's fundamental ideas were passed on to the medieval world through a variety of intermediaries, including the early Christian theologian, St. Augustine, and influenced some important scientific writers in the thirteenth and fourteenth centuries. Aristotle's works became the fundamental texts studied at medieval universities. His ideas, taken together, provided a comprehensive, coherent, and highly plausible account of the physical world which formed the basis of western scientific thinking from the twelfth century until the Scientific Revolution of the sixteenth and seventeenth centuries and even later in biology.

For Plato, for whom true reality was by definition unchanging and therefore nonmaterial, science was at best a "likely story," an approximation of an ultimate reality which could be apprehended only by freeing the mind from sense perception and all ties to the physical world. Plato believed that all knowledge was ultimately derived from the illumination of the human mind by the "Good," his name for the divine principle, or God, and therefore that ordinary observation of the physical world resulted only in transitory, faulty impressions, rather than true knowledge. Nevertheless, Plato envisioned the universe as orderly and rational and as governed by numbers and their relationships.

Aristotle, on the other hand, thought that reality was embedded in and inseparable from the concrete and specific. For Aristotle, sense perception subjected to logical analysis was the beginning of knowledge and he strongly advocated the careful observation of natural phenomena as the basis of scientific thinking. He therefore found the pursuit of qualitative information about the physical world to be an interesting and worthwhile enterprise and wrote works on most of the recognized fields of science including astronomy, meteorology, zoology, psychology, and botany. His books demonstrate a combination of empirical observations and a complex theoretical structure which tried to explain natural phenomena in terms of underlying abstract principles. The specifics of his scientific thought will be examined in more detail in later chapters.

Greek scientific thought spread throughout the ancient world in the centuries following the conquest of much of the ancient Near East by Alexander the Great, a student of Aristotle, in the fourth century B.C.E. The process of Hellenization, in which ancient Greek and Near Eastern civilizations merged to form a vibrant and energetic new culture, would have profound historical effects. Aristotle's followers, both in Athens and elsewhere, developed his ideas, sometimes testing them with simple experiments. The city of Alexandria in Egypt had a library and research center founded during the third century B.C.E. where some of the most important scientific works of the ancient world were written. Hero of Alexandria, Philo of Byzantium, Archimedes, Euclid, and Apollonius wrote treatises on mechanics and mathematics; other scientists developed the sciences of anatomy and medicine. Hellenistic astronomers systematized and refined their observations of the movements of the heavenly bodies and developed a remarkably accurate estimation of the circumference of the earth and somewhat less accurate estimations of the distances of the sun and moon. One Hellenistic astronomer, Aristarchus, even suggested, contrary to the prevailing view of a stationary earth at the center of the universe, that the earth and other heavenly bodies instead revolved around the sun. His theory, however, had few supporters and was soon forgotten. Among the most important of the later Greek scientific writers for medieval science were Ptolemy, who wrote a comprehensive survey of astronomy, and Galen of Pergamum, whose account of human physiology based on the four humors (blood, yellow bile, black bile, and phlegm) and medicine dominated western medical thinking into the early modern period.

Greek philosophy in the Hellenistic period also contributed to attitudes toward nature which strongly influenced the later development of medieval science. Stoicism, which originated in the third century B.C.E., postulated an organic, living universe permeated by a rational, life-giving force which they named *pneuma*, or breath. The idea that the world and everything in it were in some sense "alive" continued to influence western scientific thought until the completion of the Scientific Revolution in the seventeenth century. The Stoics also believed in a world purposely designed by God to be useful and serviceable to humans. Aspects of Stoic thought were later adopted by Christian thinkers in support of the idea of a "designed earth," proof of God's plan to provide for human needs and wants. The Greek Church Father Basil of Caesarea in his commentary on the account of Creation in Genesis, for example, explained how every plant and animal, even poisonous ones, had their own useful parts to play in nature. These attitudes contributed to later medieval understandings of how nature worked and a confidence that human use of nature was sanctioned by God.

Another Greek philosophy that had important effects on medieval science was Neoplatonism ("new Platonism"), which originated in the third century C.E. Neoplatonism emphasized the idea of reality as a continuing emanation from the divine principle. Its complex history will be discussed in more detail in Chapter 3.

Greek science was incorporated into subsequent European history by the Romans who, by the first century C.E., had conquered all the territory around first the western and later the eastern Mediterranean, making the Mediterranean a "Roman lake." Roman writers assimilated Greek science, often turning it to practical advantage in architecture, the military arts, geography, and medicine. But the Romans were more interested in practical things than in philosophy and gradually lost interest in the nuances of Greek thought. Over time, educated Romans began to turn to popularized versions of Greek science in the form of encyclopedias, handbooks, and even poetry rather than the more difficult original texts. Some of these works, for example, Pliny's *Natural History*, a compendium of Greek science, and an allegorical work by Martianus

Capella, *The Marriage of Philology and Mercury*, became important sources for science in the early Middle Ages.

The rise of Christianity was another important element affecting attitudes toward science in late antiquity. Over the course of several centuries, Christianity developed from a small sect of Judaism to a tightly organized and formidable religion. In 394 c.e. paganism was outlawed and Judaism and Christianity became the only legal religions of the Roman Empire. With Christianity the official state religion, the issue of the proper relationship of reason and faith became a major component of the place of science in society.

Much of the work of formulating Christian theology, ethics, and practice fell to the group of educated Christian thinkers known as the Church Fathers. Historians have widely debated the attitudes of the Church Fathers toward philosophy and science. Some have emphasized the negative attitude epitomized in the writing of Tertullian (c. 155–c. 230), who famously remarked, "What indeed has Athens to do with Jerusalem? . . . After Christ we have no need of speculation, after the Gospel no need of research."[1] Other historians have pointed out that although the Church Fathers subordinated the claims of science to the demands of faith, they rarely rejected Greco-Roman science and philosophy outright. Gregory of Nazianizus (329–89), for example, argued that the study of "the heavens and earth, and air, and all such things" helped men to appreciate the usefulness and beauty of creation and therefore of the Creator (God). Even Tertullian valued human reason in some contexts if it was used to support faith. The dominant position was somewhere between that of Tertullian and Gregory: science and human reason in general were useful to the Christian as long as knowledge about the natural world never supplanted love of God or contradicted the tenets of religious belief. According to Augustine, the most important of the Church Fathers, "If those who are called philosophers . . . have said things which are indeed true and are well accommodated to our faith, they should not be feared; rather, what they have said should be taken from them as from unjust possessors and converted to our use."[2] Yet Augustine also said, "for the Christian, it is enough to believe that the cause of all created things . . . is nothing other than the goodness of the creator, who is the one and the true God."[3] The attitude of the Fathers of the Church could be summed up in the idea that philosophy and science were "handmaidens to theology," useful up to a point but not to be considered fully independent areas of thought. This approach was passed on to the Middle Ages. Henceforth, into the modern era, debates about the extent to which scientific ideas which appeared to conflict with Christian faith should be accepted have been a major part of the history of science in the West.

In conclusion, classical thought established the basic premise that human reason was capable of uncovering the rational order which underlay the physical universe. This fundamental principle was absorbed into Christian thought, although henceforth some Christian thinkers would equally insist that scientific thought had to be ultimately subordinated to religious belief.

THE EUROPEAN EARLY MIDDLE AGES (500–1000 C.E.)

Conditions in Europe after the fall of the Roman Empire in the fifth century C.E. were not conducive to a high level of intellectual activity. Europe outside Italy was increasingly cut off from the eastern Mediterranean and the sources of Greco-Roman culture. Schools virtually vanished from the European landscape and libraries were rare, isolated, and limited in scope. Cities themselves, outside of a few rare exceptions, had shrunk and become little more than outposts run by members of the Church bureaucracy, many of whom were also wealthy landowners whose interests were more practical than intellectual. The thriving economic activity of the ancient world had been reduced in the West to a bare subsistence agricultural economy subject to frequent shortages and famines. Public services and administration largely disappeared, replaced by the competing claims of kinship ties, church patronage, dynastic loyalties, and the vagaries of violence.

Despite these unpromising conditions, the early Middle Ages demonstrated considerable creativity. As we shall see in Chapter 6, this period produced significant and important technological innovations. New forms of social and political organization also developed which set the stage for the later vitality and achievements of medieval Europe. In the area of science, however, the early Middle Ages was a period of preservation and retrenchment, rather than of new and innovative thought. Thinkers relied heavily on the "authority" of past writers, rather than on their own observations. The rudiments of classical scientific thought survived but in mostly watered-down form. The works of Plato, Aristotle, and the Hellenistic scientists were no longer accessible. Only a very few, exceptional individuals had any knowledge of Greek or any awareness of the achievements of ancient Greek scientists. Knowledge continued to be organized around the scheme developed by Roman writers of four mathematical arts (geometry, arithmetic, astronomy, and music) and three language arts (grammar, dialectic or logic, and rhetoric), collectively known as the seven liberal arts, but the scientific content of the mathematical arts and the more advanced sciences had almost entirely dropped from view.

The clearest sign of this limited perspective was the popularity of an encyclopedia by Isidore of Seville, the archbishop of Seville. Called the *Etymologies*, Isidore's work offered brief descriptions of the major topics of classical science, including each of the seven liberal arts (with an emphasis on astronomy), medicine, and mechanics as well as six books on technical subjects such as the types and parts of ships, buildings, weapons, and farm and household utensils. Isidore organized his discussion around the (usually fanciful) derivations of words. Despite its deficiencies, the *Etymologies* together with a second work by Isidore, *De naturis rerum*, passed on to their many readers the rudiments of Greek and Roman scientific thought, including the spherical shape of the earth, the motions of the heavenly bodies, the four elements, the theory of the humors, and the basics of practical medicine.

Despite the lack of progress in scientific thought in the early Middle Ages, many developments in this period were crucial for the later history of science. Perhaps most importantly, secular learning, including science, received the support of the Church. As the institutions of ancient Rome disintegrated, the Christian church had stepped into the resulting vacuum, offering a degree of protection, stability, and order to the local populace. Bishops assumed the role of city administrators. In rural areas, that is, almost all of Europe outside Italy, abbesses and abbots ran monastic institutions which gradually acquired numerous extra-religious functions, including that of repositories for wealth, schools, libraries, orphanages, and old-age homes, and sanctuaries for abused, abandoned, or runaway wives. Between the sixth and ninth centuries, many of these nunneries and monasteries gained considerable wealth and political clout and some turned their resources toward the support of learning and education.

The training provided by monastic schools had originally been narrowly religious: the reading and copying of the Bible and other religious texts, such as sermons and the writings of the Church Fathers. By the seventh century, however, this training began to be expanded to include many branches of the secular arts and sciences which were thought to aid the understanding of scripture or the performance of religious duties. Particularly important in this development were the monasteries and nunneries of England and Ireland where not only Latin grammar and style were taught but even, occasionally, Greek. The great abbesses of England and Saxony in Germany were especially noted for their learning. Among the sciences, the practical applications of astronomy, especially the computations for calculating the date of Easter, the feast days of saints, and the times for prayers, became a major part of monastic culture. Monks also valued astronomy because the invariable movements of the heavenly bodies dramatically demonstrated the nobility and order of God's creation. Medicine was also valued for its obvious utility and monasteries and nunneries early became centers for both medical practice and the collection of medical books.

Charlemagne, the great Frankish king who established a European empire in the eighth century, capitalized on these developments. Charlemagne's rule brought an increased level of peace and security and with these a modest intellectual renaissance. As part of a program to increase the level of learning among clerics (who doubled as his royal bureaucrats), Charlemagne legislated that every monastery should teach writing, computation, and grammar and that authoritative texts of important works be authenticated and copied. To promote his educational program he gathered the most learned men of Europe at his court, including Alcuin of York and Einhard, who later wrote Charlemagne's biography. Although Charlemagne himself was not very well educated (he may not have known how to write Latin) he was reputed to have enjoyed discussing scientific questions and carried on a lengthy correspondence with Alcuin and other monastic scholars on astronomical problems. Charlemagne even had a silver table made for himself which depicted the celestial spheres, the constellations, and the movements of the planets.[4]

Charlemagne was not the only ruler to promote science in the early Middle Ages. King Alfred of Wessex, the most powerful Anglo-Saxon ruler, and his circle also encouraged the importation, collection, and copying of scientific works, especially medical texts.

If the early Middle Ages were characterized by the survival of the rudiments of science rather than any originality, this period was important for setting some of the patterns that would shape later medieval science. First, education became the province of the Church. Although this may seem at first glance a disadvantage to the modern observer, in the context of medieval society it meant that science had the support of the wealthiest and most highly organized institution in Europe. Second, the continuing interest in science throughout the early Middle Ages ensured that when Europe again encountered classical thought the ground had been well prepared for progress in scientific thinking and knowledge. Finally, the practical approach to learning encouraged by the frontier-like conditions of early medieval Europe encouraged an interest in new technologies which would bear fruit in later centuries (see Chapter 6).

SCIENCE IN THE BYZANTINE EMPIRE

The Byzantine Empire was the second culture, along with medieval Europe and Islam, to replace the Roman Empire after the fifth century. Unlike Islam, the Byzantine Empire, or Byzantium, had minimal direct effect on the development of medieval science and technology. It did, however, help preserve and transmit classical texts, and for this reason we will discuss it briefly.

In some respects, the Byzantine Empire was a continuation of the Eastern Roman Empire, which never suffered the institutional and military breakdown that occurred in Europe. The eastern empire, Greek speaking with its capital at Constantinople (now Istanbul) and more economically prosperous, had gradually separated itself from the Latin-speaking West even before the fall of the western empire in the fifth century. By the time of Justinian, emperor from 527 to 565, it had emerged as Byzantium, a state that would retain its distinctive identity until its final defeat by the Ottoman Turks in 1453.

Throughout its long history, Byzantium retained links to its ancient past. Its language was Greek and it preserved the bureaucratic, legal, and political structure of the Roman Empire of late antiquity, as well as the literary traditions of classical Greece. In other ways, Byzantium developed along new lines, producing novel forms of Church organization and a unique and beautiful religious art. Increasingly on the defensive, its territory gradually whittled away by external attacks, Byzantine culture had a tendency to turn inward and was profoundly shaped by a deep interest in religious contemplation and theological questions.

Two important natural philosophers from the sixth century deserve special mention. Simplicius (d. after 533) and John Philoponus (d. c. 570) were Greek-speaking thinkers learned in both Aristotelian and Neoplatonic thought. Their attempts to revise and criticize Aristotle's natural philosophy in the light of Neoplatonic ideas influenced later medieval science when their works were translated into Arabic and Latin.

Byzantium is also credited with inventing the hospital, in the sense of an institution that supplied specialized medical care with the hope of curing patients, rather than simply providing a place of comfort to the dying, during the sixth century. Hospitals in Islam from the ninth century and the Latin West beginning in the twelfth century seem to have been influenced by Byzantine prototypes.

Byzantium's primary contribution to the history of science, however, was to preserve important texts from classical and late antiquity. Byzantine physicians and natural philosophers living in Persia, for example, are known to have translated Greek scientific texts into Syriac in the fifth and sixth centuries; in the ninth century these texts were translated into Arabic and helped stimulate and sustain the development of natural philosophy in Islam. In the same century and later, Arabic translators sought out Greek manuscripts directly from Byzantine sources. Byzantine outposts in Italy and possibly North Africa were sources for Greek medical and other texts in the sixth century and again in the eleventh and twelfth centuries. The first Latin version of Ptolemy's *Almagest*, for example, was made from a manuscript sent by the Byzantine emperor Manuel (1118–76) to the king of Sicily.[5] In the fourteenth and fifteenth centuries, emigrating Byzantine scholars brought Greek manuscripts with them to Italy, stimulating interest in classical Greek science and literature. Overall, we can say that the Byzantine Empire played an essential part in the development of medieval science through its role in the transmission of classical learning.

SCIENCE IN ISLAM

The late sixth and seventh centuries saw the rise of Islam, a new and vital culture which originated in Arabia and spread throughout much of the Near and Middle East, North Africa, Spain, and almost as far East as the border of present-day India. United through the use of Arabic as both an official and learned language, the Islamic states very early promoted scientific research. Islamic rulers not only appropriated Greek thought, making a concerted effort to translate Greek philosophical, astronomical, mathematical, and medical texts into Arabic, but they also subsidized systematic original research through the founding of astronomical observatories, libraries, and medical hospitals.

The encounter of European thinkers with Arabic science would have almost as profound effects on the development of western science as the recovery of Greek science. Arabic achievements in science were especially striking in astronomy, mathematics, optics, medicine, chemistry, and pharmacology. In these fields it would be accurate to say that between the seventh and thirteenth centuries (some historians would argue even later) Islam not only experienced a "golden age" of science but also eclipsed anything found in Christian Europe. This body of work influenced both the content of medieval science and attitudes about the relationship of scientific ideas to theological concepts. Although a full accounting of Arabic science is beyond the scope of the present work, a brief review is helpful in understanding the development of medieval European science.

The initial stages of European contact with Islamic natural philosophy took place in Spain, where, as we shall discuss later, European scholars in the twelfth century sought out texts by Greek authors unavailable in Christian Europe. Spain had been conquered by Islamic armies in the eighth century, and in the intervening period a lively, cosmopolitan, and learned culture had sprung up in which Muslim, Christian, and Jewish scholars freely mingled. These scholars made a concerted effort to make use of the whole of classical learning. By the end of the tenth century the royal library at Cordoba was said to have had over 400,000 volumes, far larger than any library in Europe outside Spain.

The comparatively advanced state of science in Spain and other parts of the Islamic world reflected in part the continuing contact Islam had had with previously Hellenized areas of the Near and Middle East. While early medieval Europe had lost access to the texts and knowledge of ancient science, the Islamic world had available an almost unbroken tradition of Greek learning. Under the leadership of the Abbasid caliphs Harun al-Rashid and al-Mamun and their successors, for example, translations of works by Aristotle, Plato, and Hellenistic scientists were produced, many under the auspices of Baghdad's "House of Wisdom," a research and translation institute founded in 830. Later Islamic scientists not only assimilated Greek science and philosophy but also compiled an enormous body of new systematic empirical data, especially in the fields of astronomy and medicine, which would later be absorbed into western medieval science. Abu Abd Allah Muhammad ibn Jabin al-Battani (c. 858–929), for example, brought together over thirty years of meticulous astronomical observations in a set of astronomical tables, translated into Latin in the twelfth century. Another astronomer, Abd al-Rahman al-Sufi (903–86), refined earlier observations of the constellations; his work provided many of the star names of Arabic origin later used in Europe. Ibn Sina (981–1037), known in the West as Avicenna, wrote a lengthy and detailed synthesis (over 1,000 pages long) of Greek and Arabic medicine called the *Canon of Medicine* which covered both theoretical issues and practical medical techniques. Other physicians identified and described as many as 2,000 distinct botanical medicines. Islamic mathematicians similarly adapted and improved upon earlier mathematics, developing the Indian arithmetic system of nine digits and a zero into what became known in the West as "Arabic numerals" and inventing new fields such as algebra and trigonometry. In many instances, Islamic scientists developed criticisms of specific assertions by Greek authorities (for example, Galen's assertion that blood passes through a hole in the wall of the heart between the right and left ventricles), refined Greek theories in order to accommodate more accurate empirical data (for example, modifications to Ptolemy's model of the universe), or significantly modified Aristotle's ideas, in part by attempts to blend aspects of Aristotelianism and Platonism. According to some historians of science, these challenges to classical scientific ideas may have been a significant factor in the genesis of the Scientific Revolution of the sixteenth and seventeenth centuries.

Much is still unknown about the history of science in Islam. Many important texts remain unedited and unstudied. Yet certain aspects of how science was practiced in medieval Islamic territories has become clearer over recent decades.

First, science and religion were generally regarded as separate, distinct enterprises. The great bulk of scientific work was carried out with the financial and institutional support of individual rulers who valued the intellectual and practical advantages of scientific knowledge. These rulers supported the practice of science, including subsidizing research and founding research institutes equipped with astronomical observatories, advanced astronomical instruments, and extensive libraries. Scientific activity, therefore, took place largely outside religious institutions and schools and most of the well-known Islamic scientists, unlike their Christian counterparts, were not also theologians or members of religious orders. At the same time, religion offered some practical incentives for scientific endeavors. All mosques, for example, were supposed to be oriented in the direction of the Kaaba in Mecca; efforts to determine the precise alignment between Mecca and individual mosques were a spur to mathematical geography and the accurate calculation of latitude and longitude.

Second, there was a wide range of attitudes toward the place and value of science current in Islamic society. Some religious scholars implicitly or explicitly opposed the pursuit of science. One theologian and philosopher, al-Ghazali (1058–1111), for example, argued in his major work, *The Incoherence of the Philosophers*, that all effects in the world, including physical ones, were caused directly and solely by God or his agents, the angels, a supposition that effectively ended the viability of ever achieving scientific knowledge of natural causation of physical events. A generation later, however, Ibn Rushd (1126–98), or Averroës, as he was known in the West, responded with a thoroughgoing defense of the scientific enterprise in his *Incoherence of the Incoherence*. Both of these views, however, were personal ones and did not represent the official, institutionalized views of any group. (In medieval Europe, on the other hand, Averroës' assertions of the primacy of reason caused an intellectual crisis, resulting in a temporary and limited ban on the teaching of some scientific texts; see Chapter 2). On balance, it is probably fair to say that "in many ways science in the Muslim world was a secular enterprise, and religion neither made an enemy of science nor championed its cause to the extreme."[6]

Third, there was a strong practical and empirical streak in Islamic science. Scientists and their sponsors pioneered in the establishment of institutions which systemically supported empirical research and its application. Rather than devoting themselves exclusively to questions of theory, Arabic scientists often explored the utilitarian benefits of scientific investigation. The physician Abu Bakr al-Razi (fl. ninth century), for example, performed a controlled experiment to test the effects of bloodletting as a treatment for brain tumor by dividing his patients into two groups, one treated with bloodletting and the other not, and recording the results. Arabic thinkers often conceptualized the different branches of science as having both theoretical and practical sides: al-Farabi (d. 950), for example, included carpentry, stoneworking, and other crafts under practical geometry, the science of weights and devices under mathematics, and medicine, agriculture, navigation, and alchemy under "physics." Arabic scientists were particularly interested in developing new and improved types of machinery and devices for use in irrigation, warfare, timekeeping, and astronomical observations. As we shall see in Chapter 6, a number of the inventions which would help transform the economy and society of western Europe during the Middle Ages seem to have had their origins in medieval Islam.

The practice of science in Islam declined after the fourteenth century for reasons that remain unclear. Nevertheless, Islamic science had a lasting impact on cultures worldwide. Specific influences on individual branches of science in medieval Europe will be discussed in other chapters. For now, a list of some of the modern English words derived from Arabic will remind us of the contributions of Islamic science: zero, algebra, chemistry, alchemy, soda, alcohol, alkali, zenith, borax.

NOTES

1. Tertullian from *Early Latin Theology: Selections from Tertullian, Cyprian, Ambrose, and Jerome* (Philadelphia: Westminster Press, 1956), p. 172.

2. Augustine, *On Christian Doctrine*, 2.40.60, trans. D. W. Robertson, the Library of Liberal Arts (Indianapolis and New York: Bobbs-Merrill, 1958), p. 75. This discussion of the Church Fathers is heavily indebted to David Lindberg, "Science as Handmaiden: Roger Bacon and the Patristic Tradition," *Isis* 78 (1987): 518–36; reprinted in *The Scientific Enterprise in Antiquity and the Middle Ages*, ed. Michael H. Shank (Chicago and London: University of Chicago Press,

2000), pp. 295–314; and David Lindberg, "Science and the Early Christian Church," *Isis* 74 (1983): 509–30, reprinted in *Scientific Enterprise*, pp. 125–46.

3. Augustine, *Enchiridion* 3.9, quoted in Lindberg, "Science as Hand-maiden," in *Scientific Enterprise*, p. 145.

4. Pierre Riché, *Education and Culture in the Barbarian West: Sixth through Eighth Centuries*, trans. John J. Contreni (Columbia: University of South Carolina Press, 1976), p. 498; Stephen C. McCluskey, *Astronomies and Cultures in Early Medieval Europe* (Cambridge, England: Cambridge University Press, 1998), pp. 132–33, 140.

5. A. A. Vasiliev, *History of the Byzantine Empire* (Madison: University of Wisconsin Press, 1952), 2:491.

6. Ahmad Dallal, "Science, Medicine, and Technology: The Making of a Scientific Culture," in *The Oxford History of Islam*, ed. John L. Esposito (Oxford and New York: Oxford University Press, 1999), p. 213.

CHAPTER 2

INSTITUTIONAL HISTORY:
THE HIGH AND LATE MIDDLE AGES

Between 1000 and 1300, Europe changed from an intellectual backwater to one of the most intellectually innovative cultures of the world. This process happened in several stages. From about the year 1000, there are numerous signs that medieval thinkers developed a new and original appreciation of nature. In the words of one important historian, twelfth- and thirteenth-century thinkers "thought of themselves as confronting an external present, intelligible, and active reality as they might confront a partner."[1] The personification of nature as a forceful and imperious goddess appeared everywhere in literature, detailed and accurate relief sculptures of local plants appeared on church exteriors, and "the natural" became a new touchstone for what was considered normal and appropriate behavior. This new awareness of nature was supported by an increasingly dynamic economy, greater social mobility, and new political, religious, and intellectual institutions. From the twelfth century onward, medieval scientists explored a vast array of scientific and related questions, ranging from the obscure ("whether light is an accidental form") to the very broad ("whether the existence of a vacuum is possible") to the seemingly bizarre ("whether aborted fetuses are resurrected").[2] Underlying this extraordinary flowering of speculative scientific thinking was the enthusiastic pursuit of the idea that nature proceeds by its own internal, rationally accessible laws, in the same way as an architect or engineer plans and executes a building (see Figure 1). The idea that nature has its own autonomous, ordered realm and does not require divine intervention for its operations is a fundamental pre-

Figure 1. God as architect of the universe. Late thirteenth century, France. This image expresses the medieval view that God created the universe in an organized and intelligent manner, endowing it with an orderly, harmonious, and rational structure. It also reflects a common description of God as a divine Craftsman. *Vienna, Österreichische Nationalbibliothek, Ms. 2554, fol.I.*

requisite for the development of science as a discipline. Although some medieval theologians objected to the enthusiasm with which natural philosophers embraced science and took issue with scientists on particular points, overall the principle that reason could explain the workings of the physical universe remained one of the basic tenets of medieval thought.

In the twelfth and thirteenth centuries, medieval science was also shaped by two key events: the recovery of classical and Arabic science and philosophy, chiefly the work of Aristotle, Ptolemy, and Galen and the Arabic commentaries on these works, and the invention of the university. These elements provided the basis for continuing achievement in all fields of science. The works of Aristotle provided a comprehensive, working body of scientific principles and knowledge; the adoption of Aristotelianism as the standard curriculum for the study of natural philosophy in the universities ensured that large numbers of students and teachers were familiar with current scientific knowledge and that science had an institutional home. These events fused with the development of scholasticism, a distinctive form of analysis which presents "pro" and "con" arguments on carefully defined questions. Scholasticism had its origins in the speculative atmosphere of the twelfth-century renaissance but soon became the basic method of intellectual argument in the universities of the twelfth and later centuries. Although scholasticism has sometimes been derided as trivializing and divorced from real-world realities, it also encouraged looking at questions from all possible sides and therefore promoted intellectual questioning. These developments made medieval science a vital and ever-evolving enterprise. At the same time, anonymous inventors and artisans both adapted old technologies, devices, and machines into more efficient and useful forms and produced new inventions. By the end of the Middle Ages, Europe had become the most technologically and scientifically advanced area of the world. In the remainder of this chapter we will follow the institutional and intellectual contexts of the development of medieval science in the crucial period from around the year 1000 to around 1300 in more detail.

REVIVAL IN THE TWELFTH CENTURY

Around the year 1000 c.e., medieval Europe entered a period of renewed security and prosperity. The attacks by Muslims, Vikings, and
Hungarians which had plagued Europe during the early Middle Ages
ceased and Europe began to go on the offensive, launching, for example,
the First Crusade in 1096. Accompanying this new sense of confidence
were the growth of cities and towns, the development of new commercial networks, the emergence of more organized governments, and a
renewed creativity and vigor in art and intellectual pursuits.

New technologies were a crucial part of this revitalization of medieval
culture. New agricultural techniques expanded the food supply, leading
to an increase of population and consequent urbanization (see Chapter
6). These economic and social developments fueled the revival of European society, including a remarkable intellectual revival often called
by historians the Renaissance of the Twelfth Century. Although we
should not overlook the continuities between the early Middle Ages and
the twelfth century, we should also recognize a new widening of intellectual horizons from the late eleventh century onward. Medieval writers
began to explore a great range of speculative ideas about the formation
of the cosmos, the fundamental elements of the physical world, and the
nature of the human organism. Underlying these efforts was a vision of
nature as a "harmonious, lawful, well-ordered, self-sufficient whole"
whose workings could be fruitfully explored by human reason.[3] During
the twelfth century, we also see a new interest in the human possibilities
of mastering nature and in making technology, now called "the mechanical arts," a recognized part of philosophy. If early medieval science
had depended almost entirely on the authority of past authors, by the
twelfth century medieval thinkers had begun to make original contributions to a scientific understanding of the world.

Especially important for the revival of scientific thought at this time
was the emergence of new educational institutions in towns and cities.
Cathedral schools (called this because they were usually attached to the
local cathedral) founded in the leading urban centers of Europe gradually
eclipsed the old monastic schools in the tenth and eleventh centuries.
The most important of these new schools were in France, in Paris, Laon,
Orleans, and Chartres, but there were also cathedral schools in cities in
Spain and Germany. These schools, which taught a great variety of

subjects ranging from grammar and literary studies to law and theology, attracted large numbers of students. In these schools we see the first evidence of new scientific thinking and speculation since the hey-day of the Roman Empire.

Although many students at the cathedral schools were more interested in ethics and "letters," by the beginning of the twelfth century some scholars had developed an intense, lively interest in the study of nature. These clerics celebrated the possibilities of human reason, even as they assumed that whatever they discovered would ultimately harmonize with Christian thought and belief. Adelard of Bath (c. 1080–1142), the author of a book on natural science and one on birds, for example, complained about his contemporaries, "these days you generally have the kind of listeners that demand no argument based on judgment, but trust only in the name of an ancient authority. For they do not understand that reason has been given to each single individual in order to discern between true and false with reason as the prime judge."[4] William of Conches (d. after 1154) more colorfully attacked those who condemned the pursuit of scientific knowledge: "Ignorant themselves of the forces of nature and wanting to have company in their ignorance, they don't want people to look into anything; they want us to believe like peasants and not to ask the reason behind things . . . but we say that the reason behind everything should be sought out. . . . If they learn that anyone is so inquiring, they shout out that he is a heretic, placing more reliance on their monkish garb than on their wisdom."[5] Most importantly, these thinkers articulated a vision of nature as harmonious, orderly, and designed for human use. Nature could not only be understood by men, it could also be used to benefit human life. Hugh of St. Victor (d. 1141), for example, promoted the idea that the different types of technology, which he named the "mechanical arts," like the arts and sciences, both demonstrated the brilliance of human reason and were part of the human task of salvation and the restoration of the lost Paradise of Adam and Eve.[6]

The twelfth century was also a period in which the tradition of learned religious women reached its greatest influence. Hildegard of Bingen (1098–1179), the celebrated abbess of Rupertsberg near Bingen, wrote highly original works on medicine, cosmology, and physics. Her insight into women's physiology was perhaps unique in the Middle Ages.[7] Heloise (1101–63), the student, lover, and wife of the philosopher Abelard, almost certainly contributed to the development of his thought. Although she is not known to have written on scientific subjects, it is perhaps significant that she named her son Astrolabe, the name of the state-of-the-art astronomical instrument of her time.

THE INSTITUTIONALIZATION OF MEDIEVAL SCIENCE

By the late twelfth century, the cathedral schools had begun to be replaced by universities. The university, a medieval invention, was the first educational institution in history to provide a required curriculum and a systematic program of study and examinations leading to the awarding of a recognized degree and professional licenses. During the same period, scientific thought in medieval Europe was slowly transformed by the rediscovery of Greek thought and science, especially the works of Aristotle. As we have seen, Arabic scholars had sought out Greek learning and science and had translated the major works of Aristotle and other Greek scientists into Arabic during the ninth century. They also had added their own ideas to those of Aristotle, sometimes challenging Aristotle, sometimes modifying his ideas. This great body of work had a profound effect on the development of medieval science. Texts by Aristotle and his Arabic commentators became the basis for the university curriculum and hence for the scientific thought of medieval Europe until the sixteenth and seventeenth centuries.

The process of rediscovery was initially rather haphazard. Medieval scholars traveled to Spain to acquire manuscripts about which they had heard but never been able to read, often hiring Jews to translate Arabic versions of ancient Greek texts into Latin. Others learned Arabic themselves. The most famous of these translators, Gerard of Cremona (c. 1114–87), single-handedly translated over seventy works, including the basic scientific works of Aristotle and Greek and Arabic astronomical, mathematical, and medical works. Sometimes works were translated from Arabic into Spanish or Hebrew, and only then into Latin, having previously been translated from Greek to Syrian to Arabic. It is not surprising that errors and shifts in meaning crept in. Awareness of these problems fueled a second wave of translations directly from the Greek beginning in the late twelfth century and continuing to the late thirteenth century. By about 1286, the bulk of this wave of translation had been completed, although medical works continued to be translated during the first half of the fourteenth century.

The medieval university provided the institutional and intellectual setting for the integration of the work of the translators into the larger framework of medieval culture. Aristotle was crucial in this development because he provided a model for investigating the natural world through both rational inquiry and empirical observation. Although much of his approach and conclusions were eventually to prove faulty, his work provided a comprehensive, plausible, and systematic explanation of the workings of virtually all aspects of the physical world. Aristotle was considered so authoritative in natural philosophy that he was referred to simply as "the Philosopher." Yet medieval scientists did not simply blindly follow his ideas and their respect did not prevent them from challenging aspects of Aristotle's thought. As we shall see in Chapter 4, for example, modifications to Aristotle's theory of motion put forth in the late Middle Ages were part of the background to the emergence of modern physics during the Scientific Revolution.

THE STRUCTURE OF THE UNIVERSITY

The name *university* is derived from the Latin term *universitas* (corporation or whole body), which meant any group of people with a common aim or function; a university was a group of masters (trained scholars) and students (apprentice scholars) formed to organize, disseminate, and expand the boundaries of knowledge. Such corporate organizations were common in the Middle Ages and they served to protect and organize the interests of their members. The guilds of merchants or craftsmen were one example of such a corporate identity; universities were another. Being a student or a master conferred certain rights and privileges, as well as status: in some contexts, scholars were considered a new order of nobility, along with the older feudal aristocracy of lords and vassals. Scholars spoke and wrote in a privileged language, Latin, and were also distinguished by being an all-male community; women were excluded by law from both the cathedral schools and the universities, although limited educational opportunities remained for a time for women within the confines of the nunnery. At least one medieval woman is known to have put on male clothing and pretended to be a man in order to get a university education. In the northern universities both students and masters were typically counted as clerics, a fact which explains the graduation robes still worn today.

The origins of individual universities are obscure. However, historians know that by the end of the twelfth century new associations based on learning had emerged in Paris and Oxford in France and England, respectively, and in Bologna and Padua in Italy. These first universities provided the models for virtually all later universities. The northern and southern universities differed in several ways. Paris and Oxford were governed by teachers in the liberal arts, most of whom were members of religious orders, and took the lead in the sciences, medicine, and mathematics during the thirteenth and fourteenth centuries. At Paris and Oxford, as well as the universities modeled after them, masters received support and time off from preaching and other religious duties in order to teach and pursue their own studies. Bologna and Padua, on the other hand, were run by the students and initially specialized in law and medicine, as well as the liberal arts. At these universities many of the masters were laymen and received a salary for teaching from the students as well as fees from their own practices in medicine and law. By the late Middle Ages from the late fourteenth through the sixteenth century, the northern universities had declined and the Italian universities had become the most important centers for scientific learning. By the end of the Middle Ages, there were over seventy universities in Europe and at least one in almost every major region.

The curriculum and teaching methods of the university had important effects on medieval ideas about the nature of science and scientific method. Knowledge was organized in a hierarchical fashion. Students pursuing a "bachelor of arts" degree followed a planned program covering first the seven liberal arts, then philosophy and natural philosophy (including metaphysics, physics, psychology, and biology), and finally moral philosophy (politics, economics, and ethics). This course of study was largely based on Aristotle and some other Greek texts, especially Ptolemy's *Almagest* and Euclid's *Elements of Geometry*, but gradually more contemporary textbooks were added. The emphasis on grammar, literature, and rhetoric was gradually reduced in importance over time but the study of logic continued in importance, as did that of mathematics and astronomy. Advanced degrees were offered in theology, medicine, and, in some universities, law. Medicine was especially important in the

Italian universities and had a strong practical as well as theoretical component.

Teaching depended heavily on the production of commentaries on authoritative works and disputations or debates on specific questions. This method, which came to be called scholasticism, grew out of twelfth-century attempts to organize knowledge and subject it to critical analysis. A typical discussion was initiated by the enunciation of a specific problem posed in yes or no format. A series of possible answers followed, in turn followed by a statement of the correct position, which was explained and developed in detail. Finally, there was a point-by-point refutation of the initial series of answers. This procedure allowed for a systematic exploration of the arguments both for and against the question being examined. You may recognize in this method the origins of modern ideas about the format of a balanced debate and some types of essay questions.

The development of scholasticism was intertwined with the foundation of two new preaching orders, the Order of Preachers founded by St. Dominic in 1216 and popularly known as Dominicans and the Order of Friar Minor, or Franciscans, founded by St. Francis of Assisi and given papal approval in 1208. The Franciscans and Dominicans gave priority to study and learning as prerequisites for effective preaching. Both became renowned for their learning and recruited many masters into their ranks. Many of the important scientists found in northern Europe during the High Middle Ages, including Albertus Magnus, Roger Bacon, and Robert Grosseteste, were either Franciscans or Dominicans.

The university curriculum and method of teaching produced students and scholars who were highly trained in the technical vocabulary of philosophical and scientific subjects and highly skilled in logic and the techniques of rational argument. As we shall discuss in more detail in the following section, this education encouraged an approach that was more theoretical than practical in its orientation and that depended on "book learning" more than firsthand observation or experimentation. This dependence on a priori reasoning, that is, reasoning which began with a premise assumed to be correct, perhaps hindered medieval scientists from making breakthroughs based on new observations of the natural world. However, university students and masters also learned skills and attitudes of mind which promoted careful, precise thinking and what one historian of science has called " 'the culture of poking around,' or the irrepressible urge to probe into many things."[8] These habits of mind had a lasting impact on the history of western science and western culture generally.

SCIENTIFIC METHOD

Like the ancient Greeks, medieval scientists conceived of science as an attempt to discover the changeless reality which lay behind sense perception and the seemingly chaotic and random changes which individual physical objects, both living and nonliving, underwent during their limited life spans on earth. In a very general sense, this remains the goal of science even today. Yet, unlike modern science, which aims to accumulate progressive knowledge to be manipulated for the benefit of mankind, medieval science, as we have seen, sought primarily to illustrate eternal truths. Medieval scientific method reflected this different understanding of the scientific enterprise, as well as different theoretical premises. Medieval scientists, for example, tended to describe natural phenomena in qualitative terms and often failed to make even simple measurements, in large part because of the overwhelming influence of Aristotle. Aristotle, unlike Plato, had ignored the potential of mathematics in understanding the natural world and, as we shall see in Chapter 3, instead emphasized the idea of inherent qualities (hot, cold, wet, dry) which determined natural processes. Although some important scientists in the fourteenth century began to pay more attention to measurement and the application of mathematics to physical processes, the full understanding that nature could be best understood through the discovery of mathematical laws was not achieved until the seventeenth century.

For the most part, medieval scientists also paid comparatively little attention to systematic empirical confirmation of scientific theories and demonstrated little awareness of the concept of controlled experimentation as a way of testing scientific ideas. In the words of Edward Grant, a noted historian of medieval science, "Medieval observations were not introduced for their own sake, namely, to learn more about the world, or to resolve arguments. They were intended rather to uphold an a priori view of the world, or to serve as an example or illustration."[9] Medieval astronomers, for example, observed comets but rejected the view that they were celestial objects because this conflicted with the assumption that the celestial realm was changeless and incorruptible. Like the ancient philosophers, medieval scientists were more concerned to explain *why* physical events happened according to underlying principles than to deduce through physical experiments *how* these events happened; instead, they often relied on "thought experiments," designed to test one logical supposition against another.

At the same time, medieval scientists did add substantially to the store of scientific knowledge available at the time and began to expand the boundaries of scientific methodology and ideas about the purpose of scientific activity. They raised myriad questions about the application of Aristotelian theory to particular issues, often refining previous answers or resolving inconsistencies. Medieval scientists made consistent efforts to observe the natural world in a precise and systematic way. Albertus Magnus, for example, discussed in the following section, reportedly made personal observations of the same eagle's nest over a period of six years while compiling information on native European birds.[10] Contemporary herbals contained hundreds of careful descriptions of local plants, their curative properties, and directions on finding and collecting them. Other natural philosophers recognized the potential and importance of mathematics, even if they failed to apply this insight in a systematic manner. In the thirteenth and early fourteenth centuries, scholars pioneered in the development of the application of mathematics to optics, especially the problem of refraction. At least one scientist, Theodoric of Freiberg (d. c. 1310), claimed to have performed experiments with prisms. In the fourteenth century, some scholars had begun to explore the notion of velocity, "impetus" (the force impressed on a moving object which caused its motion), and other questions in the field of dynamics and had attempted to formulate "a conceptual and a mathematical framework suitable for analyzing problems of motion."[11] During the twelfth and thirteenth centuries, also, many thinkers, including Hugh of St. Victor (d. 1140 or 1141), Roger Bacon (c. 1219–92), and Robert Kilwardby (d. 1279), came to include technology as an important aspect of human knowledge.

THE RELATIONSHIP OF SCIENCE AND RELIGION

Jacques Le Goff, a noted medievalist, once wrote, "nothing could become an object of conscious reflection in the Middle Ages except by way of religion."[12] In other words, medieval thinkers saw the world through religion-colored glasses and science was no exception to this rule. Science, like philosophy, was regarded as the handmaiden of theology, and ideas about science were ultimately inseparable from ideas about God. Yet this did not mean that science was shortchanged in the Middle Ages. Although some religious figures dismissed knowledge of the natural world as irrelevant to the Christian life, more often writers used religious values to justify the pursuit of scientific and technological knowledge. Even a writer such as St. Bonaventure (1221–74), a Franciscan who expressed profound distrust of philosophy as a dangerous distraction from faith, wrote a work in which he explained how knowledge of every art and science functioned for human welfare and manifested Divine Wisdom. On the whole, it is remarkable how *little* conflict there was between religion and science in the Middle Ages.

A brief look at some of the most important natural philosophers of the High Middle Ages will illustrate some of the ways in which science and religious values interacted. Robert Grosseteste (c. 1168–1253), a master at Oxford associated with the Franciscans, was influenced by both the new philosophy of Aristotle and Neoplatonic thought. Grosseteste developed the philosophical idea of knowledge as divine illumination from the Platonic and Augustinian traditions into a natural philosophy based on a theory of light as the fundamental element of creation; for Grosseteste, the mathematical and physical study of light was the key to understanding how nature worked. His student, Roger Bacon (1214–92), a Franciscan master at Oxford, argued that all knowledge, including natural science, had been given to man "by one God, to one world, for one purpose," that is, to aid faith. Among other things, Bacon was responsible for an innovative theory of optics. Bacon wrote several lengthy manifestos to the pope in which he pleaded for the implementation of a program of scientific projects to aid in the defense of Christendom against her enemies. Especially important, Bacon argued, was the study of mathematics and "experimental science," which would yield new weapons and mechanical devices including mirrors to focus the rays of the sun on enemy armies, explosives, medicines which would marvelously prolong life, cars that would move with great rapidity without the aid of animals, and flying machines. Although Bacon ultimately subordinated science to religion (one of his sources for scientific knowledge was revelation from God), he articulated a vision of scientific progress which looks remarkably modern.

Albertus Magnus and his student Thomas Aquinas took a different route. Albertus (c. 1200–1280), a Dominican, studied at Padua and the University of Paris, as well as at a Dominican school in Cologne. A master of theology, Albertus also was thoroughly learned in the works of Aristotle and wrote commentaries on virtually all of Aristotle's works, often including the results of his own scientific work based on his own observations. Albertus consistently asserted that in the study of nature one should investigate according to the "inherent powers of nature," not according to what God could, or might, do. His detailed and original descriptions of many stones, gems, the parts of plants, agricultural methods, and many animals native to northern Europe made him "perhaps the best field botanist of the entire Middle Ages."[13] His work was systematic and exact; for example, he made detailed comparative studies of the parts of plants and, like Aristotle, opened hens' eggs at various intervals to observe the developing embryo. Albertus also included accurate and precise accounts of such contemporary technologies as iron-smelting, the building of drainage ditches, and cross-plowing to avoid erosion.

Aquinas (c. 1224–74), also a Dominican, taught theology at Paris and wrote extensively on theological questions. Like Albertus, he was committed to integrating Aristotle into a Christian framework. Although his interests were less specifically focused on science than were those of Albertus, Aquinas was an effective spokesperson for the independent value of human reason, which, although it could not attain to divine mysteries, was a truthful guide to the material world.

Albertus and Aquinas, who were trained theologians, separated the practice of science from that of theology, even as they assumed that these two avenues to truth would be ultimately compatible. Other medieval scholars also sometimes put on different "hats" for different subjects, speaking primarily from a naturalistic or moralistic perspective depending upon circumstances. For example, writers discussing medical concerns might recommend sexual activity as an aid to health, even if in other contexts they upheld the Church's disapproval of sexual pleasure. Similarly, clerics trained in universities sometimes privately pursued the sciences of alchemy and astrology, despite official Church disapproval of these subjects.

Conflicts between science and religion, however, did arise in the High Middle Ages. Certain points of the Aristotelian world-system were in direct conflict with Christianity. The Aristotelian world-system asserted the eternity of the world, which conflicted with the account of creation by God in Genesis. The Aristotelian world-system also denied the mortality of the individual human soul, which contradicted the Christian promise of personal salvation and resurrection. Another potential source of difficulty was the strain of determinism in some Arabic science and philosophy which seemed to deny free will not only to human beings but also to God. These thinkers, especially Ibn Rushd, known in the West as Averroës, argued that God Himself would be constrained by natural laws, thus denying the possibility of miracles. Some Arabic writers also seemed to be arguing that human beings were so strongly influenced by the power of the stars and heavenly bodies that the existence of free will was called into question. Most European thinkers attempted to keep a balance between the claims of science and religion. They accepted Aristotle as an authority on scientific subjects while being careful to state that where Aristotle conflicted with Christian faith, the dictates of faith should be followed. However, a few thinkers, known as the Latin Averroists, were thought to follow reason to the exclusion of Christian faith and to advocate a doctrine of "double truth," that is, that something could be true according to philosophy even if not true according to faith. The tensions between the supporters and critics of the new science led to the condemnation by the bishop of Paris in 1270 and again in 1277 of a long list of propositions supposedly held by philosophers, including the eternity of the world, the mortality of the soul, the denial of God's ability to intervene in natural processes, and the influence of the heavenly bodies on the human will and everyday events. Also condemned was the idea "that there was no first man," a denial of God's creation of Adam and Eve as described in Genesis, and "that raptures and visions are caused only by nature," a denial of mystical visions sent by God.

Historians have debated the effects of the Condemnations of 1277 on the practice of science in the late Middle Ages. Most historians agree that the condemnations had some broad effects on the intellectual climate in Europe but did little to displace Aristotelianism as the basis for scientific thought. The major effect seems to have been to end the efforts of the scholastics to forge a comprehensive synthesis of Aristotelian and

Christian thought and instead to encourage the development of philosophy and science as autonomous, limited areas of knowledge distinct from theology. Some historians of science have argued that the condemnations actually furthered the cause of science because they encouraged criticism and refinement of certain aspects of Aristotelian natural philosophy. Others have pointed to a new interest in God's absolute and omnipotent power in the following centuries. The condemnations applied only to the University of Paris, although they certainly had some influence elsewhere. Although historians know little about the immediate implementation of the condemnations, we do have evidence that earlier attempts to ban the reading of Aristotle's books on natural philosophy at Paris in 1210 and 1255 had been largely ignored. In 1325 the Condemnations were partially annulled and by 1341 we have direct evidence that the natural books of Aristotle and his commentators, including Averroës, were required reading at the University of Paris and elsewhere, to be taught "except in those cases that are contrary to the faith."

THE PRACTICE OF SCIENCE OUTSIDE THE UNIVERSITIES

The university was not the only setting for the practice of science in the Middle Ages. During the early Middle Ages, as we have seen, both monasteries and royal courts were sites for the practice of sciences with a utilitarian value, especially practical astronomy and medicine and related areas such as botany and pharmacology. Although the university far surpassed these venues in the production of theoretical science, more practically oriented scientific activity continued to take place in monastic, civic, and court settings. In addition, some sciences, especially astrology and alchemy, were largely rejected by the university community but were enthusiastically pursued by both some university-trained scientists and many unknown individuals whose names have not come down to us.

The variety in types of training and settings for practice was probably greatest in medicine. Physicians might be licensed by public political authorities, craft guilds, university faculties, or even individual rulers and might practice in urban hospitals, private homes, courts, and a variety of other settings. Many "empirics," whose training was informal and largely based on word of mouth and trial by error, were not licensed at all. In northern Europe, many physicians were members of the clergy, although in Italy most were laymen. Surgeons, or barbers, were almost always members of the laity. Women also practiced medicine. A few, for example, Trotula of Salerno and Hildegard of Bingen, wrote learned treatises. Midwives formed a sizable group of women healers who had some degree of professional training and status. According to Nancy Siraisi, about 1.5 percent of the names of physicians known to us from northern Europe were women.[14] Many more practiced anonymously, probably intermittently, and left no trace in the written records. A significant proportion of both learned and empiric physicians were Jewish, especially in southern France, Italy, and Spain. A licensed Jewish woman physician is known to have attended the queen of Aragon for four months in 1381, and other records indicate that women practiced as physicians in fourteenth-century Paris.[15] Most physicians, even university professors, practiced privately and were hired by royal courts, noble households, town governments, or even individuals from more modest backgrounds. In rural communities, the most accessible health care was probably from the village empiric or *vetula* (old woman) who specialized in the use of local plants and herbs. Religious and academic methods of healing were frequently combined and the line between religious and academic methods and "magic" was often a fine one. For ordinary people, a visit to a "healer" might typically involve a combination of prayer, touch, herbal remedies, and charms, and even learned physicians resorted on occasion to magical remedies.

Alchemy and astrology were two sciences that for a variety of religious and philosophical reasons were largely rejected by the university establishment but flourished in other venues. Many royal and noble courts, for example, maintained not only a corps of physicians to attend the royal family, but also a number of astrologers and alchemists. Some physicians and other university-trained natural philosophers also pursued astrology and alchemy as part of their own scientific interests; medical astrology, which attempted to connect the movements of heavenly bodies with the outbreak and course of diseases, for example, was an important aspect of medical practice.

Alchemy was the theory and practice of changing base metals into gold or other precious metals and closely allied in its methods to chemistry and pharmacology; astrology was the science that analyzed the physical effects of the heavenly bodies on the earth and, secondarily, was concerned with the casting of horoscopes and the like. Although both alchemy and astrology are considered to be irrational and super-stitious by twentieth- and twenty-first-century scientists, in the Middle Ages there were sound philosophical and scientific reasons for accepting both as genuine sciences. Both originated in antiquity and their prac-titioners could point to a long and illustrious pedigree of masters of the art. Moreover, the principles of each were consistent with Aristotelian science as understood in the Middle Ages. Finally, both offered the possibility that the natural world and scientific knowledge might be put to practical use to benefit humankind.

Alchemy was first developed in the ancient world, was adopted by the Arabs, and hence passed to Europe. Many of the alchemical treatises known to us are anonymous or falsely attributed to well-known figures. Some alchemical writing was intentionally obscure and even written in code in order that alchemical knowledge would not fall into the "wrong" hands. Other works are fairly straightforward guides to the proper tools, chemicals, and procedures to be used in the purification of various sub-stances. Because alchemy emphasized the ability of humans to manip-ulate natural materials, it helped establish the idea that "art" or technology could provide results that went beyond the products of unaided nature. Many doctors were also alchemists, for the production of substances to prolong life, cure illnesses, and produce antidotes to poisons seems to have an important adjunct to alchemical practice. If we believe many of the accounts circulating in the Middle Ages, many clerics also took up alchemy. Along with records of serious practitioners, there were numerous stories of quacks and charlatans; in Chaucer's *Can-terbury Tales*, for example, alchemists are represented as foul-smelling con men who use sleight-of-hand tricks to fool gullible individuals.

As in the case of alchemy, astrology ran the gamut from a serious science, closely tied to astronomy, to an activity pursued mainly for its entertainment or money-making value. Astrology as a science attempted to explain how heavenly bodies exerted physical effects on earthly bod-ies. It was also thought to yield important information on the proper timing for important events, including marriages, coronations, and even, occasionally, battles. Many physicians regarded astrology as a valuable adjunct to medicine as it helped determine the timing of crises in the progress of a disease, overall conditions affecting health, and an individual's personal health risks. Astrologers therefore were a frequent presence at court, although it is difficult to always tell how seriously their predictions were taken.

THE LATE MIDDLE AGES

The continued development of scientific thinking in the late Middle Ages is more difficult to characterize than for earlier periods. The different strands in late medieval scientific thought went in many different directions and it is difficult to discern the connections among them. In addition, much of the research done on this period has been directed toward looking for connections between late medieval science and the genesis of the Scientific Revolution of the sixteenth and seventeenth centuries. While interesting and important, this emphasis has perhaps made it more difficult to see late medieval science as a whole in its own right.

One important development was a new, more mathematical approach to the study of motion. Scholars first at Merton College at Oxford University and later at the University of Paris in the fourteenth century attempted to formulate ways to quantify both motion at a constant velocity and accelerated motion. They later applied these same methods to other forms of change, including increasing intensities of heat and even changing degrees of love. Nicholas Oresme succeeded in representing velocity geometrically, using a method which has been called "a forerunner of modern graphing techniques."[16] Oresme proved what is still known as the "Merton rule" or "mean-speed theorem." This mathematical law shows that an accelerating body y travels the same distance in the same period of time as a body x moving at a constant velocity equal to the *average* speed of the accelerating body. Another mathematician in this group, John Buridan (c. 1295–c. 1358), developed a new theory of why bodies once set in motion continued to move; he supposed a natural quality of "impetus" which caused movement and depended in part upon the quantity of matter in the moving object. Oresme and Buridan also speculated about the movements of the heavenly bodies as well, both suggesting that the earth might rotate on its axis in contradiction of the long-held belief that the earth was at rest at the center of the universe.

Another center of scientific innovation in the late Middle Ages was the University of Padua in Italy in the fifteenth century. By this time, scholars at the established universities in England and France seem to have lapsed into a conservative, tradition-bound form of Aristotelianism which became famous for its triviality, sterility, and hair-splitting; when scientists such as Copernicus and Galileo articulated the new ideas of the Scientific Revolution in the sixteenth century, academic Aristotelians were among their most vocal and hostile critics. At Padua, however, a new scientific method developed which may have influenced Galileo himself when he taught at Padua in the 1590s. Scientists at Padua began to go beyond the simple observation of nature characteristic of most of previous medieval science and develop a genuine experimental method. They argued that science should proceed by a rigorous analysis of the problem of causation and that the scientist should move from specific observations to general principles (induction) and then back to an ordered body of facts (deduction). This method remains one of the backbones of today's science.

Finally, we should note that technological development continued to accelerate in the late Middle Ages (see Chapter 6). Eyeglasses, the chimney, the mechanical clock, cannon, the handgun, and moveable type (which led to printing) were among the important inventions that appeared in this period. Improvements were also made in older devices such as windmills and watermills. During the fifteenth century, medieval scientists took an increasing interest in the practical knowledge of craftsmen and craftswomen. One especially fruitful area of interchange was between medicine, alchemy, and astrology. All three of these disciplines attempted to combine theoretical knowledge with practical results. The practice of architecture, which combined theoretical training with construction techniques requiring complex machinery, also contributed to a new interchange between theory and practice. During the late Middle Ages a number of physicians also interested in astrology and alchemy explored the possibilities of new mechanical devices, including astronomical instruments, clockwork, and war machines. A closer relationship between theoretical scientific knowledge and technology was one of the hallmarks of the Scientific Revolution of the sixteenth and seventeenth centuries; the roots of this important development, however, lie in the late Middle Ages.

NOTES

1. M.-D. Chenu, *Nature, Man, and Society in the Twelfth Century: Essays in New Theological Perspectives in the Latin West*, ed. and trans. Jerome Taylor and Lester K. Little (Chicago: University of Chicago Press, 1968), p. 5.

2. Edward Grant, *God and Reason in the Middle Ages* (Cambridge, England: Cambridge University Press, 2001), pp. 268, 358; Caroline Walker Bynum, *Fragmentation and Redemption: Essays on Gender and the Human Body in Medieval Religion* (New York: Zone Books, 1992), p. 242.

3. Edward Grant, *The Foundations of Modern Science in the Middle Ages: Their Religious, Institutional, and Intellectual Contexts* (Cambridge, England: Cambridge University Press, 1996), p. 21.

4. Adelard of Bath, *Conversations with His Nephew*: On the Same and the Different, Questions on Natural Science and On Birds, ed. and trans. Charles Burnett with the collaboration of Italo Ronca, Pedro Mantas España and Baudouin van den Abeele (Cambridge, England: Cambridge University Press, 1998), p. 103.

5. Quoted in Chenu, *Nature, Man, and Society*, p. 11.

6. Hugh of St. Victor, *The* Didascalicon *of Hugh of St. Victor: A Medieval Guide to the Arts*, trans. Jerome Taylor (New York: Columbia University Press, 1961), pp. 55–56.

7. Hildegard of Bingen, *On Natural Philosophy and Medicine: Selections from the* Cause et cure, trans. Margret Berger (Cambridge, England: D. S. Brewer, 1999).

8. Grant, *God and Reason*, p. 356.

9. Grant, *God and Reason*, p. 179.

10. David C. Lindberg, *The Beginnings of Western Science: The European Scientific Tradition in Philosophical, Religious, and Institutional Context, 600 B.C. to A.D. 1450* (Chicago and London: University of Chicago Press, 1992), p. 230.

11. Lindberg, *Beginnings*, p. 307.

12. Jacques Le Goff, *Time, Work and Culture in the Middle Ages*, trans. Arthur Goldhammer (Chicago: University of Chicago Press, 1980), p. 109.

13. Lindberg, *Beginnings*, p. 230.

14. Nancy G. Siraisi, *Medieval and Early Renaissance Medicine: An Introduction to Knowledge and Practice* (Chicago and London: University of Chicago Press, 1990), p. 27.

15. Siraisi, *Medicine*, p. 31.

16. Lindberg, *Beginnings*, p. 298.

CHAPTER 3

ARISTOTLE, PLATO, AND THE MEDIEVAL SCIENTIFIC WORLDVIEW

While many achievements of medieval science and technology will be easily accessible to the contemporary student, some aspects of the medieval scientific world view are quite foreign. In this chapter we will examine some of the assumptions underlying medieval scientific thinking in order to better understand the conclusions medieval scientists came to when they considered specific kinds of scientific problems. The differences between medieval and modern ways of thinking about the natural world come through most dramatically in the consideration of such fundamental problems as why objects moved, the structure of the universe, and the nature of physical reality. This chapter will explore some of these basic questions to encourage an "insider's view" of medieval science in which we can begin to share the outlook and perspective of a medieval scientist.

First a note about terminology. *Natural philosophy* in this context refers to study of the natural world. Ancient and modern writers used the term *natural philosophy* to refer to the same activities we today would call "natural science."[1] A near synonym was physics. Whereas in modern science, the English term *physics* refers only to the science of the interaction of matter and energy, articulated in predominately mathematical terms, in the Middle Ages, the Latin *physica*, derived from the Greek *physis*, meant, simply, "natural science." In the Middle Ages, therefore, *physics* meant broadly an account of the fundamental principles that governed change in nature.

THE PLATONIC AND NEOPLATONIC TRADITIONS

Medieval philosophy was profoundly shaped by the intellectual traditions inherited from antiquity, especially the two systems of thought that originated with the Greek philosophers Plato and Aristotle. Historical circumstances in large part determined the relative importance of Aristotelianism and Platonism at different times during the Middle Ages. During the early Middle Ages, little was known directly of the works of either Aristotle or Plato. Boethius (480–525), who had planned to translate all of the works of Plato and Aristotle from Greek into Latin, died shortly after he began his grand project and was able to complete translations only of three of Aristotle's works on logic. Consequently, Aristotle had almost no impact on natural philosophy in the early Middle Ages. Of Plato's works, only a partial translation by Chalcidius of the *Timaeus*, Plato's account of the creation of the universe, was available. However, Neoplatonism ("new Platonism"), a revived and spiritualized form of Platonism which had flourished in the third century c.e., had been absorbed into the Roman and Christian tradition through the Church Fathers and other writers whose works were widely read. Chief among these was the great theologian Augustine (354–430), who brought to medieval European culture a religious and philosophical outlook which incorporated some of the basic ideas of Plotinus (205–70), a major architect of Neoplatonic thought. Another Neoplatonic thinker, Proclus (411–85), also had an influence on the West, although his writings were not known directly. Boethius also passed on a combination of Platonic and Aristotelian philosophical ideas. Another source in the early Middle Ages was Dionysius the Areopagite, a sixth-century writer believed to have been an apostle converted by Paul.

From the mid-eleventh century onward, European scholars began to expand their intellectual horizons by searching out the new Arabic learning and looking at long-available texts in new ways. Initially, one effect of this reawakening of intellectual curiosity was to stimulate a scientific interest in cosmology and the nature of creation based on Plato's *Timaeus*. The *Timaeus* described creation as the work of a Demiurge who shaped the physical world and the things in it as a craftsman shapes his materials into a finished work of art. This analogy harmonized well with the Judeo-Christian account in Genesis and the *Timaeus* remained the most important guide to cosmology until it was replaced by

Aristotle's *De caelo* (On the Heavens) in the thirteenth century. Some twelfth-century writers associated with the cathedral school of Chartres, including Thierry of Chartres (c. 1100–c. 1156) and William of Conches (1080–1160), used the *Timaeus* to explore how natural processes operated independently from divine intervention after God's initial creation. Others, such as Bernard Silvester, borrowed elements from the *Timaeus* to create an allegory of man's attempts to understand Nature, personified as the Goddess Natura, and the natural order.[2]

Platonic influences also reached Europe at this time through the writings of Arabic scientists and philosophers. Neoplatonism had continued to be an important influence on Arabic and Byzantine thought since the sixth and seventh centuries. Some of these writers tried to synthesize Platonic and Aristotelian philosophy, in part because some treatises by Plotinus and Proclus were mistakenly attributed to Aristotle. During the twelfth century, works by Arabic thinkers influenced by Plato and Neoplatonism were translated from Arabic, and some of the original works of the Neoplatonists, including commentaries on the *Timaeus*, were translated from Greek into Latin. During the thirteenth century, with the translation of the full body of Aristotle's scientific works from the original Greek, Aristotle's influence virtually overwhelmed that of Plato. Nevertheless, elements of Platonic and Neoplatonic thought continued to influence medieval understandings of the natural world and the nature of scientific inquiry. These influences emerged most clearly in thinkers who saw themselves as followers of Augustine, whose thought had been profoundly affected by Neoplatonism. While some of these writers emphasized elements within Augustine's thought that were hostile or ambivalent to the pursuit of science, others, for example, Robert Grosseteste (c. 1168–1253) and Roger Bacon (c. 1219–92), used aspects of Platonic and Neoplatonic thought to promote scientific inquiry as part of the spiritual quest for salvation. In summary, although Aristotelianism was the dominant influence on the sciences after around 1150, ideas derived from Platonism and Neoplatonism were important during the early Middle Ages into the twelfth century and had a continuing, if secondary, impact through the late Middle Ages.

The history of the reception of Plato's ideas in medieval Europe is exceedingly complex. Unlike the ideas of Aristotle, whose natural philosophy was comprehensive and internally consistent, and whose entire body of work on natural philosophy became available in medieval Europe over a relatively short period of time, Platonism reached European thinkers in a piecemeal fashion, often filtered through intermediaries who developed Plato's original ideas in different, even contradictory, directions. In addition to the *Timaeus*, there were the "Platonisms" of Augustine, of Dionysius the Areopagite, of the Neoplatonic writers of late antiquity, and of a number of important Arabic philosophers. The writings of each of these thinkers were in turn interpreted in diverse ways by individual medieval philosophers. Despite fundamental differences between the Platonic and Aristotelian approaches to the study of nature, moreover, many medieval thinkers attempted to combine elements from both systems, with complex and often inconsistent results. Not until the sixteenth century was the full body of Plato's dialogues known in the European West and an effort made to isolate Plato's original thought from the welter of additions, distortions, and interpretations made over the course of centuries.

The definitive history of how ideas and attitudes ultimately derived from Plato and the Neoplatonists affected medieval science has yet to be written. Rather than try to trace the tangled lines of the influence of specific ideas here, we will focus on a brief and admittedly incomplete account of the main themes associated with Plato and Neoplatonism and their relevance to scientific ideas before discussing Aristotle's natural philosophy.

Platonism and Aristotelianism shared many fundamental premises, but also differed markedly in several respects. These distinctions meant that natural philosophers influenced predominately by Platonism took a fundamentally different approach to natural philosophy than did those influenced predominately by Aristotelianism. In brief, Aristotelianism defined the study of the natural world as an autonomous discipline, important in and of itself, whereas Platonism and Neoplatonism regarded natural philosophy as valuable primarily as a stepping stone to the higher knowledge of metaphysics and an intellectual and emotional awareness of the power and creativity of the divine principle. In addition, the two systems of thought assessed the reliability of knowledge gained through the senses differently: Aristotelianism accepted sense perception as the necessary beginning of all knowledge, while Platonism emphasized that sense perception provided only erroneous, confused, and highly misleading impressions. Finally, Aristotle thought that four basic qualities (hotness, cold, dryness, wetness) defined the differences among substances, while Plato thought that these differences were best understood in terms of differing geometrical structures. Therefore, while Aristotle rejected mathematics as a useful scientific tool, Plato and those influenced by him thought mathematics an important method for training the mind and understanding the natural world.

Plato, unlike Aristotle, was not himself a natural philosopher. He had little interest in the concrete details of how the natural world worked, preferring to address larger issues, such as the ultimate nature of reality, the immortality of the soul, and the nature of human justice. Plato identified reality with permanence, universality, and changelessness. In much the same way as we can recognize that a circle drawn in chalk on a blackboard is an imperfect, particular copy of the universalized concept of a circle we hold in our minds, Plato regarded individual material objects as imperfect, distorted copies of the eternal, perfect immaterial idea or "form" of these objects existing in a higher realm of pure thought. In his famous "Allegory of the Cave," Plato compared our ordinary experience of physical reality with the delusions of people who have, for their whole lives, been allowed only to look at shadows; knowing nothing else, the prisoners take the shadowy images of objects for the objects themselves and dismiss reports of a higher reality as madness.[3] The physical world, which appeared to be in a constant state of flux, confusion, and change, could therefore never be truly known by the mind, and its study, according to Plato, was at best a "likely story."

Despite his orientation toward the spiritual and transcendent, Plato did contribute directly to medieval science. In the *Timaeus*, Plato described the formation of the heavenly bodies, the four elements of earth, water, air, and fire, plants and animals, and finally humans out of primordial, shapeless matter or "stuff." (His detailed account of the human body and the relationship between the body and the soul, however, was omitted in Chalcidius' translation.) Although the structure of the *Timaeus* is that of an inspiring story or myth and its content presented as at most "likely" and "probable,"[4] rather than as scientifically accurate, the work encapsulates several ideas that would have an important influence on western science in later centuries.

First, Plato describes the universe as "in very truth a living creature with soul and reason."[5] Perfect in all respects, the universe is a spherical animal, infused with intelligence and harmony, and possessed of a "world soul" or *anima mundi*. The notion of the universe as a living animal and of matter as shaped, rather than as created, by God ran counter to Christian theology, which insisted that God had created the world out of nothing (*ex nihilo*). Nevertheless, echoes of Plato's conception persisted, usually given a Christian gloss. The world soul, for example, was interpreted by some as "Nature," the source of the continued vitality of living things. Others identified the world soul with the principle of movement seemingly inherent in the planets, sun, and moon. Although almost all medieval natural philosophers ultimately denied that the celestial bodies were alive in any ordinary sense, many attributed the movements of the heavenly bodies to an associated living intelligence, sometimes referred to as an "angel."

Second, Plato passed on the idea of man as a microcosm of the universe, or macrocosm from earlier Greek thinkers. The notion of the makeup of the human body and mind as corresponding to the larger structure of the universe was influential in both the Middle Ages and the Renaissance. It contributed to the development of theories of both how man might be affected by universal forces (the medieval science of astrology) and how man might harness these forces for his own benefit (alchemy and natural magic). These ideas, in turn, supported the view that the purpose of science was not only to understand nature, but also to use nature to improve human life.

Third, Plato describes matter, despite its defective nature, as ultimately reducible to number and the creator as incorporating harmony and proportion into the structure of the universe. Building on the earlier ideas of the Pre-Socratic philosophers, Plato postulates that the four elements of water, fire, air, and earth can each be identified with four of the five regular solids (cube, tetrahedron, octahedron, icosahedron, dodecahedron), themselves reducible to right scalene and isoceles triangles.[6] Thus, according to Plato, a fundamental geometric order underlay the physical structure of the universe. This notion of a natural order grounded in mathematics remained a powerful force underlying scientific investigation throughout the Middle Ages, reaching its full development during the Renaissance and the Scientific Revolution.

Some Neoplatonists developed Plato's ideas into a systematic vision of the universe as exhibiting a continuum from the most spiritual to the most material. Like Plato, the founders of Neoplatonism were primarily metaphysicians; that is, they were interested first and foremost in the theoretical study of the nature of being. Their distinct contribution to the development of scientific ideas was to postulate that all parts of the universe partook of varying degrees of reality (identified with pure Mind) and that natural philosophy should attempt to bridge the apparent gap between the immaterial world of spirit and the material world of physical objects. This idea accentuated the emphasis on the action of unseen and immaterial powers already implicit in the *Timaeus*. While this perspective seems more mystical and religious than scientific in the light of the mechanistic philosophy of modern science, it did allow the Neoplatonists and those influenced by them to investigate the possible ways in which immaterial forces could impact physical objects in a way that Aristotelianism could not. If on the one hand this perspective leads to an intellectual justification for magic, on the other hand it provides a framework for ideas postulating that invisible but real forces might explain the movements of the heavenly bodies and the effects of these bodies on objects on earth.

Plotinus, one of the most influential Neoplatonists, envisioned a universe in which all being emanates or radiates from God (called by Plotinus "The One") in a manner analogous to the way a candle radiates light. According to Plotinus, all beings exist in a hierarchy ranging from the most spiritual (Intelligence and the world soul) through intermediary beings (which Plotinus called "daimons" and were Christianized as angels and demons) through man to the least spiritual, including the lower animals, plants, and virtually mindless beings such as rocks. Man, because he was made up of both body and soul, marked the dividing line between spiritual beings and those who were predominately made up of matter. This hierarchy, which later came to be called the Great Chain of Being, rested on the principles of plenitude (that God would create every possible form of being), continuity (that there were no gaps between created beings), and gradation (that these beings were arranged on a hierarchical scale on which some beings were "higher" than others).[7]

Together with the notions of man as microcosm and the world soul, the Great Chain of Being had a lasting effect on scientific thinking in the West. These ideas, for example, formed the basis of the medieval science of astrology, according to which the planets exerted identifiable physical effects on the weather, plants, and animals and on the human body. Medieval natural philosophers such as Roger Bacon thought rigorously about how to explain the mechanisms which enabled the stars to affect conditions on earth. Although the premises of medieval astrology were later shown to be false, Bacon and others undertook to explore this question in a genuinely rational and scientific manner. Such speculation encouraged investigation into the nature of matter and the interaction between seemingly immaterial forces and physical bodies, questions which would become an important part of the modern scientific worldview. Other natural philosophers developed the idea of light as a vital, creative force in shaping and creating the universe. Robert Grosseteste, for example, described light as the "corporeal form" of all material things and used the propagation of light through a medium as a model for other types of natural causes, including the action of heat, the effects of the stars, and mechanical forces.

Correspondences between the human body and the heavenly bodies were also an important part of medieval medicine. The stars affected the course of disease, the potency of herbal remedies, and the likelihood of epidemics. Some late medieval natural philosophers also used a combination of medical theory and the idea of vital spirits residing in animal and human bodies to explain psychological phenomena such as mystical or demonic visions and insanity. These efforts represent an attempt to explain unusual mental states and disorders of the imagination in terms of natural processes, rather than simply attributing them to the intervention of supernatural beings.

Neoplatonism also provided a philosophical basis for the practice of sympathetic and natural magic. A properly trained individual was thought to be able to manipulate the occult (hidden) powers of natural objects, linked together by unseen influences, for his own ends. Like the engineer or alchemist, the magician attempted to control the physical world for his and others' benefit. Despite the hostility of the Church, which violently condemned the calling up of demons as part of magical practice, many medieval natural philosophers made a distinction between demonic magic, which depended on the actions of demons, and natural magic, which depended on unusual or hidden natural causes. The idea of the learned magician who investigated the secrets of nature for practical purposes became especially influential in the sixteenth century with the recovery of additional Neoplatonic texts from antiquity. Some historians of science, pointing to the continued acceptance of alchemy, natural magic, and Neoplatonic conceptions of hidden influences and correspondences by important sixteenth- and seventeenth-century scientists, including Isaac Newton and Johannes Kepler, have argued that these ideas were an important catalyst for the Scientific Revolution.

Between 1200 and 1500, Aristotle's influence largely eclipsed that of Plato and Neoplatonist thought. Even writers who accepted aspects of Neoplatonism incorporated these ideas into an Aristotelian framework. Platonic and Neoplatonic thought would again become important in western science and philosophy beginning in the late fifteenth century. In the thirteenth and fourteenth centuries, however, when medieval natural philosophy reached its fullest development, Aristotle's authority was paramount. We will consider Aristotle in considerable detail because we cannot begin to understand medieval science without a grounding in his ideas.

ARISTOTELIAN NATURAL PHILOSOPHY

Aristotle's influence became paramount in the twelfth and thirteenth centuries when his writings on natural philosophy were translated into Latin, first from Arabic versions and later from the Greek originals. His works on the sciences, which included the *Physics*, *De caelo* (On the Heavens), *Meteorology*, *De generatione et corruptione* (On Generation and Corruption), among others, as well as Arabic works which incorporated Aristotelian natural philosophy, became the basis for the university curriculum in the thirteenth century. So great was Aristotle's influence that by the thirteenth century he was referred to simply as "The Philosopher."

Although medieval scientists refined, modified, and challenged Aristotelian ideas on many fronts over the course of the Middle Ages, western science did not break completely free of an Aristotelian framework in the areas of astronomy and dynamics until the seventeenth century, in biology until the eighteenth century. In part this was because Aristotle provided a comprehensive, understandable, and plausible account of how the natural world operated; in part it was because of the great authority with which Aristotle's ideas were invested. Despite numerous instances in which medieval scientists pushed Aristotle's ideas far beyond what Aristotle himself would have argued or reinterpreted Aristotle's statements in order to make them consistent with their own conclusions, they rarely directly questioned the ultimate validity of his ideas.

Aristotle's scientific ideas are complex and generally unfamiliar to modern students; because they are so important in understanding medieval scientific thought, we will spend some time explaining them. Let us begin with a broad contrast between the modern scientific and the Aristotelian and Platonic worldviews. Modern science has its origins in the Scientific Revolution of the sixteenth and seventeenth centuries which overthrew earlier scientific ideas, first in astronomy and mechanics, later in chemistry, and ultimately in biology. The new science was based on very different conceptions about the nature of physical reality than was the science of the ancient world and the Middle Ages. Although the transition from a medieval to a modern outlook on the content, nature, and purpose of science was an extremely complex and drawn-out process—and one still hotly debated by historians—we can outline certain basic differences between the old and the new scientific worldview as it emerged in the eighteenth century.

One important element of modern science was a new concept of nature and a new scientific method. According to this new method, nature was best understood not through simple observation but through mathematical analysis of data derived from controlled experiments. Galileo, for example, devised experiments to measure more exactly the motion of falling bodies by rolling balls down an inclined plane.[8] The new science also posited a world of atomic particles whose motions are governed by universal mathematical laws. This underlying reality is inaccessible to direct human experience, although it is recoverable through experiment and the use of scientific instruments. Underlying this new conception of nature was the idea that nature was best described as a machine in which change was governed by "the chance motions of material particles."[9] According to the seventeenth-century philosopher Descartes, for example, not only were animals merely sophisticated machines but even human emotions were produced by the mechanical workings of the human body.[10] This "mechanization of nature" had far-reaching implications, many of them fully realized only in the twentieth century. Among them are skepticism about the role of God in the universe, a distrust of common human experience as a key to "reality," an increasing willingness to use the natural world for human ends, and an undermining of the notions of free will and human self-determination.

A second major characteristic of modern science was that it effectively divorced the study of scientific problems from broader philosophical and theological ideas. According to H. Floris Cohen, author of a major study on the Scientific Revolution, "the new science claimed to provide an understanding of reality that did not owe its warrant to whether or not it filled in with an all-encompassing insight into the order of the world but only to the extent to which it satisfied inherent criteria of a methodical nature; quantitative precision and, above all, susceptibility to empirical checking on the level of detail."[11] This did not mean that science as such no longer implied a certain metaphysical outlook, but it did mean that scientists could define specific scientific problems for investigation without necessarily considering how the answer might fit into a total philosophical and religious worldview. As Galileo, the great seventeenth-century astronomer and scientist, memorably said, "Astronomy tells you how the heavens go, not how to go to heaven."

A third important characteristic of the new science was its provisional and dynamic character. Scientific ideas came to be framed in terms of hypotheses, to be tested and revised as necessary by new empirical data and new scientific ideas. No longer thought of as linked to absolute truths, specific scientific findings could be refined and even discarded without challenging the overall purpose of the scientific enterprise.

In contrast, Aristotelian science, and the medieval scientific worldview built on Aristotelian foundations, was in many ways inseparable from human experience and ideas about the place of human beings in the universe. According to David Lindberg, "Aristotle's world is not a world of chance and coincidence, but an orderly, organized world, a world of purpose, in which things develop toward ends determined by their natures."[12] Central to Aristotle's conception of the universe was that the physical world, like the human mind, embodied rationality and therefore that absolute, certain knowledge about the physical world in the form of abstract principles was both attainable and desirable. Aristotelian science took for granted that purpose and function were inherent in nature as they were in human life. Although Aristotle's explicit statements are ambiguous, he often speaks as if Nature had purposively brought into being a most beautiful, wonderfully varied, and well-ordered world.[13] Aristotle and his medieval followers were convinced of the overall orderliness of nature, in which all the parts appeared to work together in harmony. Ultimately, all movement and change in the physical world was directed toward what Aristotle called "the unmoved mover," and what medieval philosophers called God: the first principle toward which all things in the universe gravitated and which remained the only thing uncaused by anything else.

If modern science took the machine for the model for how nature worked, ancient and medieval science took the living organism. Aristotelian natural philosophy concentrated not, as modern science does, on the examination of the separate material elements of matter—indistinguishable whether they exist in a rock, baby, or tin can—but on the relationships among the observable qualities of natural objects and the totality of the form and purpose of the object or organism in question in relation to other natural objects.[14] Each part of nature was not an undifferentiated mass of atoms and subatomic particles, but an entity with its own essential qualities, which had to be considered in relation to all other parts. Every natural object, according to Aristotle, had its own peculiar characteristics which had to be understood both on their own terms and in terms of how they fit into the whole. A cat, for example, must be understood from the point of view of what we have observed about what it means to be and act like a cat. Aristotle conceptualized the drive to grow, survive, and reproduce, which is observable in all living things, as an inner impulse to develop this inherent nature to the fullest, to move, in his words from "potentiality" to "actuality," as a seed develops into a plant, which then produces seeds. Thus, for example, according to Aristotle, "what grows out of something proceeds to something or 'grows,' not towards that from which it starts, but that towards which it tends. Hence, its final shape is its 'nature.' "[15]

It follows from this that nature embodied value. Nature was hierarchical in that some beings were "more perfect" or "the best" and others "less perfect" as they approached the ideals of rationality and changelessness. Even though, according to Aristotle, even the most humble parts of nature were worth study and close observation, some natural objects are better than others. What was permanent and hence rational was better than what was impermanent and therefore lacking in rationality. The stars and planets, for example, were perfect because they appeared to be incorruptible or changeless, unlike the less perfect objects on earth which are subject to death and decay.[16] Regular circular motion was regarded as more perfect than irregular, rectilinear motion. Certain qualities—those associated with higher forms of life, such as hotness and rationality—were also privileged over others, for example, coldness and lack of reason. As we shall see in Chapter 5, these hierarchies were important elements in medieval medicine, including definitions of gender differences, in antiquity and the Middle Ages.

Aristotle's scientific method rested as much on a priori judgments and logical deduction as on observation. His penchant for logical deduction served him well as a means of developing a set of basic concepts and vocabulary to make sense of the variety of natural phenomena and processes which he and others saw around them. These concepts included an analysis of types of causation; a distinction between "natural" and "violent" motion; the theory of the four elements of earth, water, air, and fire and their attendant qualities; and a classification of all change into four types: (1) change of substance or when one substance becomes another, (2) change of the amount of a substance or quantitative change, (3) change in the qualities of a substance as in a change of color, and (4) change of place or local motion.[17] In the hands of medieval scientists, these ideas provided a means to systematically and consistently analyze and categorize virtually all natural phenomena.

Fundamental to Aristotle's analysis were four types of "causes," or analytical categories. Aristotle defined these as "the material, the form, the agent, [and] the 'where-for.' "[18] The first three of these are fairly straightforward: the material cause is the matter of which the thing is composed; the formal cause is a thing's shape or organizing principle which enables it to accomplish its usual activities; and, finally, the agent or efficient cause is the cause of a specific change or "coming to be" of a thing. For example, in the case of a cat, the material cause is its flesh and physical parts; the formal cause, its shape and other characteristics which define it as a cat (rather than, say, a dog); and its efficient cause, its having been born.

The fourth kind of cause, which Aristotle also called the "final cause," or "the for the sake of which," is closely related to the purposeful character of Nature referred to above. Most simply, the final cause is the purpose for which a thing exists. In the case of artificial objects, say a cup, the final cause is fairly obvious: a cup exists to be a container to hold liquids. The cup was brought into being by its efficient cause (the artisan who made the cup) so that it could fulfill its purpose of holding water or wine. Natural objects similarly exist to do what they are supposed to do, that is, to fulfill their potentiality. A kitten, for example, naturally becomes a full-grown, fully actualized cat, and its final cause would be to become that fully realized cat exhibiting its cat-like characteristics, including the rapid production of more kittens. Natural objects, moreover, have within themselves their ability to develop into their final cause, whereas artificial objects do not.[19]

The Aristotelian perspective seems intuitively plausible when applied to living organisms such as plants and animals. Aristotle's explanations of function in nature, for example, that teeth have the shape they do in order to tear or grind food, or that plants send their roots down for the sake of nourishment, seem commonsensical.[20] Even his idea that organisms seek to fulfill the potentialities of their nature and that natural processes can be described in terms of a "final cause" or purpose appears reasonable in the context of biology. A cat has the form and behavior that it does in order to maximize its unique "catness" and to reproduce its nature. The oak which grows from an acorn is the final cause of the plant's growth from a seed and exhibits the "actuality" implied by the potential of the original acorn. These concepts have echoes in the modern sciences of ecology and evolutionary biology.

When, however, the Aristotelian perspective is applied to aspects of nature which modern science defines as inorganic, such as the stars and planets, or to processes which are not uniquely associated with life, for example, the tendency of objects to fall down rather than up, it is more of a stretch. Less commonsensical, at least in this age of space travel, is the assertion of medieval scientists, following Aristotle, that the heavens and, indeed, all heavenly bodies farther from the earth than the moon were made of an entirely different, changeless element known as ether. Similarly, their view that the heavenly bodies moved in circles because uniform circular motion was the most "perfect" form of local motion seems unreasonable.

In the remainder of this chapter we will focus on Aristotelian ideas on matter, motion, and cosmology as they were understood in the Middle Ages. Discussions of precisely how to apply many of Aristotle's ideas in particular instances often became highly complex and technical and most specific examples will be left to later chapters. Here, however, we will discuss the basics of Aristotle's scientific outlook and how it was applied by medieval scientists to the fundamental problems of medieval physics, motion, and the structure of the universe. In their broad outlines, these ideas, which formed a unified and consistent system, continued to be accepted by the great majority of scientists into the sixteenth and seventeenth centuries. However, as we shall see in later chapters, it was also in these areas that the most significant challenges to the Aristotelian framework were raised.

First, we consider briefly his ideas on matter. Rejecting the theory of some of his contemporaries that matter was made of hard, invisible, massy, indivisible particles called atoms, Aristotle opted for a more empirically verifiable theory which posited four elements (water, earth, fire, and air) defined by their combination of the four fundamental qualities of matter (cold, dry, hot, and wet). These elements were not thought of as existing in pure form in nature; rather, all natural bodies were mixed or compound bodies, in which one element predominated. "Water" (by which Aristotle meant all types of liquids and some solids), for example, is cold and wet; "earth," or most solids, is cold and dry; "air," or gaseous matter, is hot and wet; "fire" is hot and dry.[21] Observable changes in material bodies were the result of transformations between these fundamental categories of matter, although exactly how these substances underwent these changes was a matter of debate among medieval scientists. Most, however, agreed that each quality drove out its contrary—that is, hot drove out or was replaced with cold, dry drove out wet, and so forth. Tracking and recording the physical properties of natural substances according to these categories was a crucial aspect of the theory and practice of many medieval sciences including medicine, zoology, botany, geology, and alchemy.

Next, we examine the foundations of Aristotelian dynamics, astronomy, and cosmology. In these areas, Aristotle attempted to explain what he and other scientists had observed about the motion of bodies on earth and in the heavens in terms of the metaphysical premises outlined previously. Whereas modern ideas on dynamics and motion depend on universal mathematical laws connecting gravity, mass, distance, and other mathematically measurable factors, Aristotelian and medieval ideas on why objects moved as they did were based on the concept that every object had a place and type of motion natural to it. Objects on earth, for example, naturally moved in straight lines, while the heavenly bodies, composed of their own distinct substance, naturally moved in constant, circular motion. Although odd-sounding to modern ears, these ideas did explain a broad range of natural phenomena in ways that were consistent with the ancient and medieval worldviews and plausible in terms of everyday human experience.

In order to appreciate why Aristotelian dynamics and cosmology remained credible into the modern period, we must begin by considering how the night sky appeared without the benefit of artificial lights and modern astronomical instruments such as the telescope. In sharp contrast to the constant variety and decay observable on earth, the heavens appeared virtually changeless. Naked-eye observations taken over centuries showed that the stars remained fixed in their position relative to each other; beyond their daily rotation around the earth, they appeared to undergo no change whatsoever. The movements of the planets, sun, and moon were more complex but still fit into constantly recurring patterns which repeated themselves endlessly over and over. Of all the types of possible change, the heavens seemed only to be susceptible to local motion. The stars, planets, sun, and moon clearly appeared to move in a vast circle as they rose and set every night; their long-term motions similarly could be resolved into a series of circular motions. Moreover, the heavenly bodies had no visible mechanism of movement but appeared to move effortlessly and naturally through eternity.

In order to account for these observations, Aristotle divided the universe into two radically different parts: a superior heavenly sphere, which contained the stars, planets, sun, and moon, and an inferior terrestrial or sublunary ("below the moon") sphere, made up of the earth and atmosphere up to the circle of the moon. At the center rested the spherical, immobile earth.[22] Although Aristotle considered the possibility of a rotating earth, he rejected this idea on the grounds of lack of observational support for the idea; late medieval natural philosophers would take up this question in considerable detail. Aristotle also asserted, on logical and philosophical grounds ("nothing can come from nothing"), that the universe must be eternal, a conclusion at odds with the scriptural account of creation in Genesis. Finding Aristotle's philosophical arguments compelling, medieval thinkers ultimately resolved the issue by declaring that the creation of the earth was a "matter of faith."

Aristotle also sketched out the structure of the universe, which he defined as a vast but finite sphere. A series of concentric crystalline spheres revolved around the earth, carrying the moon, sun, planets, and fixed stars with them (see Figure 2). Whereas matter in the sublunary realm was composed of the four elements described previously, the

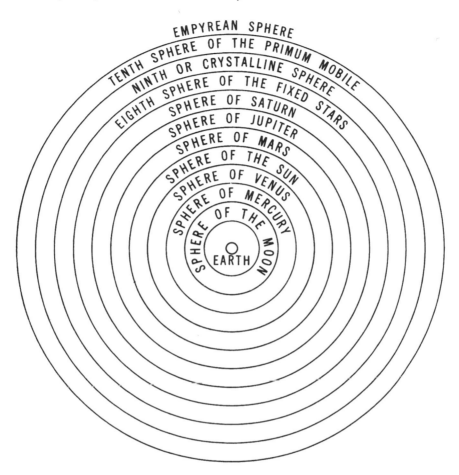

Figure 2. The structure of the cosmos in the Middle Ages. *Edward Grant, Physical Science in the Middle Ages (Cambridge, England: Cambridge University Press, 1977; reprint, 1979), figure 5, p. 72. Reprinted with the permission of Cambridge University Press.*

spheres and heavenly bodies were composed of a fifth element, the ether. Crystalline, pure, transparent, and immune to all change except for continuous circular motion, the ether was "more divine" than the elements which made up earthly matter.[23] (Because of their obvious variability, meteors, comets, and shooting stars were assigned to the sublunary sphere.)

The simplicity and plausibility of Aristotle's cosmology were somewhat compromised by his acknowledgment that it took a total of fifty-five, sometimes interlocking, spheres to account for all the complex motions of the planets. Although Aristotle seems to have thought that the spheres were solid, he did not provide any full discussion of how the spheres worked physically together, nor was he particularly interested in mathematical astronomy, that is, the working out of the calculations necessary to predict the motions of the various heavenly bodies. This problem was taken up by other astronomers, most notably Ptolemy in the Hellenistic period and the Arabic astronomers during the early Middle Ages, resulting in greatly refined and more accurate observational data. Strict application of these data to Aristotle's cosmology showed that Aristotle's simple system of concentric spheres was inadequate to fully explain the movements of the planets in mathematical terms; instead, a system of eccentric spheres and additional spheres attached to spheres, called "epicycles," was necessary to "save the appearances," that is, to explain the observed motions of the planets in terms of the requirement that they move in perfect, constant, circular motion (see Figure 3). Aristotle's explanation of what moved the spheres was also obscure; at times, he referred to the ether as "naturally so constituted as to move in a circle in virtue of its own nature"; at other times, he spoke in terms of "souls" or "intelligences" which individually moved each sphere.[24] A number of medieval astronomers translated Aristotle's "souls" into Christian "angels"; others would refer to "intelligences" or "forms" as the cause of planetary motions.

Medieval scientists continued to wrestle with the problem of reconciling the available mathematical data on the movements of the planets, sun, and moon with reasonable explanations of how the system worked in physical terms. A number of important compromises were reached which attempted to reconcile Ptolemy's mathematical model with Aristotelian cosmology and physics. Virtually every major assertion of Aristotelian cosmology and dynamics came under critical review and scrutiny. As we shall see in the following chapter, late medieval thinkers considered in detail whether the earth rotated, what caused the movements of the heavenly bodies, what mathematical laws governed the motions of moving bodies, and the number and nature of the celestial spheres. Some of this work may have influenced the efforts of Copernicus, Galileo, and Kepler in the sixteenth and seventeenth centuries to resolve these issues, initiating the Scientific Revolution.

Movement on earth was even more complicated but still depended in large part on the notion of "natural place." As stated above, Aristotle distinguished between violent and natural movement. By "violent" movement he meant any movement caused by an external agent contrary to an object's natural movement, as when a stone is flung into the air. By "natural" movement he meant movement that was an expression of an object's nature. For living beings, this included self-generated movement initiated by the soul; for inanimate objects, it meant mainly the object's tendency to return to its natural place. Heavy objects, he observed, had a natural tendency to fall down in straight lines toward the center of the earth; fire, on the other hand, had a natural tendency to move up. Each element, therefore, had its natural place toward which it tended to move in the normal course of things unless deflected or prevented. A heavy object made up mostly of the element earth, for example, would naturally come back down to earth after it has been violently propelled upward.

Aristotle also made important assertions about the nature of local motion which influenced scientific thought in the Middle Ages and into the modern period. He asserted, for example, that everything in motion is moved by something else, whether internal, as in the case of living beings, or external, as in the case of non-animate beings. The only exception to this rule was the "prime mover" or "unmoved mover," the source of all change in the universe and the philosophical equivalent of God. Aristotle had argued that unless we posit a First Principle itself not moved or brought into being by something else, we are involved in an infinite regress and cannot explain the existence of the cosmos. Thomas Aquinas, the great thirteenth-century philosopher and synthesizer of Aristotelianism and Christianity, borrowed Aristotle's argument for the unmoved mover to prove the existence of God.[25]

The cause of motion, moreover, according to Aristotle, had to be in continuous contact with the moved object, eliminating the possibility of "action at a distance." To explain why a projectile continued to move upward after being thrown, Aristotle postulated that the initial force was imparted to the air surrounding the projectile, so that as long as the resistance of the medium was less than the moving force, the object would continue its movement contrary to its natural tendency to move downward.

Aristotle also attempted to develop general quantitative relationships between the various factors which affected local motion, for example, that the speed of a falling object varies directly with its weight; that if bodies of equal weight move through different mediums, then the times required to traverse a given distance will be proportional to the densities of the mediums; and that if a force moves an object a given distance in a given time, then that force would move an object half its weight twice the distance in the same time or the same distance in half the time.[26]

Much of what Aristotle said about local motion was obscure and unclear. During the Middle Ages both Islamic and European scientists attempted to build a coherent science of kinematics (a descriptive account of motion) and dynamics (the study of the causes of motion) based on Aristotelian principles but far outstripping Aristotle in the sophistication of their reasoning. These efforts led to much creative speculation about the possibilities of measuring the intensification or diminution of qualities and about the nature of motion itself. Advances were also made in formulating mathematical laws describing acceleration. These developments will be discussed in the following chapter.

Medieval scientists never managed to break away from the fundamentals of the Aristotelian scientific worldview, nor did they develop the notion of systematic controlled experiment which was one hallmark of the emerging modern science of the sixteenth and seventeenth centuries. Nevertheless, medieval scientists effectively challenged Aristotelian doctrine on numerous specific issues, even if they did not necessarily admit that they were doing so. We will explore the ways in which medieval scientists both extended and departed from Aristotle's ideas in a variety of fields over the course of the next two chapters. Some medieval scientists moved in the direction of experiment, and many cultivated the systematic observation of nature. Certain aspects of Platonism continued to be influential in the thirteenth century and after, contributing to efforts to apply mathematics to natural phenomena. Medieval scientists also developed the idea that natural phenomena could be used for human benefit far more than Aristotle had done. These differing approaches contributed to the vitality and variety of science in the Middle Ages.

NOTES

1. The term *science* did not generally become synonymous with the natural sciences until the nineteenth century.

2. Bernard Silvester, *The Cosmographia of Bernardus Silvestris*, trans. Winthrop Wetherbee (New York: Columbia University Press, 1973).

3. Plato, *The Republic 7.514a–521b; The Republic of Plato*, trans. and with Introduction and Notes by Francis MacDonald Cornford (New York and London: Oxford University Press, 1964), pp. 227–35.

4. Plato, *Timaeus 29d; Plato's* Timaeus, trans. Francis M. Cornford and ed. Oskar Piest (Indianapolis and New York: Bobbs-Merrill, 1959), p. 18.

5. Plato, *Timaeus 30c; Plato's* Timaeus, trans. Cornford, p. 20.

6. Plato, *Timaeus 53c–56c; Plato's* Timaeus, trans. Cornford, pp. 55–61.

7. This summary is taken from William F. Bynum, "The Great Chain of Being," in *The History of Science and Religion in the Western Tradition: An Encyclopedia*, ed. Gary B. Ferngren, Edward J. Larson, Darrel W. Amundsen, and Anne-Marie E. Hakhla (New York and London: Garland Publishing, 2000), p. 444.

8. I. Bernard Cohen, *The Birth of a New Physics* (Garden City, NY: Doubleday, 1960), pp. 118–20.

9. H. Floris Cohen, *The Scientific Revolution: A Historiographical Inquiry* (Chicago and London: University of Chicago Press, 1994), p. 185.

10. René Descartes, *Treatise of Man*, French text with translation and commentary by Thomas Steele Hall (Cambridge, MA: Harvard University Press, 1972), p. 113.

11. Cohen, *Scientific Revolution*, p. 167.

12. David C. Lindberg, *The Beginnings of Western Science: The European Scientific Tradition in Philosophical, Religious, and Institutional Context, 600 B.C. to A.D. 1450* (Chicago and London: University of Chicago Press, 1992), p. 54.

13. Clarence Glacken, *Traces on the Rhodian Shore: Nature and Culture in Western Thought from Ancient Times to the End of the Eighteenth Century* (Berkeley, Los Angeles, and London: University of California Press, 1967), pp. 47–49.

14. Aristotle, *Parts of Animals*, 644a35; *De partibus animalium*, trans. William Ogle, in *The Basic Works of Aristotle*, ed. Richard McKeon (New York: Random House, 1941), pp. 646–51.

15. Aristotle, *Physics*, 193b19; *Aristotle's* Physics, trans. Richard Hope (Lincoln: University of Nebraska Press, 1961), p. 25.

16. Aristotle, *De caelo*, 270b; *De caelo*, trans. J. L. Stocks, in *Basic Works*, ed. McKeon, pp. 402–3.

17. Edward Grant, *Physical Science in the Middle Ages* (Cambridge, England and New York: Cambridge University Press, 1977), p. 36.

18. Aristotle, *Physics*, 198a25; *Aristotle's* Physics, trans. Hope, p. 35.

19. Aristotle, *Physics* 198b–200a; 192b10–193b10; *Aristotle's* Physics, trans. Hope, pp. 36–39; 22–25.

20. Aristotle, *Physics* 198b-199a; *Aristotle's* Physics, trans. Hope, pp. 36–37.

21. Aristotle, *On Generation and Corruption*, 329b–333a; *On Generation and Corruption*, trans. Harold H. Joachim, in *Basic Works*, ed. McKeon, pp. 509–17.

22. Aristotle, *De caelo*, 293a–298a; *De caelo*, trans. Stocks, in *Basic Works*, ed. McKeon, pp. 428–37.

23. Aristotle, *De caelo*, 270b–271a; G.E.R. Lloyd, *Aristotle: The Growth and Structure of His Thought* (Cambridge, England: Cambridge University Press, 1968), p. 139.

24. Aristotle, *De caelo* 269a.5–7; Edward Grant, *Planets, Stars, and Orbs: The Medieval Cosmos, 1200–1687* (Cambridge, England and New York: Cambridge University Press, 1994), p. 514.

25. Aristotle, *Physics* 258b; *Aristotle's* Physics, trans. Hope, pp. 160–61; Thomas Aquinas, *Summa Theologica*, Pt. 1 Q. 2 Art. 3; *Summa Theologica: First Complete American Edition*, trans. Fathers of the English Dominican Province (New York: Benziger Brothers, 1947), I: 13–14.

26. Lindberg, *Western Science*, p. 59. Aristotle's arguments on motion can be found in his *Physics*.

CHAPTER 4

THE EXACT
SCIENCES

This chapter will examine the medieval sciences of mathematics, astronomy, cosmology, astrology, statics, kinematics, dynamics, optics, all of which had a strong mathematical component. Despite the fact that Aristotle had emphasized qualitative change over quantitative change in his natural philosophy, medieval scientists beginning in the thirteenth century showed a passionate interest in applying mathematics to nature. This turn toward measurement and calculation had its roots in the social and cultural, as well as intellectual, environment of the late Middle Ages. During the twelfth and thirteenth centuries, the translation movement made some of the mathematical texts of antiquity, including Euclid's *Elements* and most of the works of Archimedes, newly available. Also important was the translation of Arabic mathematical texts, especially treatises by al-Khwarizmi (fl. 825) which introduced Indian (so-called Arabic) numerals and some of the techniques of algebra into the West. Europeans may also have been influenced by the growing impact of a market economy and the increased importance of money and monetary calculations, including bookkeeping, money changing, and the effects of the debasement of the coinage and price regulations, in everyday life. The increasing mechanization of daily life and new technologies, including the mechanical clock, may also have fostered a new interest in looking for mathematical relationships in natural phenomena.

By the end of the Middle Ages, medieval thinkers had increasingly begun to think about the theoretical and practical possibilities of the exact sciences in new and creative ways. Although they continued to work within an Aristotelian framework, they increasingly reworked Aristotle's ideas to fit new observations and ideas about the natural world. The questions raised, especially about the nature of movement and the structure of the universe, were an important part of the background to the later Scientific Revolution.

MATHEMATICS

Geometry and arithmetic remained the foundation of the exact sciences. In the thirteenth century, the great English scientist Roger Bacon (c. 1220–c. 92) argued that every science required mathematics, not only because mathematics was useful, necessary, and easily grasped, but also because "in mathematics alone is there certainty without doubt." He continued: "if in other sciences we should arrive at certainty without doubt and truth without error, it behooves us to place the foundations of knowledge in mathematics, in so far as disposed through it we are able to reach certainty in other sciences and truth by the exclusion of error." [1] Other writers extolled the fundamental importance of geometry and arithmetic not only for the obviously mathematical sciences of astronomy, optics, and mechanics, but also for natural philosophy as a whole and even as a tool for the literal understanding of scripture. At the same time, masons, carpenters, and other artisans made use of the techniques of practical geometry and arithmetic. In the twelfth century, the links between theoretical and practical mathematics were recognized by the philosopher Domingo Gundisalvo who, in his work on the divisions of philosophy written around 1150, included under practical arithmetic the manipulation of numbers, business math, the use of the abacus, and mathematical games and under practical geometry surveying, carpentry, masonry, iron-working, and the instruments used in these crafts.

Medieval mathematicians both continued and went beyond classical mathematics. Campanus of Novara (d. c. 1296–98), for example, cobbled together various versions of Euclid's *Elements* into a new synthesis which two centuries later in 1482 would became the first printed edition of this fundamental text in geometry.[2] In other areas, medieval mathematicians broke new ground. Stimulated by advances by Arabic mathematicians (see Chapter 2), Europeans such as Jordanus of Nemore (fl. 1230–60) and Leonardo of Pisa, known as Fibonacci (b. c. 1179–d. after 1240), applied new methods of solving algebraic equations and problems of probability and number theory. Of special interest to many was the generation of infinite series of nonrepeating numbers. According to Edward Grant, Nicole Oresme's *Algorism of Ratios*, written in the second half of the fourteenth century, was the "first extant systematic attempt to describe operational rules for the multiplication and division . . . of ratios involving integral and fractional exponents."[3]

During the fourteenth century, medieval scientists, especially those connected with Merton College at Oxford University, became increasingly interested in the possibilities of applying mathematics to natural philosophy. They investigated the relationships of physical motion, qualitative change, and quantitative measurement, which led them into what one historian has called "a near frenzy to measure everything imaginable."[4] Mathematicians in this group of "Oxford Calculators," as they are often called, tackled such problems as how to quantify changing rates of motion in falling bodies, how to measure changing intensities of heat or cold, or even how to measure degrees of "love" or "whiteness." The Merton School also influenced John Buridan and his student, Nicole Oresme, at the University of Paris; Buridan and Oresme made important contributions to the sciences of kinematics and dynamics, astronomy, monetary theory, and philosophy. During the same period, theologians seized on mathematical concepts to explain such difficult problems as the nature of angelic movement (whether angels move instantaneously or at a finite speed), God's infinite attributes, and the precise nature of the extended presence of Christ's body in the Eucharist during the miracle of transubstantiation. Despite the esoteric character of some of this discussion, underlying it were serious questions about the nature of motion, relative value, and qualitative change. Ideas developed by the Oxford Calculators carried over into discussions of the possibility of a moving earth, the relative exchange value of goods and money, and the mathematization of nature, all ideas part of the intellectual context of the Scientific Revolution.

ASTRONOMY

Astronomy was probably the most complex and philosophically meaningful of the mathematically related sciences. The majesty and beauty of the heavens had had a profound impact on the human imagination for millennia before the Middle Ages. In a world without artificial light, the night sky must have conveyed a sense of divine power and mystery difficult to recapture today. The seemingly eternal and endlessly repeating movements of the planets and stars were in stark contrast to the constant change and variability observable on earth. The sun, recognized as the source of heat and light, and hence of life, was an equally powerful stimulus to human thought and curiosity. The mysterious patterns made by the sun, moon, planets, and stars across the night sky held both religious and practical meaning. Systematic observation and recording of these movements provided the most reliable guide to the passing of time on a daily and seasonal basis. From prehistoric times, the changing position of sunrise had been used to mark seasonal changes. During the Middle Ages, observations of the sun and moon remained the basis for the calendar and the computing of important dates such as Easter and the winter and summer solstices. Early medieval monasteries used the stars to calculate the passing of time at night and even after the use of water and mechanical clocks became common (see Chapter 6), astronomical observations were essential for accurate timekeeping. Navigation, both on land and sea, also depended on knowledge of the night sky. It is small wonder, then, that the heavenly bodies were regarded as in some sense divine or, in Christian terms, as compelling reminders of the order, constancy, and beauty of God's creation.

Today, the complicated movements of the planets and other astronomical phenomena as observed by the naked eye are unfamiliar to many of us. We are rarely in the position to observe the night sky over time without the interfering effects of artificial light and have little need to keep systematic track of the changing positions of the heavenly bodies. Yet, without an effort to re-create these movements in our minds, it is impossible to understand medieval astronomy. Let us briefly then review how the universe looked from the perspective of medieval astronomers and other observers of the night sky.

The universe appears to be an enormously large, but not infinite, sphere. Using the naked eye, one sees that the fixed stars (those that do not change their position relative to one another) appear to revolve daily around the earth and also shift as a whole during the course of the year so that some constellations are visible in different parts of the night sky at different times of the year. Over much longer periods of time, the entire sphere of the fixed stars can be seen to shift about one degree every 100 years, a phenomenon known in antiquity and the Middle Ages as "the precession of the equinoxes." The planets (the name means "wandering stars"), on the other hand, look like unusually bright stars but, unlike the fixed stars, follow erratic but repeating paths as plotted against the backdrop of the fixed stars over the course of months or years, sometimes appearing to regress, at other times moving ahead. Like the sun and moon, the planets seem to revolve around a stationary spherical earth. The sun rises and sets at different points along a narrow range of the horizon over the course of a year. The planets also rise and set along a fixed band of the horizon.

During the early Middle Ages, astronomers depended solely on unaided observations and a fairly simple view of the way in which the heavens were structured. The outermost sphere of the universe, the sphere of the fixed stars, rotated daily around the earth at the center of the universe. Against this backdrop, the sun, moon, and planets (in order, the moon, Mercury, Venus, the sun, Mars, Jupiter, and Saturn) both revolved around the earth every twenty-four hours and completed a revolution around the ecliptic, a circle tilted approximately twenty-three degrees from the equator and projected onto the sphere of the fixed stars at the zodiac (the narrow band of the heavens through which the planets move, traditionally divided into 12 segments), at varying rates (see Figure 2). This latter motion explained the fact that the sun, moon, and planets rose at different points relative to the fixed stars over the course of their revolution—a period of a year for the sun but varying from a month for the moon to thirty years for Saturn. This simplified view allowed for rough calculations of the date of Easter, daily time-keeping, and a secure place for astronomy among the seven liberal arts. During the twelfth century, a period of considerable creative thought about the nature of the cosmos, more speculative ideas about the heavens appeared. These include Hildegard of Bingen's vision of an egg-shaped universe and works by William of Conches, Bernard Silvester, and Thierry of Chartres which explored the physical process of creation and emphasized the macrocosm-microcosm relationship of the cosmos and man.

By the late tenth and eleventh centuries, European astronomers had also begun to be influenced by Arabic astronomical practices and the study of astronomy became more complex. Most important, the astrolabe, an Arabic astronomical instrument and timekeeper, was introduced into the West. The astrolabe was an ingenious mechanical device which allowed for the accurate and automatic calculation of a wide range of astronomical events, including the time of day or night, the computation of the sun's position for any given date, the plotting of the positions of the planets against the fixed stars and in the zodiac, and so on. The astrolabe consisted of a spherical metal dial, the front of which was inscribed with a map of the celestial sphere, including the path of the sun, the solstices, and the equinoxes, and the back of which was inscribed with the demarcations of the signs of the zodiac. In addition, the astrolabe could be fitted with additional plates which enabled the user to correct for his particular latitude and longitude.[5]

The use of the astrolabe meant not only that astronomical calculations could be made more easily and accurately but also that precise quantitative analysis became an essential part of astronomical science. According to Stephen C. McCluskey, the first known instance of the use of the astrolabe in the West to improve astronomical predictions occurred in 1092, when the prior of the English monastery of great Malvern used it to calculate a table which gave the time of the new moon into the indefinite future.[6] The desire for more accurate data was also fueled by the translation of Arabic astronomical tables, which allowed for the easy calculation of the movements of the heavenly bodies, during the early eleventh century. The work of adapting these tables for use at European locations and developing new tables culminated around 1275 with the production of the Alfonsine tables, so called because they were produced at the court of King Alfonso X of Castile. The Alfonsine tables continued to be used into the sixteenth century.

Astronomy was further transformed beginning in the twelfth century by the translation of Ptolemy's *Syntaxis*, under the title of the *Almagest*, from Arabic into Latin by Gerard of Cremona around 1160. The *Almagest* (written mid–second century C.E.) was a comprehensive guide to mathematical astronomy and provided a clear and accurate method of calculating the movements of the heavenly bodies. During this same period, many of Aristotle's works of natural philosophy, including *De caelo*, his major work on cosmology, were also translated, first from Arabic versions and then directly from the Greek. These works by Aristotle became the core of the scientific curriculum at medieval universities. Commentaries on Aristotle and astronomical works by Arabic authors also became available.

The reception of this body of work greatly complicated the course of medieval thinking about the universe, in part because Aristotle and Ptolemy presented two quite different approaches to astronomical questions. Arabic works also added a slightly different flavor to the mix, not only because of their technical complexity but also because the Arabic astronomical tradition emphasized the influence of the heavens on the earth and human life and, consequently, contributed to the growth of astrology as a scientific discipline (see the following discussion).

Finally, medieval astronomers had to incorporate theological considerations, such as interpretations of the structure of the heavens derived from the account of creation in the Old Testament or Christian strictures against the view that the universe was eternal. For theological reasons, for example, medieval astronomers added the empyrean sphere, the immobile sphere enclosing the universe and the dwelling place of God, beyond the sphere of the fixed stars. Certain points of Aristotelian and Arabic natural philosophy came into direct conflict with Christian theology, in particular, the assertion of the eternity of the world, the idea that the heavens controlled human will, and the implied view that God did not have the absolute power to suspend natural laws and principles. In response to this tension, in 1277 Etienne Tempier, the bishop of Paris, issued a list of 219 propositions, some of which had relevance to astronomy, which could not be held or taught on pain of excommunication (see Chapter 3). Paradoxically, the Condemnations of 1277, rather than restricting astronomical thought, seem to have encouraged speculation about what God's power might effect in the natural world, even in violation of Aristotelian principles. For example, after 1277 the question whether God could have created a plurality of worlds or a void beyond the cosmos became a serious point of discussion for the first time.

The task of medieval astronomers, therefore, became reconciling these authoritative but different scientific, religious, and philosophical perspectives. This need to deal with divergent traditions meant that medieval scientists could not merely passively accept and pass on received astronomical knowledge. Instead, medieval scientists actively explored an extraordinary variety of issues, questions, and problems, pushing the boundaries of available knowledge to the limit. Not infrequently, their conclusions ran contrary to aspects of Aristotelian natural philosophy, although these discrepancies were often not acknowledged.

The two main traditions influencing medieval astronomy by the thirteenth century were those of Aristotle and Ptolemy. Aristotle's account of the structure of the universe was an integral part of his ideas about local and celestial motion: the incorruptible, spherical heavens moved in perfect, constant, circular motion around an immobile, spherical earth, the center of the cosmos. Heavy objects on earth fell down precisely because of their natural tendency to move in a straight line toward the center of the earth.

Because Aristotle was interested in articulating a view of the universe that was intelligible in terms of his understanding of how and why objects moved as they did, his ideas on physics could not be separated from his ideas on astronomy; his writings offered a comprehensive worldview encompassing both astronomy and dynamics. Ptolemy's primary aim in the *Almagest*, on the other hand, was much narrower: to develop a mathematical system to explain and predict with accuracy the motions of the heavenly bodies. Using far more voluminous records of the movements of the sun, moon, and planets than were available to Aristotle, Ptolemy had recognized that the system of concentric spheres outlined by Aristotle was inadequate to accurately account for these movements mathematically.[7] Ptolemy, therefore, devised an ingenious system in which a complex series of circles could be combined for each planet to account for its observed movements without violating the principle of constant circular motion. Each planet, he said, was carried on an epicycle, a sphere with its center on the larger sphere of that planet. The larger sphere was itself eccentric with respect to the earth (see Figure 3). By adjusting the sizes and positions of the epicycles and eccentrics, Ptolemy was able to predict the complex movements of the planets with a very high rate of accuracy. Simplified versions of the Ptolemaic system were presented and explained in the *Sphere* of Johannes de Sacrobosco, also known as John of Holywood (mid-thirteenth century) and the *Theorica planetarum* (Theory of the Planets) by Campanus of Novara, written between 1255 and 1259. Campanus' work also contains the first western description of the equatorium, an astronomical instrument long known to Arabic astronomers. Combined with astronomical tables, Ptolemy's geometrical diagrams of planetary movements also allowed for the calculation of the absolute distances of the planets from the earth. Unfortunately, his scheme made little sense in terms of Aristotelian physics because it posited that the planets, sun, and moon moved around imaginary points eccentric to the earth's position at the center of the universe. As Arabic astronomers critical of Ptolemy had often pointed out,

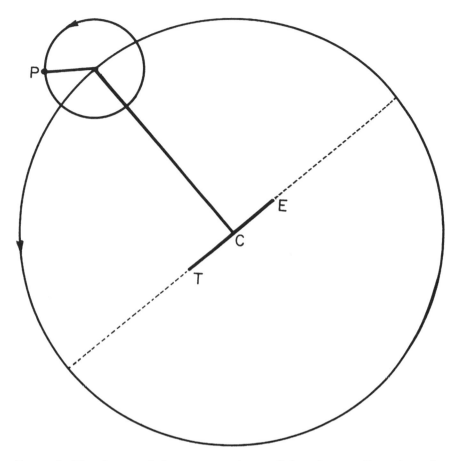

Figure 3. The theory of the superior planets (Mars, Jupiter, Saturn) in the Ptolemaic system. The planet (P) is carried on an epicycle which moves uniformly around its center. The center of the epicycle in turn is carried by a circle with its center at C, the earth at the center of the universe. However, the motion of the epicycle's center on this circle is measured as uniform with respect to a point eccentric to C, called the equant (E). *Olaf Pedersen, "Astronomy," in David C. Lindberg, ed.,* Science in the Middle Ages *(Chicago and London: University of Chicago Press, 1978), figure 19, p. 317.*

a system that seemed to ignore the physical reality of the heavens left much to be desired.

Medieval natural philosophers recognized the advantages and disadvantages of both the Aristotelian and Ptolemaic systems and, on the whole, made a concerted effort to combine the best features of each. A new theory which retained the concentric spheres of Aristotle but added at least three eccentric orbs and epicycles within each concentric sphere as necessary to accurately calculate the position of the planet was first described by Roger Bacon in the 1260s (see Figure 4). Dubbed the "great compromise" by historian Edward Grant, it was widely, if not universally, adopted in the late Middle Ages.[8] This "three-orb" system worked well because it preserved the system of concentric spheres and the eccentrics and epicycles are clearly meant as real, physical entities, not mere mathematical constructs designed to save the appearances. Nevertheless, as a few thinkers acknowledged, if eccentric orbs were physically real, their existence violated Aristotle's premise that all the heavenly bodies moved around the geometric center of the universe.

A willingness to ask questions and explore possible answers led medieval writers on cosmological and astronomical subjects to an extraordinary range of topics. Grant has catalogued the most important astronomical questions in medieval scholastic texts; even a short selection shows the range and complexity of their thought:

4. Whether the universe is eternal.

26. Whether the world was truly made and created from nothing by God.

54. Whether there is something [that is, body, void, imaginary space, or animate creatures] beyond the sky [or heavens].

62. Whether there are, or could be, more worlds.

91. Whether all celestial spheres and all stars, both wandering [that is, the planets] and fixed, are of the same ultimate species.

97. On the number of spheres, whether there be eight or nine, or more or less.

126. Whether the heaven is spherical in shape.

128. Whether the heavens are animated.

135. Whether the heavens are fluid or solid.

141. Whether the spots appearing on the Moon arise from differences in parts of the Moon or from something eternal.

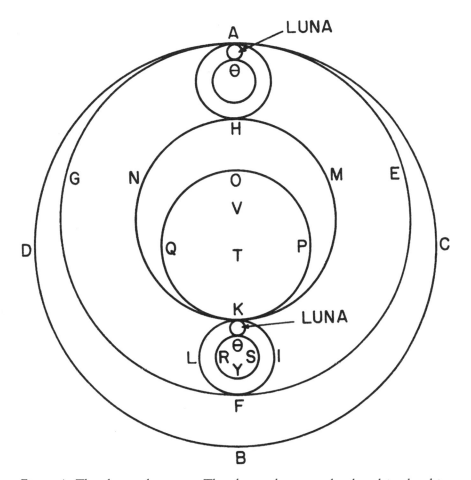

Figure 4. The three-orb system. The three-orb system developed in the thirteenth century as a compromise between the concentric spheres of Aristotle
and the eccentric circles and epicycles of the Ptolemaic system. Eccentrics and
epicycles are added within each concentric sphere as necessary to accurately
calculate the position of the planet. In this diagram, the moon (Luna) is shown
moving on its epicycle carried between two eccentric spheres (AGFE and
HNKM) with their centers at V, while this whole system is enclosed within
two concentric circles (ADBC and OQKP) with their centers at T. This system
preserved the system of concentric spheres and the eccentrics and epicycles are
clearly meant as real, physical entities, not mere mathematical constructs designed to save the appearances. *Edward Grant, "Cosmology," in David C. Lindberg, ed.,* Science in the Middle Ages *(Chicago and London: University of Chicago
Press, 1978), figure 16, p. 282.*

195. Whether the heavens or planets are moved by intelligences or intrinsically by a proper form or nature.

220. Whether for saving the celestial motions of the planets it is necessary to assume eccentrics and epicycles.

231. Whether all the planets, except the Sun, receive their light from the Sun or from themselves.

237. Whether or not celestial bodies act on the sublunar world.

308. Whether it is possible that a vacuum can exist naturally.

325. Whether, if a vacuum existed, a heavy body could be moved in it.

383. Whether the whole earth is spherical.

389. Whether the earth always rests or is always moved in the middle [or center] of the heavens or world.[9]

One of the most important debates was on the causes of celestial motions. Natural philosophers agreed that motion in the heavens could not be explained in the same mechanical and natural terms applied to motions on earth. Were the planets then moved by angels (often referred to as "intelligences"), some kind of internal form or soul peculiar to each celestial body, or the natural motion of the orbs themselves? Most medieval thinkers opted for angels, a view current into the seventeenth century. By "angels," however, natural philosophers meant not so much personal, individualized spiritual entities, as impersonal forces which acted on the heavens much as a mechanical force might.

Other discussions were devoted to the nature of the ether which composed the celestial spheres and orbs, including whether different regions or parts of the heavens might have different densities, whether the orbs were fluid or hard, and whether the concave surface of one sphere was identical with the convex surface of the sphere below it or distinct but touching at every point. More speculative thought concerned the possibility of multiple worlds and whether an infinite void filled with God's presence existed beyond the world.

The most innovative writers on astronomical questions were John Buridan and his student, Nicole Oresme. Buridan (c. 1295–c. 1358) and

Oresme (c. 1320–82) were both members of a circle of thinkers around the University of Paris active in the mid to late fourteenth century. They and some of their contemporaries around Paris and Oxford were responsible for some of the most creative and groundbreaking thought in astronomy, dynamics, and mathematics in the Middle Ages. Their contributions to kinematics and dynamics will be discussed later. In astronomy, Buridan and Oresme are distinguished by their discussion of the possibility of the daily rotation of the earth on its axis.

The immobility of the earth at the center of the universe was a crucial premise of both Aristotelian and Ptolemaic astronomy and physics. Nevertheless, Ptolemy reported in passing that "some people"[10] had argued that the movements of the stars would look the same if the earth rotated on its axis from west to east every day than if the sphere of the fixed stars rotated daily. Buridan and Oresme took up this possibility in their commentaries on Aristotle's *De caelo* and deduced numerous reasons for its superiority to the traditional view of an immobile earth. Ultimately, however, both Buridan and Oresme return to the traditional view that the earth is immobile, Buridan because of certain problems he saw in explaining local motion on earth and Oresme, who was a theologian as well as a scientist, for religious reasons. Oresme's final comment reveals both his recognition of the limits of scientific proof in this question as well as his assertion of the primacy of faith: "For God hath established the world which shall not be moved, in spite of contrary reasons because they are not conclusive persuasions. . . . What I have said by way of diversion or intellectual exercise can in this manner serve as a valuable means of refuting and checking those who would like to impugn our faith by argument."[11]

Buridan's and Oresme's arguments are quite similar, although Oresme's discussion is more detailed and more systematic. Both begin by pointing out the relativity of our perception of motion; if the earth turned while the spheres of the planets and stars were at rest, Buridan asserts, "all the celestial phenomena would appear to us just as they now appear."[12] Both also discuss whether motion might be seen as natural to the earth. Buridan and Oresme both turn Aristotelian logic on its head, pointing out that if rest is more excellent and philosophically preferable to motion, then it would be more appropriate for the earth, "the vilest element," to move than for the heavens to move. Oresme adduces additional arguments to show that the earth's rotation would not affect the motions of the heavenly bodies. Both also invoke the principle of simplicity and economy, arguing that it would be easier for the relatively small earth to rotate daily on its axis than for the comparatively vast heavens to rotate "excessively" fast every twenty-four hours.[13] Finally, Buridan and Oresme deal with two well-known and long-lived empirical arguments against the motion of the earth: (1) that if the earth moved, an arrow shot upward would return to earth at a point far from its original setting off point and objects above the earth's surface (for example, clouds) would also be left behind; and (2) that the motion of the earth would create a continual wind perceptible to our senses. Both respond that these objections can be answered if we posit that the air surrounding the earth, and everything in it, is carried along with the rotating earth.

Many questions raised by medieval astronomers remained important through the Scientific Revolution. Parts of Buridan's and Oresme's arguments for a rotating earth, for example, appear in Copernicus' *De revolutionibus* (1543), the first persuasive demonstration of a moving earth and the heliocentric solar system. In this and other respects, the continued efforts of natural philosophers to apply Aristotle's ideas to astronomical and other problems led to a tendency to "tweak" Aristotelian principles to the point of outright denial. This implicit questioning of the Aristotelian paradigm is part of the background for the advances made in the mathematical sciences during the sixteenth and seventeenth centuries.

ASTROLOGY

Astrology in the Middle Ages was intimately associated with astronomy, so much so that the terms *astronomer* and *astrologer* were often used almost interchangeably. Astrology had two distinct but related aspects. The first was what we generally mean by astrology today: the prediction of the future on the basis of the positions of the heavenly bodies, whether storms, wars, floods, or the course of an individual's life. This predictive or "judicial" astrology, when applied to human life and actions, was controversial and often criticized as contradicting the idea of free will, as being unsupported by empirical evidence, and as having too close an association with demonic magic. Nevertheless, it was widely practiced and the line between it and scientific astrology, which might involve predicting the movements of physical bodies, was often blurred. The second aspect of astrology was the scientific study of the physical influences of the heavens on the earth and was regarded as a respected part of natural philosophy. John North, a historian of astronomy, has compared the relationship of scientific astrology to popular astrology and divination as that of a professional economist and a crystal ball: "neither is wholly reliable, and both may be wrongly motivated, but there is a world of difference between their techniques."[14]

Scientific astrology acquired a new intellectual framework in the West with the translation in the 1130s of the *Tetrabiblos*, an astrological work by Ptolemy, and Abu Ma'shar's (787–886) *Greater Introduction to the Science of Astrology*. This understanding of astrology was backed up by a wealth of seemingly scientific evidence and was perfectly consistent with the premises of astronomy and other of the sciences. It considered the physical effects of the heavenly bodies, especially the sun and moon, on the earth and studied their effects on weather, climate, the tides, natural cycles of birth and death, illnesses, and animal and human behavior.

The superiority of the incorruptible heavens over the corruptible sub-lunary sphere was taken as a sufficient explanation for the influence of the celestial bodies over the earth. Scientific astrology depended on the idea that the ether which made up the heavens exuded "a certain power" which affected the fire and air surrounding the earth; these atmospheric effects in turn influenced the earth itself and the animals and plants which lived on it. The effects of the stars on terrestrial events were thought to be manifold and constant. Many natural philosophers argued that if celestial motions ceased, all change on earth would also cease and the world would be destroyed. In general, the planets were thought to transmit the qualities of hotness, dryness, moistness, and coldness (the four fundamental qualities according to Aristotle), through motion, light, and invisible influences or "species" which traveled from the planet to the earth and made literal impressions on earthly materials.

The effects of the sun and moon were the first model for the action of celestial influences on the earth. The movements of the sun obviously caused the seasons and affected the degrees of heat, moisture, dryness, and coldness on earth, which in turn affected the productiveness of plants, the generation of animals, the flowing of rivers, and such. Because of the sun's special association with generation, it was also thought to generate metals and gems within the earth. The moon also obviously affected the earth, the most dramatic example being the tides.

Because of the powers of the sun and moon to affect the growth and other attributes of plants, scientific astrology was an important part of the study of herbs and herbal remedies. Similarly, because the moon was thought to influence liquids, the phases of the moon were associated with critical days of illness. Most medieval scientists, many of whom were also theologians, agreed that the heavens could not affect human souls, for any form of astrological determinism was thought to violate human free will. Nevertheless, the planets were thought to have an influence over the human body, which might in turn affect a person's emotions, personality, and behavior. The planets, for example, determined the sex of a fetus. For this reason, astrology was an important part of medieval medicine.

From antiquity, the Middle Ages inherited a complex system of "correspondences" between individual planets and specific effects on earth, including effects on human physiology and psychology. Jupiter, for example, usually considered the most noble of the planets after the sun, was thought to be hot and wet and was associated with benevolence, wisdom, masculine beauty, springtime, the metal tin, blood (the noblest of the body's humors), and a sanguine temperament. Saturn, on the other hand, was thought of as cold and dry and was associated with sadness, timidity, a dark or pale complexion, winter, old age, the metal lead, black bile (a potentially dangerous humor liable to cause physical and mental illness), and a melancholic temperament. The moon, not surprisingly, was connected to water, infancy, silver, phlegm, and madness, and was thought of as feminine.

Over time, these correspondences became a fully developed theory of personality which became absorbed into the philosophical, medical, and literary culture of the Middle Ages and the Renaissance. Echoes of these beliefs are still observable in our language today, as when we refer to a "sanguine" person as easy-going or use the term "lunatic" for an insane person.

Predictive or judicial astrology attempted to "read" the precise positions of the planets in the heavens in terms of influences directly and indirectly affecting human events. The process of reading horoscopes was quite complex and might involve elaborate determinations of the positions of the planets in relationship to the zodiac, the position of the sun, and the place of the planets in one of twelve "houses" into which the night sky was divided. Judicial astrology, therefore, qualified as a mathematical science and may have functioned as a motivation for the collection of more accurate astronomical observations.

Judicial astrologers typically attempted to determine the probable effects of the stars on human behavior, in particular the type of personality an individual would have based on time and date of birth, the probable outcome of an important decision or event (for example, marriage or a decision to go to war) given the time it was to take place, or, conversely, the determination of the best time to undertake a specific action. Many royal and noble courts during the Middle Ages had a resident astrologer, although it is difficult to judge the extent to which astrology was used to determine or merely to justify the timing of executive decisions. Lest we assume that the practice of astrology merely reflects medieval irrationality and superstition, we should remember that both scientific and judicial astrology flourished during the Scientific Revolution and that Johannes Kepler, the great seventeenth-century astronomer who discovered the elliptical orbits of the planets, was the official astrologer for the court of Emperor Rudolf II. One of the most cogent critiques of judicial astrology from the Middle Ages was written by Oresme, who points out that reason, memory, and judgment provide better tools for predicting the future than do the works of astrologers.

STATICS, KINEMATICS, AND DYNAMICS

Medieval statics (the science of weights), kinematics (the mathematics of motion), and dynamics (the study of the causes of motion) were all closely based on Aristotelian concepts of local, natural, and violent motion (see Chapter 3). Basic to Aristotle's understanding of motion was the maxim "Each thing that is moved is moved by a mover" and that all motion took place in and through a medium, such as air. Aristotle himself had made little effort to quantify motion beyond suggesting (1) that in a naturally falling body the speed is directly proportional to the weight of the body and inversely proportional to the density of the medium and (2) in violent motion the speed is directly proportional to the force applied and inversely proportional to the mass of the moved body.[15] Since applying these proportions to movement in a void would result in an infinitely great speed, for this and other reasons Aristotle also concluded that motion in a void was impossible.

As was the case with astronomy, medieval natural philosophers questioned and qualified many of Aristotle's specific assertions, although they never overthrew the Aristotelian paradigm as a whole. Perhaps their greatest achievements were the attempts in the late Middle Ages to redefine and quantify the concepts of velocity and acceleration, efforts which many historians believe had a direct or indirect influence on Galileo, the great seventeenth-century scientist who invented the modern science of dynamics.

The sciences of statics, kinematics, and dynamics scarcely existed in the early Middle Ages. Prior to the translation and assimilation of the works of Aristotle, as well as those of other Greek and Arabic scientists, there was little effort to treat these topics in a scientific fashion. "Mechanics" is listed in early medieval classifications of the arts and sciences, but seems to have meant no more than "physics" or natural philosophy. Even after Aristotle began to be known in the West, the level of medieval thought on mechanics remained rudimentary. Some "textbook" accounts retained the flavor of a worldview of a cosmos suffused with purpose, value, and natural essences, but did little to further a scientific understanding of local motion. Here, for example, is how the twelfth-century scientist Adelard of Bath explains why heavy objects fall toward the earth to his inquiring but ignorant nephew:

> We know that the earth is heavy. . . . What is heavy stays best in the lowest position. Each thing loves what preserves its life. But it tends towards that which it loves. Therefore it is necessary that every earthy thing tends towards the lowest of all positions. But in a spherical shape it is obvious that what is in the middle is also the lowest. Thus, whatever is earthy tends towards the middle position. The middle position is a simple point which is indivisible and has a place. . . . Where individual weights hurry to, towards that place they also fall. For the falling of weights is nothing other than their hastening to a middle position. When they fall, they do not cease to keep still, unless some force is brought to bear on any of them, as a result of which they are pushed away from their natural tendency.[16]

In the thirteenth and fourteenth centuries, however, a number of medieval thinkers explored how to apply mathematics to the problem of motion and other instances of change. They also reexamined what motion was and what caused it. Their work was often very abstract and highly technical, a challenge to modern students. Yet before we dismiss their efforts as impossibly rarefied, we should remember both the difficulty of the task of analyzing the many factors which affect motion as it exists in everyday life and the fact that late medieval scientists lacked such basic scientific instruments as thermometers, accurate clocks, and slide rules. To a large extent, medieval philosophers got around their lack of precision instruments by concentrating on measurement in the form of ratios and proportions, rather than in absolute numbers. Much of their work was couched in a "What if . . ." format and fell into something like the category of what Galileo would later call "thought experiments." (For these late medieval thinkers, however, unlike Galileo, the aim was to test the limits of logical possibility rather than to find applications to real life situations.) Paradoxically, the history of the Scientific Revolution shows us that a move away from ordinary experience and commonsense toward a more abstract view of nature was a prerequisite to the development of the experimental method (see Chapter 3). The work of these late medieval mathematicians and natural philosophers was a step, if an indirect one, in this direction.

The earliest of this group was Gerard of Brussels (fl. thirteenth century) who, perhaps influenced by the newly translated works of Euclid and Archimedes, attempted to mathematically reduce variations in the velocity of points and lines on revolving solids to uniform rectilinear velocities. About the same time Jordanus of Nemore (fl. 1230–60) wrote a treatise, *De ratione ponderis*, demonstrating the basic rules governing the ratios of weight and length of the arms on both sides of a balance beam (for example, "when the beam of a balance of equal arms is in the horizontal position, then if equal weights are suspended from its extremities, it will not leave the horizontal position").[17]

By the fourteenth century, discussion had become considerably more sophisticated. One line of thought examined what motion was and whether there was such a thing as motion separate from the thing moving. Arising from a somewhat muddled reading of a passage from Aristotle's *Physics* and commentaries on it, many natural philosophers concluded that motion was in fact something distinct from the object that was moving. This view was held by John Buridan, among others. William of Ockham (c. 1285–1347), the great philosopher known for his intellectual rigor, held the opposite view. He argued that since we can describe a moving object without adding a separate entity "motion" by talking about the body and its place at successive times, that "motion" as distinct from moving objects was superfluous; in other words, motion is not a thing but a concept.

Kinematics, the application of mathematics to motion, emerged during the first half of the fourteenth century in the work of a remarkable group of mathematicians associated with Merton College, Oxford, known as the Oxford Calculators. Thomas Bradwardine (c. 1290–1349), William Heytesbury (fl. 1335), Richard Swineshead (fl. 1340–55), and John Dumbleton (d. c. 1349) began with a general project to quantify the intensification and diminution of the qualities (or "forms" in medieval terminology), such as "hotness" or "whiteness," of physical objects. They also developed a distinction between the *intensity* of a quality in an object and the total *quantity* of that quality in a given object: for example, they distinguished between the "hotness" of an object as reflected in its temperature and its overall quantity of heat, depending in part on the size of the object. The Oxford Calculators deliberately couched their analysis in purely logical terms with no reference to tangible objects and had no practical means of making actual measurements. Nevertheless, their work had practical applications, for example, in attempts to calculate the efficacy of medicines and in the development of ideas about the working of a monetary economy. This work also had implications for chemistry and the science of matter, in that it raised the question of whether "qualities" should be considered as existing in a continuum or in terms of discrete units of intensity (see Chapter 5).

The next step toward the mathematization of motion was to develop a method of representing increases and decreases in qualities, including speed and acceleration. Perhaps using the merchant's abacus as a model, the Oxford Calculators did this by conceiving qualitative change to "occur over a qualitative 'distance' open to quantification."[18] Nicole Oresme turned this idea into a simple and elegant geometrical representation of the relationships between the acceleration of a moving body, the distance traveled, and the time elapsed. Oresme used a base line to represent the extension of time. From that base line, the intensity of a quality of the object—say, velocity—at any one point in time was represented by a perpendicular line from the base line with changing intensities recorded as proportionally longer or shorter perpendicular lines. By connecting the tops of the perpendicular lines, the mathematical relationships between time and velocity would be represented geometrically. Thus, uniform velocity of an object would be graphed as two parallel lines, a uniformly accelerated velocity (defined as equal increments of velocity acquired in equal periods of time) from a zero point by the hypotenuse of a right triangle, and a nonuniform velocity by whatever figure resulted from graphing the velocity against time (see Figure 5).[19]

The final step taken was to begin the process of quantifying velocity by establishing the relationships between different "quantities" of speed, time, and distance for the same body or bodies of equal weights. In 1328 Thomas Bradwardine, working from Aristotle's view that velocity is related to resistance through a medium, postulated that if a specific velocity of a moving body is produced by a specific proportion of force to resistance, then if the ratio of force to resistance is squared, the velocity will be doubled.[20] Richard Swineshead subsequently experimented with varying parts of this formula and calculating what the resulting changes would be. William Heytesbury first formulated what came to be known as the "Merton mean-speed theorem." This theorem stipulated that a body moving at a uniformly accelerated speed will travel the same distance in a given time as a body moving at a uniform speed equal to the average speed of the accelerating body. A related theorem formulated by the Oxford Calculators said that in a body moving with a uniformly accelerated velocity, the distance covered in the first half of the movement will be one-third of the distance covered in the second half of the movement. Finally, Oresme developed geometrical proofs for both theorems. Both theorems are easily recognized as true if the uniformly accelerated movement is represented as the hypotenuse of a right triangle with the horizontal base line representing time, the perpendicular side representing velocity, and the area representing the resultant distance traveled (see Figure 6).[21] Galileo used the mean-speed theorem in his own work.

Late medieval natural philosophers were also innovative on the question of the causes of movement. Aristotle, as we have said, argued that in forced motion every moving object is moved by a mover. This meant in practice that there was no such thing as "action at a distance" and

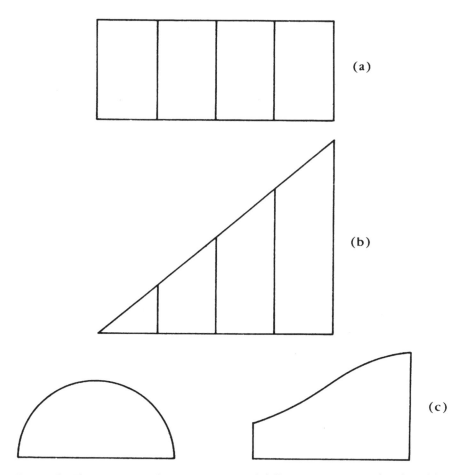

(a)

(b)

(c)

Figure 5. The geometrical representation of different motions as developed by late medieval mathematicians. The base line represents the extension of time. The intensity of a quality of the object at any one point in time was represented by a perpendicular line from the base line with changing intensities recorded as proportionally longer or shorter perpendicular lines. Connecting the tops of the perpendicular lines was a simple way to represent the relationship between time and velocity. Two parallel lines (a) represented an object moving at a uniform velocity. A uniformly accelerated velocity was graphed as the hypotenuse of a right triangle (b) and a nonuniform velocity by various figures resulting from graphing the velocity against time (c). *David C. Lindberg*, The Beginnings of Western Science: The European Scientific tradition in Philosophical, Religious, and Institutional Context, 600 B.C. to A.D. 1450 (*Chicago and London: University of Chicago Press, 1992*), *figure 12.7, p. 299.*

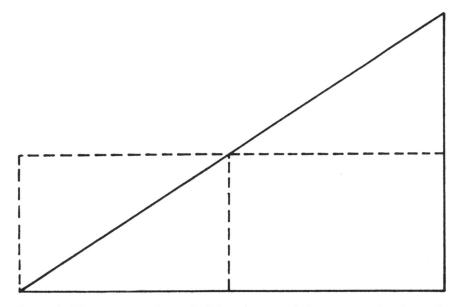

Figure 6. The geometrical proof of the mean-speed theorem. Uniformly accelerated movement is represented as the hypotenuse of a right triangle with the
horizontal base line representing time, the perpendicular side representing velocity and the area representing the resultant distance traveled. The area of the
triangle is clearly equal to the area of a rectangle whose area represents the
distance traveled by a body moving uniformly with a speed equal to the mean
speed of the uniformly accelerated body. *John E. Murdoch and Edith D. Sylla,
"The Science of Motion," in David C. Lindberg, ed.,* Science in the Middle Ages
(Chicago and London: University of Chicago Press, 1978), figure 12, p. 240.

"the mover" had to be in continuous physical contact with the moving
object. Local, forced motion, according to Aristotle, therefore depends
on the power to transmit movement being transferred from the original
mover to the surrounding medium so that there is continuous contact
between the moving object and a force making it move. That is, when
an arrow is shot into the air, the bow transmits power to the air, which
transmits power to the air further on, and so on, until the resistance of
the air overcomes the diminishing power of the transmitted motive
power to keep the object moving, and it begins to fall back to earth.

Difficulties had been raised about this theory since antiquity, among
them how a medium could simultaneously act as resistance to, and trans-
mitter of, motion. Building on earlier ideas by Arabic and European

scientists, Buridan attempted to improve on Aristotle by positing that the bow or other projector transmitted or impressed a natural "incorporeal motive force," which he called "impetus," to the projectile. Buridan thus eliminated the need to posit a medium to explain motion, opening up the possibility of motion in a void. (William of Ockham, in another context, also argued for "action at a distance," in this case that light might impress an image on the eye without any effect on the intervening medium.) Impetus continued to make the projectile move until some sort of resistance or counterforce intervened, its strength determined by the quantity of matter of the body in which it was impressed. Buridan also suggested that additionally generated impetus explained why freely falling bodies accelerate and that an initial burst of impetus delivered by God at the creation was the cause of the eternal circular motions of the heavenly bodies. This latter idea was important, in part because it suggested a purely mechanical explanation for the movements of the celestial bodies. It was also significant because it implied the possibility that motion in a resistance-less environment would continue indefinitely.

Some historians of science, including Grant and Herbert Butterfield, have suggested that Buridan's notion of impetus, like the mean-speed theorem, had an important influence on the early thinking of Galileo on dynamics and the later development of the idea of inertia.[22] Others have emphasized that Buridan's concept lacks the fundamental idea of inertia—that a body, once at rest or set in motion, needs no additional force to continue in that state.

OPTICS

Optics, known by contemporaries as *perspectiva*, was a multifaceted science which included not only the mathematical study of light and its behavior (for example, reflection, refraction, and perspective) but also the meteorological effects of light (as in rainbows), the use of lenses, and the anatomy and physiology of the eye. From the thirteenth century onward, medieval scientists attempted to formulate a comprehensive theory of light which would take into account the geometrical properties of reflection and refraction and provide an explanation of sight in both mathematical and physical terms. Optics, like astronomy, thus had one foot in the mathematical sciences and the other in natural philosophy.

Optics also had a strong practical aspect. Arabic physicians had taken a particular interest in medical knowledge about the eye and eye diseases, information passed on to European doctors and natural philosophers. Experimentation with the practical uses of lenses, ranging from the invention of eyeglasses in the late thirteenth century to speculation about the uses of magnifying lenses and "burning" mirrors as weapons of war, was also part of medieval optics.

Finally, optics drew on a deep-seated philosophical tradition which identified light with spiritual revelation. In the Platonic and Neoplatonic traditions, absorbed into Christian thought through St. Augustine, light was a powerful metaphor for the process by which an individual came to an awareness of divine truth, that is, became "enlightened." Robert Grosseteste (d. 1253), a natural philosopher associated with Oxford and also bishop of Lincoln, for example, thought that the cosmos had originated in a point of light which then diffused itself into the material creation.

Optics first emerged as a unified field of study in the work of the eleventh-century Arabic scientist Ibn al-Haytham, known in the West as Alhazen (c. 965–c. 1039). Alhazen inherited two divergent theories of sight perception from his predecessors, and his achievement was to utilize and reconcile the most satisfying elements of each. Alhazen's ideas as assimilated and revised by the European scientists Roger Bacon (c. 1220–c. 92), John Pecham (d. 1292), and Witelo (d. after 1281) were the basis for the mathematical treatment of western optics until the seventeenth century.

Ancient science took for granted that only physical images could produce sense perception in the sense organs and that physical effects could take place only through some medium or mode of transmission. A major problem in explaining sight, therefore, had been to account for a mechanism of physical contact between the eye and the object that is seen. The atomists of the ancient world had suggested that visual perception occurs as objects emit a sort of film or outline of the same color and shape as the object itself; this "simulacrum," or image, enters the eye, triggering the perception of the object. Aristotle concurred that vision took place because of images emitted from the seen object, but he modified this theory to emphasize the role of the transparent medium in transmitting the qualities of the seen object. This idea, the "intromission" theory, explained the physical process of visual perception in plausible terms but failed to explain why the eye received a clear image of the world rather than a confused jumble of overlapping images. Another influential explanation, however, the "extramission" theory, was that the eye itself emitted "a visual power" or "species" which, when intercepted by an opaque object, registered perception of the object. This visual power was seen as a pyramid, the apex of which is in the eye and the base of which is on all parts of the visible object. Although this theory had some obvious flaws (for example, it made it difficult to understand how far distant objects such as the fixed stars could be seen apparently instantaneously, did little to explain how the emitted rays affected the eye they had left, and could not explain how strong light could physically injure the eye), it was superior in explaining how the eye was able to clearly register the distinct distance, location, size, and shape of seen objects and also provided a clear basis for a mathematical treatment of light. This theory was also implicitly supported by Galenic medicine which, based on the physiology of the brain, optic nerve, and eye, suggested that a "vital spirit" reaches out from the eye to the surrounding air and to the object.

Alhazen's innovation was to understand the "intromission" theory in such a way as to make it useful for a geometrical analysis of the behavior of light. Opponents of the theory asked how, if simulacra are emitted from objects, does the eye keep straight all the incoming images? Do they not interfere with one another? How are objects able to emit images so that the same object can be seen by thousands of people at the same time? Alhazen solved these problems by positing that while objects may be emitting images in all directions, only one image would enter the eye exactly perpendicular to the convex surface of the eye. It was this image alone which would trigger perception; all other images, those entering at other than a ninety-degree angle, would fall away and not register on the eye.

In working out mathematical descriptions of the behavior of light, Bacon, Pecham, and Witelo adopted versions of Alhazen's intromission theory. Also following Alhazen, they assumed that light traveled in straight lines. On this basis, they were able to derive accurate geometrical formulations of the laws of reflection and refraction and pinpoint where a reflected image would appear in differently curved mirrors. Perhaps the most sophisticated application of these laws was Theodoric of Freiberg's (d. c. 1310) analysis of the rainbow. Theodoric's analysis demonstrates that light is refracted in an individual raindrop, then reflected back by the back of the raindrop, and then refracted a second time as it leaves the raindrop, producing the perception of a rainbow. This understanding of how light functions in a rainbow is essentially the modern one.

In tackling the more difficult problem of what exactly light and color were, however, medieval scientists were on shakier ground. Bacon understood light to be a "species" or "form" radiating in a straight line from a body. In the words of David Lindberg, "It was agreed by virtually everybody who touched on the matter . . . that both light . . . and color propagate their forms or likenesses through transparent media to observers."[23] Yet scientists were unsure whether the species of light should be considered to be corporeal, noncorporeal, or in some way intermediate between these states (perhaps not surprising considering that modern notions of light consider it as both a particle and a wave). There was also discussion of whether light was propagated instantaneously or merely very quickly.

CONCLUSION

The exact sciences contained some of the most creative and original scientific thought of the Middle Ages. Although medieval natural philosophers continued to work within the framework of Aristotelian thought, in many specific instances they went far beyond standard Aristotelian responses to scientific questions. In discussing such issues as the possibility of a rotating earth, the structure of the universe, the path of light through a raindrop, or the relationship between velocity, time, and distance for a freely falling body, medieval scientists showed an interest in looking at natural phenomena in new and original ways.

Several observations are in order here. First, medieval philosophers did not passively accept an inherited body of thought from their classical and Arabic predecessors. Instead, they questioned, redefined, modified, and even—occasionally—rejected the statements of Aristotle and other authorities. It follows from this that the sciences discussed in this chapter were not monolithic or static bodies of information and thought. Within the general scope of Aristotelian natural philosophy, there was ample room for differences of opinion and emphasis.

Second, the systematic efforts of late medieval scientists to apply mathematics to natural phenomena was an important step toward the ultimate success of modern science. This in itself was a departure from Aristotelian natural philosophy, which emphasized qualitative over quantitative assessment of change in nature. Although they failed to arrive at a unified theory of dynamics, the Oxford Calculators and Buridan and Orseme, their successors at the University of Paris, did begin a project for formulating the mathematical laws which underlay the workings of nature.

Finally, the main advances made in the exact sciences were conceptual rather than advances in the collection of data or the empirical observation of data. The main exception to this generalization was astronomical observation, which did become more comprehensive and more accurate. However, the insights into the nature and causes of local motion, the relativistic character of our perceptions of the movements of celestial bodies, and the nature of sight were based more on conceptual leaps than on new facts. This is partly the result of the subjects addressed by these sciences: astronomical phenomena, light, and motion are by their nature difficult to observe, especially without the precision instruments we take for granted today. However, it also reflects the nature of much of late medieval science in these areas, which was speculative and closely tied to the disciplines of philosophy and logic.

To recognize this last point, however, is not to denigrate the efforts of late medieval natural philosophers. Science progresses as much by new ideas as by new factual information; indeed, new concepts are often a prerequisite for finding fresh empirical evidence. If the extraordinary achievement of the Scientific Revolution was to bring together for the first time in human history new ideas with new empirical data through the development of a true experimental method, then medieval work in the exact sciences was part of the essential background and preparation for this accomplishment.

NOTES

1. Roger Bacon, The Opus majus of Roger Bacon, trans. Robert Belle Burke (New York: Russell and Russell, 1962), p. 124.

2. Edward Grant, ed., A Source Book in Medieval Science (Cambridge, MA: Harvard University Press, 1974), p. 136, n. 1.

3. Grant, Source Book, p. 150, n. 1.

4. John Murdoch, "From Social into Intellectual Factors: An Aspect of the Unitary Character of Late Medieval Learning," in John Murdoch and Edith Sylla, eds., *The Cultural Context of Medieval Learning* (Dordrecht and Boston: D. Reidal, 1975), p. 287.

5. Stephen C. McCluskey, *Astronomies and Cultures in Early Medieval Europe* (Cambridge, England: Cambridge University Press, 1998), pp. 171–74.

6. McCluskey, *Astronomies*, p. 180.

7. The problem arises because as was shown by Johannes Kepler in 1609, the orbits of the planets around the sun are in fact elliptical and, for each planet, in equal time intervals, a line from the planet to the sun sweeps out equal areas.

8. Edward Grant, *Planets, Stars, and Orbs: The Medieval Cosmos, 1200–1687* (Cambridge, England: Cambridge University Press, 1994), p. 284.

9. Grant, *Planets, Stars, and Orbs*, pp. 682–741.

10. Ptolemy was referring to two Hellenistic astronomers, Heraclides of Pontus and Aristarchus of Samos. Aristarchus argued not only for the daily rotation of the earth on its axis, but also for the revolution of the earth around the sun.

11. Nicole Oresme, *Le Livre du ciel et du monde*, ed. Albert D. Menut and Alexander J. Denomy, trans. with an Introduction by Albert D. Menut (Madison: University of Wisconsin Press, 1968), pp. 537, 539.

12. John Buridan, "The Compatibility of the Earth's Diurnal Rotation with Astronomical Phenomena," in Grant, *Source Book*, p. 501.

13. Oresme, *Le Livre du ciel et du monde*, p. 535.

14. John North, *The Norton History of Astronomy and Cosmology* (New York and London: W. W. Norton, 1995), p. 121.

15. G.E.R. Lloyd, *Aristotle: The Growth and Structure of His Thought* (Cambridge, England: Cambridge University Press, 1968), p. 176.

16. Adelard of Bath, *Adelard of Bath, Conversations with His Nephew: On the Same and the Different, Questions on Natural Science, and On Birds*, ed. and trans. Charles Burnett, with the collaboration of Italo Ronca, Pedro Mantuas España, and Baudouin van den Abeele (Cambridge, England: Cambridge University Press, 1998), p. 181.

17. Jordanes of Nemore, *De ratione ponderis* in Grant, *Source Book*, p. 214.

18. Joel Kaye, *Economy and Nature in the Fourteenth Century: Money, Market Exchange, and the Emergence of Scientific Thought* (Cambridge, England: Cambridge University Press, 1998), pp. 190, 202.

19. This discussion is heavily indebted to David C. Lindberg, *The Beginnings of Western Science: The European Scientific Tradition in Philosophical, Religious, and Institutional Context, 600 B.C. to A.D. 1450* (Chicago and London: University of Chicago Press, 1992), pp. 298–300.

20. John E. Murdoch and Edith D. Sylla, "The Science of Motion," in *Science in the Middle Ages*, ed. David C. Lindberg (Chicago and London: University of Chicago Press, 1978), pp. 224–26. In order for the mathematical laws governing falling bodies to be successfully formulated, motion had to be imagined as occurring in a void, so that the effect of air resistance could be discounted. This step was first taken by Galileo. Eventually, Galileo would recognize that the velocity of a freely falling body is uniformly accelerated proportionally to time and that the distance fallen is directly proportional to the square of its time of fall.

21. The foregoing discussion is heavily indebted to Lindberg, *Beginnings*, pp. 296–300 and Murdoch and Sylla, "Motion," pp. 224–40.

22. Edward Grant, *Physical Science in the Middle Ages* (Cambridge, England: Cambridge University Press, 1977), pp. 53–54, 58; Herbert Butterfield, *The Origins of Modern Science 1300–1800* (New York: The Free Press, 1965), pp. 22–26.

23. David C. Lindberg, "The Science of Optics," in *Science in the Middle Ages*, ed. Lindberg, p. 357.

CHAPTER 5

THE BIOLOGICAL AND EARTH SCIENCES

This chapter discusses the biological and earth sciences, including chemistry, alchemy, medicine, zoology, botany, geology, meteorology, and geography, as they were known in the Middle Ages. Although some of these sciences might be classed as "minor," alchemy and medicine were among the most historically significant of all the medieval sciences. As was the case with astronomy and the other mathematical sciences reviewed in the previous chapter, these sciences were based on Aristotle's natural philosophy, even though Aristotle's ideas were often filtered through the work of Hellenistic and Arabic scientists and sometimes colored with aspects of Platonism. We can make some general comments about this group of sciences. First, scientific description and explanation in these sciences was qualitative rather than quantitative and made use of the Aristotelian definition of the four fundamental qualities (hot, cold, wet, and dry). Overall, little use was made of mathematics. Second, although medieval scientists continued to accept fundamental Aristotelian theory in these sciences, they did not hesitate to go beyond or even reject Aristotle on specific points on the basis of their own experience. Third, there is a utilitarian bent to medieval practice of many of these sciences. This tendency to look for the practical benefits afforded by these sciences fed into medieval development of technology.

THE SCIENCE OF MATTER (CHEMISTRY AND ALCHEMY)

A unified science of chemistry in the modern sense did not exist in the Middle Ages. Rather, several different areas of inquiry coexisted which together might be said to make up the medieval sciences of matter. First, there was considerable theoretical discussion of the nature of matter and how to define what happens when matter is transformed—for example, when water, through evaporation, seems to become air. This discussion was couched in terms of Aristotelian concepts of "substance" and "form," which medieval writers elaborated upon with considerable detail and subtlety. Second, medieval writers had a lively interest in cataloging and improving upon methods of producing useful chemical substances such as pigments to be used in book production and stained glass as well as the production and refinement of metals and medicines. Medieval scientists recorded this kind of information in recipe books, sometimes presented in quite straightforward terms, at other times dressed up as "Books of Secrets" in order to protect professional knowledge and intellectual property from theft as well as to provide an aura of religious and philosophical truth. An important example is the twelfth-century work *On Diverse Arts* by a monk known as Theophilus. Theophilus, who emphasizes the virtuous nature of his craft, provides detailed instructions on glass-making, metalwork, paint-making, bell-casting, and the construction of an organ. Over the next three centuries, recipe books continued to be written, becoming more specialized and often registering technical innovations. Finally, there was alchemy, which was practiced both as a practical discipline designed to produce substances useful for human life and as a theoretical and spiritual discipline accompanied by elaborate symbolism and mystical overtones.

Discussion of the nature of matter led medieval natural philosophers in several different directions. On the one hand, some investigated whether there were different kinds of matter, whether there was such a thing as "spiritual matter," and whether matter existed in "natural minima," that is, in the smallest pieces that retained the qualities of a particular substance. Atomism, or the idea that matter existed in discrete, indivisible particles, was also discussed, although only one thinker, Nicholas of Autrecourt (b. c. 1300; d. after 1350), is known to have accepted it. On the other hand, there was considerable attention to how materials, especially metals, could be transformed in terms of the four Aristotelian elements of earth, water, fire, and air. This discussion often shaded into the practice of alchemy.

The empirical and practical side of the medieval science of matter is illustrated not only in recipe books but also in works specifically on alchemy, many of which contained a wealth of practical information on chemical processes.

Alchemy had its origins in the ancient world. It was brought to Europe first by way of Arabic Spain and later by translations of other Arabic alchemical texts by Abu Bakr al-Razi (c. 865–between 932 and 935) and others. The most famous of these texts were those attributed to "Geber," who was perhaps the Arabic alchemist Jabir ibn Hayyan (fl. eighth century). Albertus Magnus (c. 1193–1280), Roger Bacon (c. 1219–92), Arnald of Villanova (c. 1240–1311), Paul of Taranto (thirteenth century), and Petrus Bonus, author of "The New Pearl of Great Price" (written c. 1330), were among the important European natural philosophers who treated alchemical subjects. Later medieval alchemy tended to become increasingly focused on the spiritual and magical; the high point of this type of alchemy was reached in the sixteenth century during the Scientific Revolution.

The ultimate aim of alchemy was to discover so-called "elixirs," substances which could transmute metals into gold and prolong human life. Alchemists attempted to reduce matter to its primal condition and then build it up again in the desired form, that is, gold or life-enhancing medicines. The theoretical basis for this effort was Aristotle's idea that matter had no qualities until form was imposed on it and that the four elements could be transformed into each other. To this, some alchemists added the influence of celestial forces. Critics, and there were many during the Middle Ages, charged that only God could transmute species and that alchemists were either scoundrels or fools. Alchemists responded that their craft was difficult but not impossible, that it was based on scientific principles, and that human art, properly applied, can equal or even outdo nature.

Alchemy, despite its mystical overtones, had important scientific consequences. First, in the hands of some of its practitioners, alchemy represented one of the earliest attempts to construe scientific methodology in terms of creating a science that would allow human technology to improve upon nature. Roger Bacon, for example, asserted that alchemy was the primary science because it deals with elementary matter. According to Bacon, "experimental science," of which alchemy was a major part, would bring things of "wonderful utility" to the Church, to the state, and to individuals. Another thirteenth-century alchemist, Paul of Taranto, argued that the alchemist, who had true scientific knowledge of matter and its qualities, could manipulate materials on the most basic level. Although alchemists may have overestimated what they could actually accomplish, they did assert something very much like the modern concept of applied science.[1] Late medieval and Renaissance alchemists also tended to emphasize how alchemy could improve man's material condition.

Second, alchemists laid many of the foundations of the later science of chemistry. Practical alchemy included knowledge of techniques of distillation, condensation, sublimation, the heating of corrosive materials to high temperatures, and the smelting of metals. Essential to these techniques was the development of more effective apparatus, and alchemists pioneered in the use and improvement of the still, the balance for weighing substances, glass beakers, and furnaces. The distillation of pure alcohol, often used in medicine, was first achieved during the twelfth century. Of particular importance was the production and identification of nitric, hydrochloric, and sulfuric acids, which could be used in a variety of chemical processes. In addition, mercury was used to dissolve metals and sodium chloride to corrode them. Alchemists were also the first in the West to mention saltpeter (potassium nitrate), the active ingredient in gunpowder.

MEDICINE

Medicine had a more direct, intimate, and far-reaching impact on medieval people's lives than the other sciences we have discussed. Given the wretched health conditions prevalent in the Middle Ages, including high infant mortality, poor diet, often dangerous working conditions, and common but deadly diseases, almost everyone must have had recourse to some sort of healer at some point in their lives. Medicine, therefore, had an immediate relevance to daily life which cut across social classes and had a more than academic importance for both medical practitioners and their patients.

Medicine, moreover, by its nature interacted with society at large. As Nancy G. Siraisi, the noted historian of medieval and Renaissance medicine, has pointed out, "the history of medicine, perhaps more than that of any other discipline or skilled occupation, illuminates broad social and cultural patterns of the period."[2] Medical knowledge, for example, both reflected and reinforced attitudes about sexuality, reproduction, and appropriate behavior for men and women. Echoes of medical ideas on the sexual differences between men and women appeared in advice manuals and ecclesiastical pronouncements on sexual morality and proper gender roles. Medical authors supplied methods for testing whether a woman was a virgin (her urine would be clear rather than cloudy) and suggested that women's relative weakness could be explained by their greater coldness and humidity. On the other hand, some medieval medical writers were remarkably independent, for example, recommending sexual intercourse, even for adolescent girls, for health reasons although this ran counter to the Church's moral strictures on sexuality.

Medicine also intersected with ideas about magic and the supernatural. Illness without an obvious cause might be attributed to the work of a demon, a spirit, or even a vengeful saint as punishment for sin, necessitating a cure by exorcism or magical remedies rather than medical treatment. Conversely, physicians were, on occasion, called in to determine if the healing miracles attributed to a candidate for sainthood were in fact miraculous, rather than natural, cures. In this way, physicians were to some extent the rivals of both magicians and religious healers.

In this section, we will concentrate on learned medicine in the Middle Ages, that is, medical theory and treatments as they appear in texts produced by educated individuals. We should keep in mind, however, that much of the medicine practiced in the Middle Ages was performed by various types of practitioners with varying degrees of formal learning. Relatively little is known about these people or their methods of treatment. Many village healers were almost certainly illiterate and undoubtedly used a combination of observation, commonsense, and folk remedies. Other individuals, commonly referred to as "empirics" (because they relied more on practical training than on book-learning), combined a practice of surgery or medical treatment with other trades or crafts. In the early Middle Ages, monasteries were centers of medical practice although few monks or nuns had much formal medical training. Despite the fact that they left few traces in the historical record, many women also undoubtedly helped the sick on a part-time, informal basis, either as part of their domestic duties or as acts of charity.

During the early Middle Ages, medicine seems to have been largely therapeutic, based on herbal prescriptions and traditional techniques such as bloodletting. Some of the rudiments of classical medicine were known through the survival of a few classical texts and compendia derived from them, especially herbals and a few works by Galen. This knowledge seems to have fused with local Germanic practices and folk remedies. Early medieval medical books, such as the Anglo-Saxon *Leechbook*, include a bewildering collection of remedies using herbs, animal parts, and ground up stones, to be taken internally or placed on the skin as poultices. These were often combined with incantations, prayers, and the use of these same substances in amulets worn around the neck, making it difficult to clearly distinguish medical healing from magic. Other recipes used herbs and foodstuffs in a completely naturalistic manner, for example, the use of barley-water in a restorative diet. Although it is difficult to judge the efficacy of herbal remedies, it is known that many plants do have profound pharmacological properties and, in addition, a placebo effect may have operated, causing an improvement in symptoms.

Medicine, like many of the other sciences, was transformed during the twelfth and thirteenth centuries from a practical and relatively unsophisticated enterprise into a highly structured and rigorous system of thought. The translation of the body of Greek and Arabic medical texts for the first time provided a clear scientific framework for medical practice. During the twelfth century, many of the works of Galen, the great Hellenistic physician whose ideas formed the basis of Greek, Arabic, and European medieval medicine, became available. Equally important was the translation of Avicenna's *Canon*, a massive 1,000 page encyclopedia of medical knowledge, works by the Arabic physician and alchemist al-Razi, and a host of lesser-known works.

Increased economic growth together with the expansion of cities, the founding of universities, and more organized church and secular governments from the late eleventh century onward also had an impact on the practice of medicine. A center for medical practice, serving both men and women, seems to have developed at Salerno in southern Italy as early as the mid-tenth century. The most celebrated product associated with Salerno was a collection of texts on the diseases of and treatments for women known as the *Trotula* and dated from shortly after 1100. Widely read into the sixteenth century, the *Trotula* has been called "the most popular assembly of materials on women's medicine from the late twelfth through the fifteenth centuries."[3] Of uncertain authorship, parts of the *Trotula* were probably written by a woman physician, or written about an actual woman's practice.

The revival of a more theoretically oriented science of medicine also appeared in twelfth-century works associated with cathedral schools and monastic centers. Particularly interesting are the writings of Hildegard of Bingen (1098–1179), abbess of Rupertsberg and later Eibingen in north central Germany. Hildegard, a prolific writer of letters, sermons, visionary works, dramatic productions, and liturgical music, was also the author of two works on medicine and natural philosophy, the *Physica* and the *Causa et curae* (Causes and Cures). In these works, Hildegard pays special attention to the medicinal uses of plants, remedies for common ailments, and human physiology. Among the illnesses she discusses are headaches, fevers, rashes, abscesses, intestinal worms, sterility, and baldness. Particularly striking are her remarks on sexuality, which highlight female desire and pleasure in sex.

During the twelfth and thirteenth centuries, medical training was incorporated into the university curriculum, with the most prestigious faculties emerging at the universities of Bologna, Montpellier, and Paris and by the fifteenth century, Padua. The curriculum included the major Arabic and Greek authors and led to a doctorate in medicine. Most of the students were also exposed to the scientific works of Aristotle. The course of study included not only the study of texts but some degree of hands-on experience, including accompanying a senior physician on rounds, some independent practice, and attendance at public dissections of human bodies.[4] Autopsies on human bodies were done for training purposes by the beginning of the fourteenth century. Most university-trained physicians devoted at least some time to actual attendance on patients, not only out of interest and a sense of duty but also as a lucrative source of income. Even the most educated physician recognized the limitations of what could be offered patients, and it is sobering to reflect on Siraisi's assessment that "no means existed whereby medicine could alter the course of acute, life-threatening, or serious chronic disease."[5]

The institutionalization of medical education within universities had several effects. First, it reinforced a social and professional hierarchy of medical practitioners. University-trained physicians had the most prestige and commanded the highest fees, yet this group seems to have encompassed overall no more than half of the known medical practitioners between the twelfth and fifteenth centuries. Other medical practitioners might be literate, even if not university educated, and were often licensed by guilds, city governments, or other public authorities. A subset of medical practitioners were surgeons—who specialized in treating injuries and their complications by physical manipulation, cutting, cautery, and external medications—and barber-surgeons, who often performed bloodletting. Like doctors in general, surgeons as a group ran the gamut from highly educated individuals to illiterate, itinerant empirics. Although women were excluded from universities, female physicians sometimes surface in historical records, often because they were charged with practicing without proper training. Women also appear as barbers and surgeons. Midwives were the largest group of female medical practitioners, for until the early modern period male physicians typically only attended births of the upper classes (an exception being difficult births when surgery was being considered). Midwifery involved considerable skill and judgment, although we know little about midwife training until the early modern period.

A second result of the establishment of academic medicine was to promote a theoretically oriented medicine which depended heavily on a synthesis of Galenic medicine and Aristotelian natural philosophy. Although actual diagnosis and treatment must have depended heavily on experience and were flexible and pragmatic, simplified versions of these medical ideas were extraordinarily long-lived and left their traces in literature, philosophy, and common attitudes into the twentieth century.

Three fundamental concepts underlay medieval medical theory: the idea of "complexion" (*complexio*), or temperaments, the closely related idea of the four humors, and the "faculties" or functions of the major organs in bodily processes. Medical astrology, which was pervasive in late medieval medicine, also was an important part of medieval medical knowledge.

"Complexion" referred to the balance of hot, cold, dry, and wet—the four qualities fundamental to Aristotelian natural philosophy—in living beings. Not only each individual person, but every type of plant, animal, food, medicine, and organ within the body had its own natural and appropriate complexion. The heart, for example, was naturally hot, the brain cold. Similarly, almonds and lentils were cold, mandrake root cold and dry, the herbs feverwort and wormwood hot and dry.

Complexion, however, was always relative to some degree. A particular substance might be "hot" with respect to the human body but "cold" with respect to other animals. Moreover, complexion varied naturally with respect to age, region, and gender. Age made people colder and drier, people from northern climates were naturally colder and moister than those from hot, dry regions, and women were in general colder and moister than men.

Galenic theory also supposed that the body produced four distinctive fluids or humors from ingested food: blood, phlegm, yellow or red bile, and black bile. Health depended on the proper balance of the humors within the body according to the person's natural complexion and was affected by diet, personal habits, and emotional states. Each humor had its own functions and qualities which contributed to the health of the person and produced its own characteristic illnesses if there were either too much or too little of that particular humor circulating in the body. The humors were produced through a series of digestions or "concoctions" which transformed food by the action of internal heat first in the stomach, then in the liver, and finally in the veins and members. At each stage, both good and healthful humors were produced as well as bad residual humors, which needed to be expelled from the body in the form of perspiration and menstruation, as well as in the urine and feces and other bodily excretions.

Humoral theory presupposed that physical and mental health were closely related. The balance of humors affected the emotions and the mind as well as the body; conversely, emotional states were recognized as affecting a person's physical condition. Of the four humors, blood was primary: it supplied the body with nourishment and was the main product of concoction in the liver. Hot and wet, blood was associated with growth and life. As it traveled around the body, it was further refined, in women becoming breast milk and in men, semen. A person in whom blood predominated would be agreeable and well proportioned and would have abundant body hair. Phlegm (which included all colorless and whitish secretions except breast milk and semen) was judged to be cold and wet. Thought to be an "imperfectly matured blood," it also supplied nourishment, was present as a secondary fluid in the blood and was associated with the brain. Phlegmatic individuals were plump, lazy, stupid, and pale. Yellow or red bile, described as hot and dry, also served to nourish the body (especially the gallbladder), but its special functions were to thin the blood so that it might travel into the smallest parts of the body and to cleanse the intestines. People dominated by yellow bile were graceful but often angry. Black bile was the most dangerous of the humors. Cold and dry, it nourished the bones and the spleen, thickened the blood, and strengthened the stomach. Excess black bile, however, resulted in melancholy and was associated with depression and insanity.

Medical theory also posited three systems of organs and their functions within the body. The vital faculty, associated with the heart, thoracic cavity, and arteries, transported blood and "spiritus" (life force or breath) and provided for the fundamentals of life, including respiration, the pulse, and the beating of the heart. The natural faculty accounted for the processes of nutrition, growth, and reproduction and was associated with the digestive organs, the liver, and the veins. (The veins and arteries were not recognized as connected in ancient and medieval medicine and were thought to serve different functions, the veins supplying nourishment, the arteries breath.) Finally, the animal faculty, so called because *anima* was the word for soul, provided for movement, sensation, and mental activity and was located in the brain, spinal cord, and nervous system.

In diagnosing a patient, physicians were expected to note the patient's general appearance, take a history of the illness, and, especially, observe the condition of the patient's urine and pulse. One text distinguishes among over forty different types of unhealthy urine based on variations of color, thickness, quantity, and other qualities and a urine flask was a standard part of the physician's equipment (see Figure 7). Treatment was divided into diet, medicines, and surgery. The latter often meant bloodletting, which was regarded as a particularly efficacious treatment. (Figure 8 shows a patient undergoing bloodletting, or phlebotomy.) Wine and distilled alcohol were used to clean wounds and as pain relievers. Recommendations for diet were often based on common experience, for example, prunes for constipation and chicken broth for strength, but they also followed the humoral idea that "contraries drive out contraries." Therefore, if a patient had been diagnosed as suffering from an excess of black bile, which is cold and dry, foods that were considered hot and wet would be recommended. Medicines, which might be given by mouth or used as ointments, were usually composed of herbs and animal products and followed a similar pattern. To rid the body of bad humors, substances that caused vomiting or diarrhea were often administered. An additional source of information for diagnosis and treatment was medical astrology, which taught that illnesses, espe-

Figure 7. A deathbed scene from the 1430s. Note the physician holding his urine flask on the left in the background and the monk and nun praying in the foreground. *The Pierpont Morgan Library, NY, Ms. M. 917, Book of Hours of Catherine of Cleves, f. 180. The Pierpont Morgan Library / Art Resource, NY.*

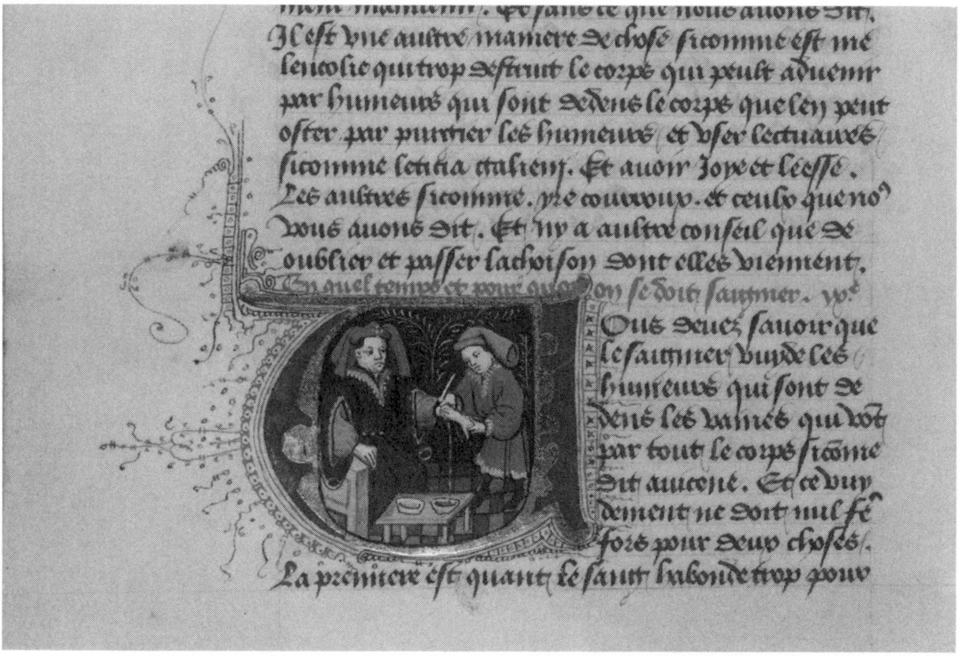

Figure 8. Bloodletting. Bloodletting, or phlebotomy, was a major form of therapy in the Middle Ages. Believed to help restore the proper balance within the body by removing excess humors, bloodletting also allowed the physician to examine the patient's blood, collected in a basin, for diagnostic purposes. Medical manuals included detailed information on when and how patients should be bled; generally, it was thought that children, pregnant women, the very sick and old people should not be bled. Although leeches were occasionally used for bloodletting, more typically, physicians used surgical methods, as shown here. *The Pierpont Morgan Library, NY, Ms. M. 165*, Le Regime du Corps *by Aldobrandino da Siena (fl. 1256–1287), France, 15th century, f.19v. The Pierpont Morgan Library / Art Resource, NY.*

cially fevers, had specific "critical days," or turning points determined by the phases of the moon.

Medieval physicians also wrote case histories and observed and cataloged the symptoms and course of many individual diseases. Although many of these were general or formulaic, some diseases, such as smallpox, bubonic plague, and syphilis (first recognized as a new disease in the 1490s), were described with considerable detail and accuracy. The Black Death, which killed roughly one-third of the population of Europe in 1348–50, was known to be contagious, and public health measures included quarantines.

Texts describing women's diseases not surprisingly emphasized problems such as lack of menstruation, infertility, problems in childbirth, and miscarriage. The uterus, or womb, was seen as the source of many female illnesses, although medieval physicians, unlike those in the nineteenth and early twentieth centuries, did not think that a malfunctioning uterus caused hysteria and mental illness. Menstrual retention was regarded as a serious problem, for regular menstruation was thought to rid a woman's body of "bad and superfluous" humors, which in men were excreted through perspiration and the growth of beards. Recipes for purported contraceptives and methods to cause abortion also appear in various contexts, despite the Church's disapproval of such techniques. Physicians and natural philosophers also supplied remedies for impotence and sterility, ranging from techniques to increase sexual pleasure (a woman's orgasm was thought by some to be necessary to guarantee conception) to the use of spells.

BOTANY AND ZOOLOGY

Medieval botany and zoology were a mixture of fantasy, moral edification, and detailed and accurate observations of plants and animals. Descriptions of animals were typically collected in bestiaries, which were compilations of short accounts of the appearance and habits of various animals, ranging from the imaginary (unicorns were usually included) to indigenous species. Herbals, compiled for practical purposes for use in medicine, were one important source for information on plants. Incidental descriptions of domestic and wild plants and animals appear in travel literature, treatises on agriculture, and other texts, and manuscript illuminations and church sculptures often depicted animals and plants

Figure 9. Realistically detailed depictions of animals and plants were often incorporated into medieval manuscript illuminations. In this example, Saint Ambrose, an important fifth-century religious leader, is shown surrounded by eleven mussels and a crab, all meticulously rendered, even showing barnacles on the shell of one mussel on the right. The illumination is from a Dutch compendium of devotional texts, or Book of Hours, dating from the early fifteenth century and made for Catherine of Cleves, the Dutchess of Guelders. Why the artist chose to accompany St. Ambrose with mussels is not known. *The Pierpont Morgan Library, NY, Ms. M. 917, Book of Hours of Catherine of Cleves, f. 244. The Pierpont Morgan Library / Art Resource, NY.*

in an accurate and naturalistic manner (see Figure 9). In addition, some medieval natural philosophers attempted to give a more scientific account of animals and plants, which they largely based on the work of classical authorities, but also often included personal observations.

The aim of the bestiary was not scientific knowledge but moral instruction and entertainment. The ultimate source for almost all medieval bestiaries was the *Physiologus*, originally written in Greek, probably between the second and fourth centuries C.E., and translated into Latin before the ninth century. Medieval writers, however, made significant modifications to the original text, perhaps to make bestiaries more useful reference works for examples to be used in sermons. Bestiaries, which were extremely popular, are excellent sources for folklore and the symbolism attributed to animals in the Middle Ages, but they tell us little about what medieval philosophers thought about the natural world.

An example from a twelfth-century English bestiary should illustrate this point:

> Vulpis the fox gets his name from the person who winds wool (volupis)—for he is a creature with circuitous pug marks who never runs straight but goes on his way with torturous windings. He is a fraudulent and ingenious animal. When he is hungry and nothing turns up for him to devour, he rolls himself in red mud so that he looks as if he were stained with blood. Then he throws himself on the ground and holds his breath, so that he positively does not seem to breathe. The birds, seeing that he is not breathing, and that he looks as if he were covered with blood with his tongue hanging out, think he is dead and come down to sit on him. Well, thus he grabs them and gobbles them up. The Devil has the nature of this same. With all those who are living according to the flesh he feigns himself to be dead until he get them in the gullet and punishes them. But for spiritual men of faith he is truly dead and reduced to nothing.[6]

Other fables from the bestiaries that had a long, rich life in literature were that bears lick their newborn cubs, born formless, into shape; that unicorns can only be trapped by a virgin girl; that lions are compassionate; and that beavers, when pursued by a hunter, bite off their own testicles and fling them in their pursuer's face to escape.[7]

Medieval texts written to provide scientific rather than moral information about animals, however, are quite different. Two books stand out in this respect: *On the Art of Hunting with Birds* by the German emperor Frederick II (1194–1250), written between 1244 and 1250, and the *De animalibus* (On Animals) of Albertus Magnus (c. 1193–1280), written around 1260.

On the Art of Hunting with Birds has been called "one of the great scientific treatises of the Middle Ages."[8] Frederick II was justly famous in his own time for his support of science at his court in Sicily, where he encouraged exchanges on scientific problems between not only Christian but also Jewish and Arabic scholars. Frederick, who was particularly interested in animals, had a personal menagerie, including elephants, camels, panthers, lions, leopards, and monkeys, and also commissioned the earliest known European work on veterinary medicine for horses. His *Art of Hunting* reflects his personal passion for both falconry and firsthand investigation into scientific questions.

The book begins with a detailed and systematic account of the types, anatomy, and habits of birds based largely on Frederick's own observations. He knows Aristotle's writings on animals but makes a point of saying that in the light of his personal experiences, Aristotle is "not entirely to be relied upon."[9] The remainder gives practical and detailed information on falcons and their capture, the training of hunting birds, and equipment. Among other things, Frederick compares his own experience with methods from different parts of the world and relates how he tested whether vultures use sight or smell to find their food by sealing their eyes while leaving their nostrils open. Equally remarkable are the over 900 illustrations of birds attributed to Frederick's son, Manfred, which appear in some manuscripts and are described by historian of science Charles Haskins as "accurate and minute, even to details of plumage, while the representation of birds in flight has an almost photographic quality."[10]

Albertus Magnus, a Dominican friar who taught theology at the University of Paris, wrote extensively on many scientific topics, including botany, alchemy, meteorology, and natural philosophy, and is considered one of the most important scientists of the Middle Ages. The *De animalibus* is a systematic discussion of all topics relevant to the physiology and natural history of animals, including human anatomy and reproduction. Like many of Albertus' works, it is in the form of a commentary on Aristotle and represents a thoughtful synthesis of current knowledge from a variety of sources, including the great Roman naturalist Pliny the Elder, the Arabic philosopher Avicenna, and Albertus' own remarks.

Over 1,700 pages in English translation, the *De animalibus* defies a quick summary. However, we can note some of its important characteristics. First, Albertus combines extensive book learning with direct observation. Although he adopts many of the basic tenets of Aristotelian natural philosophy, he does not hesitate to correct Aristotle on the basis of his own experience as needed and describes many instances in which he tested out commonly held ideas about animals with simple experiments of his own. Among other examples, he describes how he dissected a mole, a cricket, and developing hen's eggs and checked the supposition that "cold" animals were impervious to fire by frying a spider on a grill and throwing another into a candle (the spiders did not survive). He is the first known European naturalist to describe the weasel, the rat, the common dormouse, and the polar bear. Second, Albertus shows a strong interest in the practical uses of animals. He mentions methods of hunting wild boar, aurochs, deer, whale, and various types of birds. He also describes the uses and habits of domestic animals and provides an extended account of the training and veterinary care of dogs, falcons, and horses. Finally, we should note that Albertus matter-of-factly includes discussion of the human body and discusses human sexuality with great frankness, including physical changes and the awakening of sexual desire in both girls and boys at puberty.

Botany had a somewhat different history than zoology in the Middle Ages because of the overriding importance of herbs in medicine. The great classical authorities on plants were *On Plants* (attributed to Aristotle but actually a Latin translation of an Arabic text based on the work of Aristotle's student Theophrastus (c. 372–c. 288 B.C.E.) and the *De materia medica* of Dioscorides (first century C.E.). Although Dioscorides remained an authority on herbal remedies for almost 1,500 years, medieval herbals partially superseded his *De materia medica* over time, adding new information about the medicinal uses of the plant and instructions on gathering and drying specific plants. In general, medieval herbalists seem to have taken an active role in promoting empirical knowledge of plants. For example, Linda Voigts has suggested that the presence of Mediterranean plants in early medieval Anglo-Saxon herbals does not reflect a slavish copying of Dioscorides but the fact that a warmer, drier climate allowed these plants to be cultivated in northern

Europe until the thirteenth century.[11] As befitting their function as reference works used for utilitarian purposes, plants in medieval herbals are usually listed alphabetically by common name rather than by any theoretical taxonomic scheme. Herbals also illustrate the overlap between medicine, religion, and magic, for many plants are accorded exceptional properties to heal if ritually worn around the neck or if blessed.

Theoretical botany is largely confined to Albertus Magnus' *De vegetabilibus* (On Plants). As in his work on animals, in *De vegetabilibus* Albertus combines a theoretical discussion based on Aristotle with his own descriptions of specific plants. Albertus reviews the parts of plants, their physiology, and their reproduction. He was especially interested in why plants are so diverse in their structure and appearance and recorded many specific details about the more than 400 species that he described, many from firsthand examination. On occasion, he includes not only the most obvious aspects of a plant's appearance but also its smell, taste, and habitat. He also includes a section on agriculture and horticulture.

GEOLOGY AND METEOROLOGY

Geology as such did not exist in the Middle Ages. Rather, stones and minerals were discussed in "lapidaries," reference works describing the useful properties of various stones, roughly equivalent to herbals for plants and, like the herbals, often ascribing magical properties to stones. On the other hand, such events as changes in the earth's surface, the formation of rivers and mountains, fossils, weather, and earthquakes were discussed under the title "meteorology." As we have seen, Aristotle divided the cosmos into an eternal, unchanging heaven and a constantly mutable sphere "below the moon." This sublunary sphere included not only the earth itself but also the concentric layers of water, air, and fire which were thought to encircle the earth. Transformations and movements of the four elements in the atmosphere and within the earth were thought to be responsible for a broad range of phenomena, including earthquakes, the weather, lightning, and the generation of metals within the earth. Because they were obviously changeable and temporary, comets, shooting stars, and meteors were thought to exist in the upper atmosphere rather than in the heavens.

Medieval writers were particularly interested in the formation of stones, metals, and mountains and significantly expanded on what Aristotle had written on a number of meteorological topics. Avicenna and later John Buridan wrote detailed accounts of how stones were formed from sediment or precipitated from water. Avicenna suggested that mountains were formed by land being thrust up by earthquakes or the eroding effects of water and wind on land. Buridan also suggests that mountains were formed by the weathering away of softer stones or the shifting of the earth's center of gravity.

One of the few subjects *not* covered by Aristotle had been mineralogy. This gap was filled by Albertus Magnus, who has been credited with being the founder of this science. Albertus considers in detail differing types of stones, their different degrees of hardness, and which are most useful for building. He is particularly interested in metals and provides numerous firsthand observations of mining, smelting, and the process of making steel from iron. He also describes meteorites.

Medieval scientists significantly expanded on a number of meteorological topics. Following Aristotle, but writing with more precision and detail, they explained how "exhalations" drawn up by the heat of the sun from the four elements produced a variety of changes: air drawn up to the sphere of fire ignites and results in comets and meteors; water drawn up from the sea into the air produces clouds, rain, and snow; air drawn up from the earth causes earthquakes; and so on. The natural philosopher Robert Grosseteste (c. 1168–1263), among others, recognized that the tides were caused by the moon. A treatise by Peter Peregrinus, also known as Peter of Maricourt (fl. 1269) is the earliest known systematic description of the magnet and magnetic polarity and includes an account of a mariner's compass, as well as perhaps the first scientific attempt to construct a perpetual motion machine.

GEOGRAPHY

Geographical writing and travel literature were lively genres in the Middle Ages. Scientific geography was a part of astronomy and included such topics as proofs of the spherical shape of the earth, the size of the earth, the shape and location of the three continents (Europe, Asia, and Africa), and speculation about whether a fourth, unknown continent existed on the other side of the earth. Travel literature, of which the most famous examples are Marco Polo's *Travels* (1298) and Sir John

Mandeville's *Travels* (c. 1360), blended descriptions of far-off lands, anthropology, and fabulous tales.

Medieval geography is of special interest because of its connection to the voyages of Christopher Columbus. Columbus is known to have used and annotated a fifteenth-century printed copy of a work written in 1410 by Pierre d'Ailly (1350–1420), the *Ymago Mundi*. D'Ailly, a French theologian, assumes that the world is round, as did every educated person in the Middle Ages. There is even some evidence that uneducated people knew the earth was round, and many texts refer to the earth as round like an apple, the yolk of an egg, or a ball. Among natural philosophers, several proofs of the spherical nature of the earth were commonly mentioned, including the circular shape of the earth's shadow during a lunar eclipse, the fact that when a ship approaches the horizon the hull disappears before the top of the mast, and the changing positions of the constellations as an observer traveled south. The legend that medieval people thought the world was flat seems to have been invented in the nineteenth century and has been perpetuated by twentieth-century writers.

Columbus may have been influenced by other aspects of medieval geography. Although the great Hellenistic scientist Eratosthenes (c. 276–194 B.C.E.) had correctly calculated the earth's circumference at the equator as about 24,000 miles, most medieval scientists, following Ptolemy, thought the earth was considerably smaller. Moreover, some medieval writers, including d'Ailly, thought that the earth was covered by much more land than water and that therefore the Atlantic ocean was not large. Some medieval authors had entertained the theoretical possibility of circumventing the globe since the thirteenth century and in 1297 two Portuguese ships had attempted to sail around Africa. Advances in cartography during the late Middle Ages are also part of the background to Columbus' voyage. Portolan charts, invented in the second half of the thirteenth century, made use of knowledge gained by sailors to draw accurate coastlines and used intersecting radiating lines to represent distances and directions between any two points. The increasing use of the compass also encouraged sea travel.

There was also considerable interest in travel literature. Land travel around Europe and to the Near East was common in the Middle Ages, and traveling merchants, pilgrims, crusaders, and itinerant poets and scholars reported on their experiences. Scandinavian clerics compiled descriptions of Greenland, Iceland, and northern Atlantic islands such as the Orkneys.

Other aspects of medieval travel writing reflected religious and cultural preoccupations. Traditional geography divided the world into a torrid southern zone, frigid zones at the poles, and two temperate zones. Medieval world maps (*mappaemundi*), however, represented the world as a circle, often divided into three parts with "Asia" to the top, "Europe" on the left, and "Africa" on the right, so that the divisions looked like a T inscribed in a circle. The garden of Eden was usually positioned at the top and Jerusalem at the center as the "navel of the world." No effort was made to indicate distances or the shapes of the continents. Rather, the map was meant as a schematic representation of world biblical history and the creation story. Some were illustrated with fabulous animals and peoples, including cannibals, satyrs, and races without heads, with enormous ears or with backward feet. Such hybrid monstrous races, like the ones the twelfth-century, half Anglo-Norman, half Welsh writer Giraldus Cambrensis describes as living in Wales, or the cannibalistic Indians described by Columbus and other European explorers, served to project anxieties onto a monstrous "other" and deflect them from the writers and their audience.

NOTES

1. This point is taken from William Newman, "Technology and Alchemical Debate in the Late Middle Ages," in *The Scientific Enterprise in Antiquity and the Middle Ages*, ed. Michael H. Shank (Chicago and London: University of Chicago Press, 2000), pp. 282–85.

2. Nancy G. Siraisi, *Medieval and Early Renaissance Medicine: An Introduction to Knowledge and Practice* (Chicago and London: University of Chicago Press, 1990), p. ix.

3. Monica H. Green, "Introduction," in *The Trotula: A Medieval Compendium of Women's Medicine*, ed. and trans. Monica H. Green (Philadelphia: University of Pennsylvania Press, 2001), p. xi.

4. For this and other information I am much indebted to Siraisi, *Medieval and Early Renaissance Medicine*.

5. Siraisi, *Medieval and Early Renaissance Medicine*, p. 118.

6. *The Bestiary: A Book of Beasts, being a Translation from a Latin Bestiary of the Twelfth Century*, ed. and trans. T. H. White (New York: G. P. Putnam's Sons, 1960), pp. 53–54.

7. This last tale depends on a clever pun on the Latin name for beaver (*castor*) and the word *castrare* (to castrate).

8. Edward Grant, ed., *A Source Book in Medieval Science* (Cambridge, MA: Harvard University Press, 1974), p. 657.

9. Frederick II, "On the Structure and Habits of Birds," trans. and annotated by Casey A. Wood and F. Marjorie Fyfe in *A Source Book in Medieval Science*, ed. Grant, p. 658.

10. Charles Homer Haskins, *Studies in the History of Mediaeval Science* (New York: Frederick Ungar, 1924), p. 306.

11. Linda Voigts, "Anglo-Saxon Plant Remedies and the Anglo-Saxons," in *Scientific Enterprise*, ed. Shank, pp. 174–76.

CHAPTER 6

MEDIEVAL TECHNOLOGY

The study of medieval technology, unlike that of medieval science, is quite recent. Over the past forty years, historians have increasingly recognized that technological development "took off" in the medieval and early modern West in a way that it had not in the ancient world and did not in contemporary China and the Islamic regions. The "dry" compass, mechanical clock, firearms, and the printing press—all medieval inventions—helped set the stage for European world dominance in the modern age. More mundane inventions, including new agricultural methods, the wheelbarrow, the spinning wheel, the chimney, and eyeglasses, had significant and long-lasting effects on European society. Medieval people also adapted older technologies, such as the watermill and windmill, the stirrup, and gunpowder, to new uses. Yet there is considerable scholarly debate about why, and even if, the Middle Ages as a whole was a period characterized by rapid technological change. In this chapter we will review the most important technological innovations of the Middle Ages and also consider some of the scholarly arguments on the causes and extent of medieval technological development.

MEDIEVAL TECHNOLOGY AND THE WRITTEN RECORD

Medieval technology and medieval science were largely separate enterprises. Medieval science, as we have seen, was highly theoretical and aimed at understanding the natural world rather than changing it. Most natural philosophers learned and communicated through written texts, and, with the exception of alchemists, astrologers, and physicians, they showed little interest in applying scientific knowledge to technological problems. Indeed, praise for technology, or the "mechanical arts," as technology was called in the Middle Ages, was more likely to occur in religious and philosophical contexts than in scientific ones.

Technology, on the other hand, was largely practiced by itinerant artisans, craftsmen and women, monks and peasants who had little or no scientific training but possessed an avid interest in the practical problems of life. In the twelfth and thirteenth centuries, even master architects—the most highly educated craftsmen—worked through on-site experimentation and observation, using practical geometry and arithmetic rather than mathematical theory. Only at the very end of the Middle Ages did the gap between theoretical science and practical knowledge of techniques begin to narrow significantly.

The process of technological invention in the Middle Ages, therefore, has left few traces in the written historical record. Only in the fourteenth and fifteenth centuries did some learned men and a few artisans begin to write treatises on technological subjects. The artisans responsible for many of the great inventions of the Middle Ages typically did not know Latin (although some seem to have known how to read and write in the vernacular) and proceeded largely by trial and error, intuition, hands-on training, and oral transmission of knowledge. Master craftsmen and skilled workers were quite mobile during the Middle Ages, and if most did not record their expertise in writing, it may not have been only because many were not literate but also because they found person-to-person communication more effective. In the late Middle Ages technical treatises become more common; artisans, however, sometimes continued to be reluctant to record technical knowledge out of fear that it would be stolen by professional rivals.[1]

These circumstances have complicated the historian's task considerably. Historians can find indirect traces of technological change in manuscript illuminations, archaeological finds, account books, archival records, and occasional comments in other kinds of documents, but documentation is spotty and almost never records the actual method of invention. Pictorial representation of techniques also typically postdated the actual use of new devices by many years. Consequently, we do not know who was responsible for even the most important of medieval inventions or much about the diffusion of devices and techniques. Recent in-depth studies of the use of particular technologies in specific localities have begun to remedy this deficiency but there is still much more work to be done. Much of this work has suggested that new techniques were not automatically adopted, as some historians had previously assumed, but that a variety of economic, social, and cultural factors came into play which sometimes encouraged and at other times discouraged technological change.

Nevertheless, numerous sources testify to the value accorded technology by medieval people. The sheer number and variety of technological innovations in the Middle Ages is noteworthy and itself supports the view that the cultural and social environment of the Middle Ages in some ways favored technological growth and innovation. Praise for technological achievement appears in religious writing, philosophical works, and manuscript illuminations. During the twelfth and thirteenth centuries, natural philosophers for the first time included the mechanical arts as a valued and respected part of human knowledge in their classifications of the arts and sciences. From the twelfth century on, medieval people seem to have increasingly imagined technological solutions to practical problems. Other evidence indicates that possession of the latest and largest technological innovation, such as a public clock, city fountain, cathedral, or mill, conveyed prestige on communities and individuals by demonstrating the command of resources, labor, and expertise. Finally, late medieval writing on some technological subjects, especially architecture, military technology, engineering and metallurgy, fed into the increased prestige of technology in the Renaissance.[2]

THE SOCIAL, CULTURAL, AND ECONOMIC SETTING OF MEDIEVAL TECHNOLOGY

The development of medieval technology, as we have indicated above, took place almost entirely outside the university and, at least until the fifteenth century, what we would call today the "scientific community." Much more needs to be learned about how and why technological change took place, with special attention to local and regional variations over time. Economic relationships in the Middle Ages were extremely complex, existing within a convoluted web of communal and personal privileges, customary rights, gender relations, and intricate power relationships. Social attitudes toward technology were complicated by the coexistence of many different sets of values about manual labor, the making of money, and the relationship of humans to the natural world. The technological progress of the modern industrialized world is clearly closely related to the development of capitalism; unfortunately, for the Middle Ages it is still unclear whether cultural attitudes promoting technological innovation drove the development of a more capitalistic economy or whether the reverse was the case.

Modern scholars have generally agreed upon certain very basic assessments while disputing their significance and meaning. There was sustained economic growth in medieval Europe between the eleventh and the thirteenth centuries and again from the late fourteenth through the fifteenth century although whether the terms "medieval industrial revolution" or "proto-capitalism" are applicable to this economic development is debated. Technological innovation and the diffusion of already developed technologies were features of medieval society, even though medieval enthusiasm for technology may not have been as pervasive as once thought. Religious values and institutions were closely tied to the development of technology and its representation as "morally virtuous," although whether Christian values caused medieval technological advance or merely reflected developments taking place for other reasons is highly contested.

A detailed review of these large and complex questions is beyond the scope of the present book. At the end of this chapter we will briefly address some of the arguments which have been made about the causes and extent of medieval technological development. First, however, we will review the basic technological achievements of the Middle Ages.

THE AGRICULTURAL REVOLUTION OF THE MIDDLE AGES

Agriculture was the foundation of medieval society. During the early Middle Ages there was little commercial activity, and Europe existed at the level of a peasant, subsistence economy. Between the ninth and thirteenth centuries, however, new and adapted agricultural techniques, as well as the bringing of new land under cultivation, significantly raised agricultural productivity and allowed the population to rise from about 42 million in the year 1000 to 73 million in 1300. This agricultural revolution provided the economic basis for the commercial, urban, and intellectual expansion of the High Middle Ages. In the late Middle Ages, some regions of Europe, especially the Netherlands and Germany, also increased agricultural productivity by applying known techniques in a more intensive fashion. Throughout the Middle Ages, farming and related activities were a family enterprise, in which the labor of women and children was essential.

The most important agricultural innovation was the introduction of the "three-field system" of crop rotation. The new crop rotation encouraged the cultivation of more land and the planting of more nutritious crops. Previously, half the cultivated land each year had had to be left fallow (unplanted) and used as pasture in order to replenish the soil. The new system allowed two-thirds of the land to be cultivated at any one time: one-third was left fallow, one-third planted with grain (rye, oats, or barley), and one-third with nitrogen-fixing crops such as legumes and beans which returned nutrients to the soil.

The three-field system simultaneously provided highly nutritious crops and helped mitigate the perennial problem of declining fertility of the soil. Combined with new types of equipment, including a new, heavy-wheeled plough, which was better suited to the heavier, wetter soil of northern Europe, and the harrow, as well as more intensive use of manure, the new system may have increased productivity by as much as 30 percent and, according to some historians, produced yields in some areas that would not be superseded until the eighteenth century.

One agricultural innovation which has received considerable scholarly attention was the rigid, padded horse collar. The harness used by the Romans was well suited to oxen but in horses pressed into the arteries in the neck, cutting off blood to the brain and making it difficult, if not impossible, for the horse to pull with its full strength. The new collar rested on the horse's shoulders, bypassing this problem. Historians currently disagree about the extent to which horses replaced oxen for plowing in the Middle Ages. The horse was faster and more efficient than the ox, but also more expensive to feed and more delicate. The invention of the horse collar, however, provided medieval peasants with a new option. The introduction of horseshoes allowed horses to be used in a variety of terrains and climates. Horses also seem to have been used to power small mills for grinding grain.

Sheep raising was another important agricultural activity. Sheep were used for food, their skins were used to make parchment for writing, and, most importantly, their wool was the basis for the production of wool cloth, one of the most profitable medieval industries (see the later section in this chapter on textiles). Most prized was English wool; by the thirteenth century, the Cistercian monastic order in England was the largest exporter of wool in Europe. Wine, ale, and salted herring were other agricultural products with large export markets.

WATER AND WIND POWER

One of the most visible examples of medieval technology was watermills. Although waterwheels were well known in the ancient world and contemporary Islamic regions, their use seems to have been largely confined to grinding grain and irrigation. By the end of the Middle Ages, perhaps encouraged by the abundance of fast-flowing streams and rivers, however, the watermill had also been adapted to a myriad of industrial and other purposes.

Watermills proliferated in the Middle Ages. As early as the late eleventh century, southern England had over 5,600 mills in approximately 3,000 communities. By about 1300, England had over 9,000 watermills and at least 3,000 windmills. A tributary of the Seine River in France had two mills in the tenth century, four in the eleventh, and ten in the thirteenth. Similarly, one district of France had fourteen mills in the eleventh century, sixty in the twelfth, and over 200 in the fourteenth. By the fourteenth century, Paris had sixty-eight mills less than a mile from the center of the city. Comparable figures could be produced for Germany and Italy.

To some extent the proliferation of watermills may have simply reflected the growth in population from the tenth to the beginning of the fourteenth century. Most of these mills were probably used for the traditional purpose of grinding grain. At the same time, it is significant that medieval people experimented with many different types of mechanization, with both overshot waterwheels (in which the water hits the top of the mill, turning it in the direction of the flow) and undershot wheels (in which the water hits the underside of the wheel). During the High and late Middle Ages, water-driven mills were adapted to pound hemp, saw wood, make paper, grind grain and pigments, sift flour, strip bark, press grapes for wine and olives for oil, tan leather, forge iron, prepare cloth, and power bellows used in furnaces. Of these, fulling cloth, the process which cleaned, strengthened, and tightened the weave of woolen or linen cloth, probably had the most sustained economic impact (see the later section in this chapter on textiles). Some modern calculations indicate that medieval improvements increased the power output of waterwheels by as much as 100 to 200 percent over ancient waterwheels. (The greatest limitation of medieval watermills was that they were made of wood.) Other innovations were the invention of the tidal mill, the use of dams to increase water flow, and the invention of the camshaft, which allowed the gears of the mill to drive hammers vertically up and down as well as in a circular motion.

Windmills were used first to grind wheat and later to pump water for drainage. Although the windmill was probably not a European invention, medieval Europeans made significant improvements. The medieval post-mill, for example, could pivot its sails to take advantage of the typically constantly shifting winds found in Europe. Fifteenth-century windmills were larger, more stable, and more efficient than earlier versions.

To what extent did water and wind power replace human muscle in the Middle Ages? This question is still largely unanswered. Human labor undoubtedly remained the primary method of producing goods throughout the Middle Ages, as it would until the nineteenth century. Mills were expensive to build and maintain. Nevertheless, the use of water and wind power had significant effects on medieval life. As we shall see in the following sections, water wheels had a major impact on the medieval industries of iron and cloth production. Even though grain could often be ground by hand more cheaply, watermills and windmills produced a finer, whiter flour which was in demand. Experiments with gearing in mills also probably contributed to innovative methods of gearing in other contexts, such as hoists and war machines.

MINING AND METALLURGY

Mining and metallurgy were major industries in the Middle Ages. Demand was high for iron, which was used in a wide range of items ranging from farm implements and woodworking tools to domestic items such as needles, door hinges and latches, and bells to armor and swords and, by the fourteenth century, cannon, cannon balls, and clockworks.

Especially important were nails and horseshoes: Richard I is said to have ordered 50,000 horseshoes in preparation for the Third Crusade. Iron armor and chain "mail" were in use by the eighth century (when Charlemagne's army was described as "men of iron"); by the fourteenth century knights were typically equipped with full body armor. Other metals had more specialized uses: lead for making water pipes, in stained glass windows, and, in the thirteenth century, in church roofs; silver in coinage and fine decorative objects; steel in swords and, at the end of the Middle Ages, in armor. Bronze, an alloy of tin and copper, was used for making bells and, sometimes, cannon; pewter, an alloy of tin and lead, was used to make tableware. Gold, which was relatively scarce in Europe, was generally reserved during the early Middle Ages for decoration of sacred objects such as crowns, chalices, reliquaries, and gold foils for manuscript illuminations; only after the mid-thirteenth century were gold coins minted.

Although mining took place all over Europe, we know most about production in Germany and eastern Europe (a center for silver), France (known for iron production), and England, which had tin, silver, lead, copper, and zinc mines. In many areas, monastic orders were in the forefront of mining operations. Between the thirteenth and the seventeenth centuries, for example, the Cistercians were the leading producers of iron in the Champagne region of France.

The history of iron production during the Middle Ages foreshadows the later industrialization of Europe. The processing and working of silver, gold, tin, and bronze continued to be done by hand and methods remained virtually unchanged. In contrast, iron production was revolutionized at the end of the Middle Ages by two technological innovations: the use of water power at almost every stage of production and the invention of the blast furnace. In consequence, between the eleventh and sixteenth centuries iron production gradually moved from a small-scale handicraft to a thoroughly mechanized industry. Women and older children, as well as men, worked in mining, although their role tended to diminish as mining became more large-scale and specialized.

Crucial to this shift was the invention of the blast furnace sometime in the mid-fourteenth century. The blast furnace used water-powered bellows to boost the draft and, therefore, the temperature of the furnace. It could not only produce much more iron in a shorter amount of time with less labor than earlier types of furnaces, but it also enabled workers to produce either cast iron, which was relatively weak but could be molded, or the much stronger wrought iron, which had to be shaped while hot by hammering. By the end of the Middle Ages, pieces of wrought iron weighing almost 300 pounds were routinely produced.

Also essential to iron production was the adaptation of watermills. In addition to powering bellows, water power was used to crush and wash iron ore and to hammer the wrought iron. Mills were also used in more specialized operations, such as drawing wire.

The expansion of the iron industry had negative as well as positive effects. The demand for charcoal to run furnaces resulted in such aggressive cutting of forests that deforestation resulted on some areas. Later the burning of coal led to air pollution. Water pollution from this and other increasingly industrialized manufacturing activities became a serious problem in the later Middle Ages.

ENGINEERING AND CONSTRUCTION

Construction was also a major industry in the Middle Ages. The most innovative techniques can be found in the building of churches, which befits the immense importance of religion in medieval society. Improvements can also be found in buildings with military and economic importance such as palaces, castles, government buildings, and bridges. Private homes, with the exception of castles, were generally simple and usually made of wood. A particularly interesting and important subset of engineering techniques can be found in the water systems constructed for cities and monasteries.

Medieval cathedrals have justly been called the embodiment of Christian knowledge and faith.[3] The Gothic cathedral integrates stone, light, and space to create the impression of a divine presence on earth while, in the words of architecture historian Lynn T. Courteney, "pushing building technology to unprecedented heights."[4]

The hallmark of the medieval cathedral was ingenious engineering in which every element contributed to the stability and functionality of the structure as well as to its aesthetic qualities. Two twelfth-century innovations made the Gothic style possible: the pointed arch and the flying buttress. Earlier techniques had allowed for the building of massive Romanesque churches. The abbey church at the monastery of Cluny, for example, begun in 1088, could hold thousands of people and was the largest church in Europe until the sixteenth century. For structural reasons, however, Romanesque churches had only very small windows, leaving the interior dark. The use of the pointed arch and flying buttress, along with other architectural innovations, however, allowed the high walls of the Gothic church to be almost completely filled with stained glass windows.

Gothic churches were built with exceedingly high vaults in proportion to their width: by the thirteenth century, cathedral vaults might reach over 140 feet. The pointed arch, whose width could be varied while the height remained constant, allowed the downward thrust of the weight of stone to be distributed to slender columns, leaving the expanse of wall free from structural demands. The flying buttress, added to the exterior of the building, balanced the outward thrust of the walls. An additional upper flying buttress was added to help stabilize the building in strong winds. Slender stone and timber spires reinforced the effect of height. The spire of Salisbury Cathedral reached 404 feet, that of Strasbourg 468 feet.

Other typical features exhibit a similar technical resourcefulness. The stone tracery in the windows which held stained glass in Carlisle Cathedral in England, for example, were "so ingeniously jointed and arranged that any one of the [86] blocks of stone can be cut out for repair or replacement without endangering the stability of the whole wonderful fabric."[5] Cathedrals also had numerous interior passageways, which allowed for easy movement across and up and down within the structure, crucial in the case of fire and to facilitate construction and repairs.

The second major type of building in the Middle Ages was military fortifications. Castles were massive fortresses designed to withstand sieges and provide a measure of offensive capability. Between the ninth and thirteenth centuries, fortifications developed from rather simple structures, which consisted of a barracks built on a raised mound of earth and surrounded by a ditch and enclosed yard known as a motte-and-bailey castle, to elaborate stone complexes. By the thirteenth century castles typically included a large circular keep, which served as a main residence and might be as much as four or more stories high, a large interior courtyard, and as many as eight additional towers, used as barracks and firing galleries, the whole of which was enclosed by massive stone walls, twelve or more feet thick, and a moat.

Some of the innovations in castle design, including numerous openings in the walls and ramparts through which arrows could be fired or boiling liquids dropped, were borrowed from the Arabs. Indigenous innovations included the moat and drawbridge and the fireplace (twelfth century) and chimney (thirteenth century). The chimney for the first time allowed for multiple fireplaces in different rooms to replace a single, central hearth and, it has been suggested, encouraged the development of a new appreciation of privacy in western culture.

Like cathedrals, castles required enormous resources to build. Windsor Castle, for example, constructed in the fourteenth century, required no less than 3,944 oaks, in addition to massive amounts of stone. Labor costs were also high. One thirteenth-century castle required the labor of 400 masons, 200 quarrymen, thirty smiths and carpenters, and over 2,000 laborers. Architects were widely respected for their knowledge and consequently well paid. Masons, likewise, were recognized as being highly skilled. Laborers, however, were poorly and often irregularly paid. There are many colorful stories of work disputes between and among workers, architects, and employers, sometimes ending in violence.

Towns were also sites for major construction projects. Complex water systems, employing sophisticated hydraulic technology, were another type of project demanding a high investment of labor and money. Gravity-fed water systems were adopted by cities and large communities, such as the larger and more prestigious monastic houses, from the twelfth century onward and by the late Middle Ages were beginning to be supplemented by systems using waterwheels and pumps. These systems supplied not only drinking water but also water for washing and laundry, as well as for the *necessarium* (privy). In cities, elaborate fountains provided drinking water and were a mark of civic pride and honor. Some cities also had public toilets and public troughs for washing clothes.

Towns were also increasingly fortified with stone and earth walls. Within towns, bridges became more numerous and increasingly became sites for civic activities; late medieval bridges were often equipped with shops, hospitals, lecture halls, and churches, as well as tower fortifications. Mills and fishponds were often built near or under bridges. Employing new construction techniques, late medieval bridges were often impressively large. A bridge built in northern Italy in the 1370s reached a span of 236 feet, the largest single-arch bridge until the eighteenth century. The world's largest stone arch bridge was completed in Prague in 1503 and reached almost 2,000 feet.[6]

Finally, we can briefly note that during the late Middle Ages, medieval engineers made increasingly large-scale attempts to alter the course of rivers and connect them through canals.

TEXTILES

Textile production, largely of woolen cloth but also of silk, cotton, and linen, was perhaps the largest of all medieval industries. Clothing represented a much higher percentage of family wealth in the Middle Ages than it generally does in the industrialized world today. Fashion also became a factor in clothing design after the thirteenth century. Concentrated in Italy and Flanders, the high volume of trade in both luxury and more ordinary cloth and the consequent high profits fueled commercial development beginning in the High Middle Ages. This so-called commercial revolution produced significant innovations in commerce and banking, including new forms of business partnerships, "bills of exchange" (the forerunner of the check), insurance, new techniques for providing credit, and, around 1340, double-entry bookkeeping.

The scope of textile production was made possible by the mechanization of a number of the key processes in producing cloth. Perhaps the most important innovations in this respect were the horizontal loom and the application of water power to the process of fulling. Fulling had traditionally been done by hand, or, more literally, by feet which pounded the cloth in a solution of water, lye, soap, and urine. By the thirteenth century, however, water-powered mills using heavy hammers had largely mechanized the process.

The horizontal loom, which beginning in the twelfth century gradually replaced the older vertical loom, quickened the weaving process by allowing the operator to sit while working the loom using foot treadles, leaving his hands free to guide the thread. (By this date, weavers were almost always men.) Other improvements in looms made it possible to weave more complex patterns. The medieval spinning wheel equipped with flyer and bobbin, which appeared around 1400, also made the spinning of yarn more efficient. The reeling and throwing of silk was also mechanized between the thirteenth and fourteenth centuries, and by 1500 water-powered silk-throwing mills had appeared in Italy. According to one historian of textile manufacture, these new machines allowed two or three operators to replace the work of several hundred workers.[7]

Other more minor innovations included a carding instrument made with metal teeth, the toothed warper, and a device for breaking down the fibers of flax.

The textile industry supported other industries in addition to banking. Linen rags could be economically turned into paper (a Chinese invention), and the first paper mills appeared in Italy in the thirteenth century. The demand for wool and other agricultural products also supported commercial farming in England and elsewhere.

TRANSPORT

The growing commercial activity of the High and late Middle Ages was obviously related to possibilities for transport of goods and the movement of merchants. Although people in the Middle Ages traveled surprisingly frequently, land travel remained often dangerous and slow. Some improvements were made in land transport, but the major changes occurred in sea travel.

Among the most important developments were improved navigational techniques. The arrival of the mariner's compass first invented in China and known in Europe by the end of the twelfth century, together with more seaworthy ships, made year-round sailing in the Mediterranean possible. Later in the Middle Ages the use of portolan charts (see Chapter 5), better maps, improved compasses, and astrolabes aboard ships allowed new Atlantic routes to be developed.

Ships were also continually diversified, although this tended to result from more imaginative uses of existing techniques than from new inventions.[8] Crusader ships could carry up to 600 tons of warriors, horses, and supplies by the mid-thirteenth century. Merchant ships were made larger and more defensible if attacked. By around 1250, Italian cargo ships sailing the Mediterranean used two side steering rudders and two pairs of steering oars, had several decks, and might reach more than 470 tons. Northern European cargo ships, called cogs, used a heavy keel, a sternpost rudder, and more efficient masts and rigging to become true ocean-going vessels. By the fifteenth century, the cog's successor, the carrack, routinely reached 700 to 1,000 tons. By this time also merchant ships, as well as war galleys, were usually equipped with cannon and firearms. Another closely related type, the caravel, was smaller but more maneuverable and used an improved rudder and several sails of various types. According to Richard Unger, "the full-rigged ship was the great invention of European ship-design in the Middle Ages."[9] The full-rigged ship as it appeared in the late fifteenth century combined the best features of earlier ships with three masts carrying several different types of sails, allowing greater speed and control. Columbus used one full-rigged carrack, the *Santa Maria*, and two full-rigged caravels, the *Niña* and the *Pinta*, in his first voyage west.

Improvements in land transportation were less dramatic. After the twelfth century, city streets began to be paved. Carriages benefited from improved design, including suspensions and iron "tires" in the fourteenth century. Postal service improved in the late Middle Ages, although it does not seem to have surpassed the service available in the ancient world. We know of several attempts to build bridges across mountain passes.

MILITARY TECHNOLOGY

Considerable attention was paid to military technology in the Middle Ages. Indeed, the invention of the musket and wheel-lock pistol at the very end of the Middle Ages represents one of the most effective and sustained efforts to improve existing techniques until the Industrial Revolution.

The earliest example of new military technology, however, comes from the early Middle Ages. Between the eighth and eleventh centuries, aristocrats combined the use of the stirrup (perhaps first invented in China) with new types of saddles, horseshoes, the use of spurs and curb bits, chain mail, and the breeding of exceptionally large and heavy horses to create a new kind of warrior, the armored knight on horseback. By the thirteenth century, armor was typically full body armor and, by the early fifteenth century, often made of steel and polished to a blinding brilliance. Horses also were increasingly armored. These techniques converted the knight and horse to a sort of animate "fighting machine," which embodied the prestige and power of the medieval nobility.

The use of projectiles against enemy forces, both as handheld devices and in siege warfare, goes back at least to the ancient world. The longbow, probably invented by the Welsh before the thirteenth century, could project an arrow for twice the distance and with greater impact (enough to pierce chain mail) than the previously used short bow. It was quickly superseded, however, by the crossbow, a mechanical bow which was at least as powerful as the long bow and required much less training to be used. The crossbow continued to be improved throughout the High and late Middle Ages by a number of sophisticated devices which increased the tension on the bowstring while reducing the strength needed by the human operator. By the fifteenth century the bowstring was commonly made of steel, further increasing the crossbow's power.

Various sorts of siege machines, that is, engines rigged to throw large stones against a stationary target such as a town or castle wall, were also improved in the Middle Ages. The trebuchet, a massive slingshot first developed in China, was powered by a team of as many as 100 men. The counter-weight trebuchet, which used the controlled fall of three-ton weights for power, was used into the fifteenth century. It could throw a 300 pound stone 900 feet with enough force to do significant damage. (Other techniques used to bring down besieged cities included throwing incendiaries and the dead bodies of diseased animals or even body parts of the besieged inhabitants, when available, over the city walls.)

These methods, however, were eclipsed by the invention of cannon and firearms. Gunpowder had been invented in China probably in the eighth or ninth century, where it was used primarily as an explosive. It was first known in Europe in the thirteenth century. The first use of gunpowder in weapons in Europe dates from the early fourteenth century, when cannon were used on the battlefield to "cause panic."[10] Crucial to the further development of firearms was the discovery of how to make saltpeter, an essential component of gunpowder, cheaply from decaying organic matter. By the end of the century, iron cannon were effectively used in siege warfare, although their use on the battlefield was limited due to their slowness of firing, immobility, and tendency to blow up their handlers. By the late fifteenth century, cannon, called "bombards," might weigh up to thirty-five tons. Massive cannon such as these were used by the Ottoman Turks to capture Constantinople in 1453, a city which had stood virtually impregnable for over a thousand years.

The invention of the handgun represents a triumph of the emerging "arms race" of the late medieval and early modern periods. Bert Hall has argued that small arms probably developed in south German cities, in a "fertile exchange" between city militias with a need to improve town defenses and skilled urban craftsmen. There the availability of raw materials, technical expertise, and effective communal organization resulted in German cities becoming "hotbeds of technical innovation."[11]

The first evidence of handheld firearms dates from the 1420s and 1430s. Small arms benefited from improvements in the processing of gunpowder which made it burn more rapidly. Guns could be made larger, as in the case of bombards, but they also could be miniaturized.[12] During the late fifteenth century, firearms became increasingly portable and easy to fire. By 1500 guns were commonplace in militias. A final innovation, the wheel-lock pistol, which allowed a fully primed, ready-to-shoot weapon to be carried in a holster, appeared by 1505.

The successful production of guns was made possible by a determined effort to overcome the technical obstacles which made the earliest firearms inaccurate, slow, and dangerous to the user. Another key element was the need to make weapons which might require skill to produce but were easy to use. The democratization of lethal weapons helped, ultimately, to end the military and political power of the medieval aristocracy.

INFORMATION TECHNOLOGY—THE MECHANICAL CLOCK AND THE PRINTING PRESS

The mechanical clock and the printing press were probably the most significant of all medieval inventions. The printing press made possible the rapid diffusion of written material for the first time in history, with enormous intellectual, political, and social results for the modern world. The mechanical clock has been called the "key machine of the modern industrial age" and its use "the symbol of the process of European modernization,"[13] in part because it subordinates human lived experience to the demands of an abstract reckoning of time produced by a machine.

Despite intense study by historians, the origins of the mechanical clock remain obscure. Part of the difficulty lies in the original sources, which are often unclear and leave out (to us) essential information. Another problem is the use of the same term to cover a variety of different types of devices; thus the term *horologium* (clock) might refer to a water clock, a mechanical clock, or even a sundial. In addition, the term was sometimes applied in the early Middle Ages to astronomical instruments, even when they had no specific time-telling function.

The German historian Gerhard Dohrn-van Rossum has done the most to clarify these difficulties.[14] Dohrn-van Rossum points out that what seems to have impressed contemporaries most was the emergence around 1340 in the Italian cities of Milan and Padua of tower clocks which struck the hours; that is, they struck a bell once in the first hour, twice in the second, and so on for the twenty-four hours of the day and night.

In order to appreciate the significance of this apparently simple innovation, we must briefly review the history of timekeeping. During the early Middle Ages, the only people interested in keeping track of the "hours" were monks and nuns whose religious duties included communal prayer at regular times of the day and night, determined in part by the season and duration of darkness and daylight and in part by the length of the liturgy. Particularly important was making sure that the monks were awakened for night prayers.

Monasteries used various methods to keep track of time, including observations of the stars, sundials, burning candles calibrated by weight and length, and even assigning one member of the community to sing psalms at a set rate. Other people during the early Middle Ages had little use for keeping exact track of time; in an age with few artificial sources of light, what mattered was getting done what had to be done between sunrise and sunset.

The most technologically developed timekeeping device used by monasteries and nunneries was the water clock. Well known in antiquity, in its simplest form the water clock measured time by calibrating the flow of water from a cistern into a smaller basin. By the twelfth and thirteenth centuries, water clocks seem to have often been connected to an "alarm" system which automatically rang bells at set times, although we know almost nothing about how these systems were constructed.

In keeping with the rhythms of an agricultural society without electricity, virtually all water clocks seem to have been calibrated in "unequal" hours. That is, the period from sunrise to sunset was divided into twelve equal hours and the period of night also divided into twelve hours. Naturally, the length of an "hour" varied daily according to the season and whether it was an hour of night or day, hence the term "unequal" hours.

Urban tower clocks which struck the hours appear for the first time in Italian cities around 1340. Initially objects of awe and civic prestige, clocks gradually came to be seen as a necessary embodiment of communal identity and town life. Unfortunately, it is not clear whether these very early clocks were true mechanical clocks or other sorts of devices. As in the case of guns, the earliest mechanical clocks were less accurate than preexisting technologies, and had to be set using a water clock or sundial.

The essential element in the mechanical clock as it clearly emerged in the late fourteenth century was the "verge-and-foliot escapement" (see Figure 10). This device worked to control the motion of a weight-driven axle through a self-regulating mechanism (the verge), which could be set to make the axle turn at a predetermined uniform speed. The axle in turn moved a balance (the foliot) back and forth in an oscillating motion, whose duration could be regulated by weights set at the ends of the balance.

It remains unclear whether the verge-and-foliot escapement developed out of the increasingly elaborate bell-striking mechanisms used in monasteries or from the even more elaborate astronomical "clocks" whose primary purpose was to represent the movements of the heavenly bodies. The most famous example of the latter is the astrarium of the physician Giovanni Dondi finished in 1365, which included separate dials for each of the five planets and a perpetual calendar giving the date of Easter.

Not only town governments but also territorial rulers across Europe, including the pope, supported the building and maintenance of city clocks, not only for their prestige value but also as a symbol of political control. Clocks were typically installed on communal towers and functioned as highly visible and audible expressions of communal authority. Similarly, the chapters of cathedrals and large urban monastic houses donated money and other forms of support for the building of public clocks. Significantly, towns wanted mechanical clocks even when they proved to be less accurate than traditional timekeeping devices (mechanical clocks continued to be set using a water clock or sundial into the sixteenth century). Early mechanical clocks were also not much good at measuring small intervals of time, and times of an hour or less were usually reckoned by using a sand or hourglass. Figure 11 shows the variety of timekeeping devices in use by the mid-fifteenth century.

As mechanical clocks proliferated during the fourteenth and fifteenth

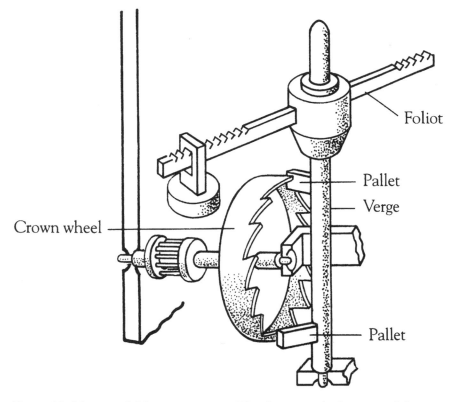

Figure 10. Verge-and-foliot escapement. This device worked to control the motion of a weight-driven axle through a self-regulating mechanism (the verge) which could be set to make the axle turn at a predetermined uniform speed. The axle in turn moved a balance (the foliot) back and forth in an oscillating motion, whose duration could be regulated by weights set at the ends of the balance. *Francis Gies and Joseph Gies*, Cathedral, Forge, and Waterwheel: Technology and Invention in the Middle Ages *(New York: HarperPerennial, 1994), p. 212. Reprinted with permission of HarperCollins Publishers, Inc.*

centuries, the psychological and institutional effects were profound. Civic events such as the meeting of town councils, class times in urban schools, the beginning and end of the work day, and the opening and closing of town markets came to be increasingly regulated according to clock time. Offenders were penalized for not being "on time," and advice manuals increasingly warned against "wasting time." Moreover, the modern system of "equal" hours more and more substituted for the traditional system of "unequal" hours. Although the mechanical clock could theoretically be calibrated to the old system, the process was cumbersome

Figure 11. Timekeeping devices in the fifteenth century. French, c. 1450. Depicted are a large clock-work on the far left, with an astrolabe at its base; a bell-striking mechanism (designed to be placed on top of the clock) in the middle; and on or hanging from the table a small sundial, a quarter-circle equatorium, a table clock, and a more elaborate sundial. In addition to revealing the avid interest in measuring time in the late Middle Ages, these precision instruments demonstrate advances in metallurgy and instrument-making by the fifteenth century. *Henri Suso, L'Horloge de sapience, Bruxelles, Bibliothèque Royale de Belgique Ms. IV III, fol. 13v.*

and time consuming, requiring mechanically resetting the clock every day. Over time, it came to be seen as far more useful and efficient to keep track of time using the modern hour system, even if it conflicted with the more flexible rhythms of natural time or the liturgical time used by the Church.

Human consciousness of time, therefore, gradually shifted from one based on natural rhythms and human experience to one based on the abstract notion of dividing the day into twenty-four equal hours. Business and personal documents also increasingly used the modern hour system, referring to "the ninth hour" of the evening, for example, with no reference to sundown or the time Mass was said. By the end of the fourteenth century, public clocks began to be equipped with dials, further mechanizing the process of keeping track of time. By the end of the fifteenth century, clocks were made portable and about the same time began to be worn or carried in a handbag.

The printing press had equally important effects but had a far simpler history. Prior to the invention of the printing press, the copying of books onto vellum or parchment was done by hand; it was both expensive and extremely time consuming. In addition, hand copying was a source of error as copyists inadvertently or deliberately changed the text they were working on. Paper, made from old linen and cotton rags, was cheaper and easier to produce than parchment and began to be available in the fourteenth century. Block printing was known first in China and was used in Europe from the early fifteenth century for illustrations. Moveable type, in which individual letters were printed from cast metal type, was introduced in the 1450s by Johann Gutenberg. Gutenberg developed an oil-based ink borrowed from contemporary painting, adapted the wine press to a new use, and himself found the best metal alloy for making type. He also took advantage of the increasing availability of paper and recognized the pent-up demand for more and cheaper reading matter.

Early printed books were extremely successful; many still exist and can be read today with ease. Although the history of the impact of printing belongs to the early modern period, rather than the Middle Ages, we can note that about nine million books were printed between the 1450s and 1500. The new rapidity with which ideas could spread contributed to the success of Protestantism and the acceptance of the new science of the Scientific Revolution.

THE TECHNOLOGICAL IMAGINATION

As important as the concrete achievements of medieval artisans out-lined in the preceding sections was the emergence of a technological way of thinking. Increasingly, medieval people noted with admiration the invention of new arts. Giordano da Pisa, a Dominican preacher, for example, said in 1305:

> It is not yet twenty years since they discovered the art of making eyeglasses, which let one see clearly, which is one of the finest and most necessary arts the world has, and it is such a short time since they were discovered: a new art, that never was before.[15]

By the fifteenth century, approving lists of new inventions became common, as did manuscript illuminations which associated mechanical inventions with the virtue of Temperance. One such image, for example, shows Temperance as a woman sitting with her feet on a windmill, holding eyeglasses in her right hand, with spurs on her heels, a bit and bridle in her mouth, and a clock on her head (see Figure 12). The accompanying verse reads in part:

> He who is mindful of the clock
> Is punctual in all his acts. . . .
> He who puts glasses to his eyes
> See better what's around him. . . .
> The mill which sustains our bodies
> Never is immoderate.[16]

Indications of an enthusiasm for imagining technological innovations can be seen as early as the eleventh, twelfth, and thirteenth centuries. Historian of medieval technology Lynn White, jr., for example, identifies an eleventh-century Benedictine monk named Eilmer who attempted to fly by constructing wings for his hands and feet, climbing to the top of a tower, and jumping off. He flew for over 600 feet before crashing, breaking both his legs. According to the chronicler, he attributed his failure to forgetting to add a tail on his back.[17]

In later centuries examples of "the technological imagination" be-come more common. Both the thirteenth-century draftsman Villard de

et fauur. Encores me rend plus

Figure 12. The virtue of Temperance, shown as a woman sitting on a windmill, with spurs on her feet, a bridle in her mouth, eyeglasses in her right hand and a clock on her head. Fifteenth century. This image shows how technology came to be identified with the religious virtue of Temperance or moderation and was given a high moral value. *Allegory of Temperantia. From De quattuor virtutibus cardinalibus by Pseudo-Seneca. Dresden, Sächsische Landesbibliothek, Ms. Oc. 79, fol. 68 v. Deutsche Fotothek.*

Honnecourt and his contemporary, Peter Peregrinus (fl. 1269), imagined a perpetual motion machine based on the power of the magnet. Roger Bacon (c. 1219–92), who pioneered in the science of optics, envisioned massive mirrors set up on mountain tops to intensify the rays of the sun and burn up the invading armies of the Anti-Christ. He also spoke of lenses that would enable people to see far-off objects as if they were close and wrote of flying machines, submarines to explore the bottom of the sea, and carriages that would move by themselves.

Technology also gradually acquired a new intellectual respectability. The classical Greek tradition had tended to view technology more as physical labor than as a mental activity requiring intelligence. During the twelfth and thirteenth centuries, however, technology, under the rubric "the mechanical arts," became a recognized part of human knowledge. Moreover, the view, derived from Aristotle, that human art or craftsmanship could only offer an inferior imitation of natural processes was gradually eroded over the course of the Middle Ages.

In the fifteenth century, there seems to have been a growing convergence between engineering and more theoretical disciplines. Several late medieval physicians, among them Conrad Kyeser and Giovanni Fontana, experimented with the design of novel machines, including a windmill-powered, armored "tank" and a parachute. Mariano Taccola (1382–c. 1453), an engineer employed in various capacities by the Italian city of Siena, drew pictures and wrote brief descriptions of many machines, some known and some imaginary, such as siphons which could carry water over mountains and amphibious vessels driven by wind or animals.

Such flights of technological imagination may be partly inspired by literary tales of fabulous wonders, which were popular in the Middle Ages. Nevertheless, they seem to reflect a playful enthusiasm for technological innovation. Popular pleasure in automatic clockworks mounted in church towers, which presented cocks flapping their wings and crowing or processions of monks, reflect a similar sentiment, as do pageantry automata and medieval "amusement parks" equipped with devices that automatically played music and moved mechanical trees.

During the fifteenth century, technology also came to be increasingly seen as an important adjunct of political power and social status. According to Pamela O. Long, fifteenth-century rulers increasingly valued building projects, military technology, and decorative arts as ways of displaying and legitimizing their power, while some elites began to appreciate craftsmanship as the source of objects of conspicuous consumption.[18] This new elevation of technical knowledge had its roots in a new convergence of interests among learned humanists, artisans, and patrons and princes. A key effect was to spur the writing of technical treatises which, as Long has argued, began to transform craft know-how into discursive knowledge "about the world itself," promoting the empirical methodologies characteristic of the science of the Scientific Revolution.[19]

WHY DID THE MIDDLE AGES VALUE TECHNOLOGY?

What aspects of medieval society and culture promoted the enthusiasm shown by medieval people for technology? This thorny question has prompted more discussion than any other connected with medieval technology.

One line of thought attributes medieval pursuit of technology directly to the values of western Christianity. No scholar has done more to argue and popularize this view than Lynn White, jr. (1907–87). White, who virtually founded the study of medieval technology in the United States, marshaled a great deal of iconographic and other evidence that religious communities in the Middle Ages supported technological development. He pointed out that early medieval monasteries made manual work an essential part of daily life and suggested that the uniquely "activist" character of medieval religion made the pursuit of technology morally virtuous. White also argued that the fact that western Christian churches, in contrast to Byzantine churches, typically possessed both clocks and organs demonstrated Latin Christianity's commitment to technological innovation. Finally, he noted that the Cistercians were often in the forefront of medieval technology, equipping their domains and buildings with "state-of-the-art" technologies such as water-powered mills adapted to a variety of purposes. In one article, "The Historical Roots of Our Ecologic Crisis" (1967), which reached an exceedingly wide readership, White went even further, arguing that medieval Christianity inculcated an "exploitative" attitude toward nature and therefore bore "a great burden of guilt" for the current environmental crisis.[20]

Critics have challenged what has come to be called the "Lynn White Thesis," on several fronts. One group of scholars interested in the intersection of religion and attitudes toward the environment have agreed that Christianity supports technology but have denied that it encourages an "exploitative" attitude toward nature; instead, they say, Christianity mandates an attitude of "stewardship." Some historians of medieval technology have accused White of "technological determinism," that is, of assuming without adequate evidence that technology was an overriding factor in medieval society. Most recently, microstudies of how specific technologies were used in specific places have shown that medieval peasants did not necessarily enthusiastically pursue new technological methods; rather, a variety of complex social and economic factors came into play which helped determine if and how technological innovations were adopted. Some of these authors also challenge White's view that mechanization replaced human muscle power to a significant degree in the Middle Ages. They argue, instead, that hand labor was often preferred even when mechanized alternatives were possible and that agriculture remained productive only when it continued to be labor intensive.[21]

Intellectual and cultural historians have questioned many of the finer points of White's thesis and on the whole have argued that medieval culture, including religious communities, was far more ambivalent toward technological progress than White admitted. Some have also pointed out that everyone in the Middle Ages saw the world through "religion-colored glasses"[22] and, therefore, that religious approval of technology might be a reflection, rather than a cause, of technological development.

Another line of argument emphasizes the social and economic climate of the late Middle Ages in the emergence of technology as a valued type of human knowledge and endeavor. The late medieval world was increasingly urbanized and increasingly dependent on an emerging commercial capitalism; as machines, buildings, art objects, and other products of technological know-how came to be seen as valuable in supporting the political power and prestige of secular elites, the status of technology itself was elevated.[23]

No scholarly consensus on what promoted technological development during the Middle Ages exists at present. To date, work on this topic has often been overly general and too dependent on value judgments about the meaning of technology, religion, and capitalism in the present as well as the past. Future research of a more focused kind should shed light on the complex relations of local variations in land holding, the availability of markets, and power relations between different social groups as they affect technological development and innovation. The results of this work would then need to be integrated with the history of the representation of technology and manual labor in the Middle Ages. Such research, which gives full attention to the details of lived existence, will give us a fuller picture of medieval technology in its cultural and social context than we now have.

NOTES

1. Pamela O. Long, *Openness, Secrecy, Authorship: Technical Arts and the Culture of Knowledge from Antiquity to the Renaissance* (Baltimore and London: Johns Hopkins University Press, 2001), pp. 89–93.

2. Long, *Openness*, pp. 208–11, 243.

3. Erwin Panofsky, *Gothic Architecture and Scholasticism* (New York: Meridian Books, 1957), p. 44.

4. Lynn T. Courtenay, "Introduction," in *The Engineering of Medieval Cathedrals*, ed. Lynn T. Courtenay, Studies in the History of Civil Engineering, 1 (Aldershot, England: Ashgate, 1997), p. xv.

5. Martin S. Briggs, "Building-Construction," in *A History of Technology*, ed. Charles Singer, E. J. Holmyard, A. R. Hall, and Trevor I. Williams, vol. 2 (Oxford: Clarendon Press, 1957), p. 437.

6. Francis Gies and Joseph Gies, *Cathedral, Forge, and Waterwheel: Technology and Invention in the Middle Ages* (New York: HarperPerennial, 1994), p. 217.

7. R. Patterson, "Spinning and Weaving," in Singer et al., eds., *History of Technology*, p. 207.

8. Richard W. Unger, *The Ship in the Medieval Economy 600–1600* (London: Croom Helm and Montreal: McGill-Queen's University Press, 1980), p. 22.

9. Unger, *Ship*, p. 216.

10. Kelly DeVries, *Medieval Military Technology* (Peterborough, Ontario, Orchard Park, New York and Hadleigh, Essex: Broadview Press, 1992; rpt. 1998), p. 145.

11. Bert Hall, "Weapons of War and Late Medieval Cities: Technological Innovation and Tactical Changes," in *Technology and Resource Use in Medieval Europe: Cathedrals, Mills, and Mines*, ed. Elizabeth Bradford Smith and Michael Wolfe (Aldershot, England: Ashgate, 1997), pp. 207–8.

12. DeVries, *Medieval Military Technology*, p. 149; Hall, "Weapons of War," p. 205.

13. Lewis Mumford, *Technics and Civilization* (New York: Harcourt Brace, 1939), pp. 14–15; Gerhard Dohrn-van Rossum, *The History of the Hour: Clocks and Modern Temporal Orders*, trans. Thomas Dunlap (Chicago and London: University of Chicago Press, 1996), p. 3.

14. The following account is heavily indebted to Dohrn-van Rossum, *History of the Hour*.

15. Quoted in Chiara Frugoni, *Books, Banks, Buttons and Other Inventions from the Middle Ages*, trans. William McCuaig (New York: Columbia University Press, 2003), p. 2.

16. Lynn White, jr., "The Iconography of *Temperantia* and the Virtuousness of Technology," in *Medieval Religion and Technology: Collected Essays* (Berkeley, Los Angeles, and London: University of California Press, 1978), pp. 198–99.

17. Lynn White, jr., "Eilmer of Malmesbury, an Eleventh Century Aviator: A Case Study of Technological Innovation, Its Context and Tradition," in *Medieval Religion and Technology*, pp. 59–74.

18. Long, *Openness*, p. 141.

19. Long, *Openness*, pp. 247–49.

20. Lynn White, jr., "The Historical Roots of Our Ecologic Crisis," in *Dynamo and Virgin Reconsidered: Essays in the Dynamism of Western Culture* (Cambridge, MA: MIT Press, 1971), p. 90. First published in *Science* 155 (1967): 1203–7, this article has been widely reprinted. *Dynamo and Virgin Reconsidered* was first published by MIT Press under the title *Machina ex Deo: Essays in the Dynamism of Western Culture* (1968). For a review of the impact of this article and criticisms of its arguments by historians and others, see Elspeth Whitney, "Lynn White, Ecotheology, and History," *Environmental Ethics* 15 (1993): pp. 151–69.

21. See, especially, articles by David Crossley, Paolo Squatritti, Richard Holt, and Michael Toch in *Technology and Resource Use*, ed. Smith and Wolfe.

22. Jacques Le Goff, *Time, Work, and Culture in the Middle Ages*, trans. Arthur Goldhammer (Chicago and London: University of Chicago Press, 1980) pp. 107–10.

23. Long, *Openness*, p. 245.

CHAPTER 7

THE IMPACT OF MEDIEVAL SCIENCE AND TECHNOLOGY

In assessing the impact of past events, we are often inclined to look for those aspects of past history which seem to lead directly to the present. While this process is valuable, it is also important to appreciate the past in and of itself and on its own terms. We will look at the impact of medieval science and technology as they helped create the modern world; first, however, we will consider briefly what medieval science and technology tell us about a world that is very different from ours.

Medieval scientists regarded science as part of a broad philosophical and religious understanding of the world. Although they gave preference to naturalistic explanations over supernatural ones, they also assumed that science was part of a larger worldview which ultimately included God and His manifestations in the world. Unlike most modern scientists, therefore, medieval scientists did not wish to wholly separate scientific questions from religious ones. It is also significant that medieval universities were ecclesiastical institutions and almost all medieval natural philosophers were clerics. Although this does not seem to have had a constricting effect on the technical content of science in the Middle Ages, it does mean that medieval scientists were often interested in different types of questions than are modern scientists. For one thing, science as it was understood within the university was almost entirely theoretical science. Following the Aristotelian model, the purpose of knowledge was to understand, rather than to make use of, nature. Even though medieval philosophers during and after the twelfth century included the mechanical arts as part of the recognized arts, few of them would have thought that the mechanical arts should be a part of a university education. Medieval universities did not have laboratories, nor did most university-trained scientists seek opportunities to apply their findings in practical ways.

There were important exceptions to the above. Exceptional individuals like Adelard of Bath, Frederick II, and Peter Peregrinus wrote important scientific works with practical implications outside a university context. Alchemy, perhaps because of religious scruples about infringing on God's unique capacity to create, was also developed outside the university, even when studied by university-trained clerics. For the most part, however, science and technology were practiced by entirely different groups of people; only in the late fourteenth and fifteenth centuries do we begin to find learned people—usually physicians, astrologers, or alchemists—who seem to have actually tried to design and build machines, or, conversely, engineers and clock makers who brought learning in the liberal arts and philosophy to bear on their mechanical activities. The deliberate bringing together of theoretical science with practical problems in engineering was one of the novel aspects of the new science practiced by Galileo and others in the seventeenth century.

If medieval science was so different from modern science, were there any connections between them? One view, which has its origins in the eighteenth and nineteenth centuries, would respond that medieval science was a dead end because it was too abstract and too dominated by religion. One influential history of science published in 1837, for example, summed up physical science in the Middle Ages as an "almost complete blank"; even today, it is not uncommon for the Middle Ages in the popular press to be simply referred to as the "Dark Ages."[1] Since the mid-twentieth century, however, this view has been almost completely supplanted among scholars by a more nuanced assessment which argues that while medieval science was not the *same* as modern science, it did provide the necessary preconditions and structure for modern science to emerge.

Why the Scientific Revolution took place over the sixteenth and seventeenth centuries in Europe and not in the ancient world or the Middle Ages, or elsewhere in China or the Islamic regions, is an extremely complex question; a recent, important book on the various arguments historians have had on this issue is over 650 pages long.[2] Clearly, we cannot fully address this question here. We can, however, point out that almost all of the characteristics associated with science during the Scientific Revolution, including the close observation of nature, the application of mathematics to scientific problems, a social investment in the pursuit of science and technology, and the systematic asking of scientific questions, appeared in at least partial or rudimentary form between 1100 and 1500.

Although they might disagree on how much to emphasize each characteristic, historians have generally agreed upon the following as associated with science during the Scientific Revolution: a strong interest in close and accurate observations, the application of mathematics to natural phenomena, the idea of testing natural processes through experiment, an interest in using nature for human benefit, an idea of scientific and technological progress, and a view that science and technology were worth supporting financially and institutionally. During the Scientific Revolution these values were applied energetically, creatively, and in a broad range of contexts, eventually destroying the Aristotelian worldview of medieval science.

Nevertheless, it is significant that each one of these values shows up somewhere during the practice of medieval science. Albertus Magnus and others carefully observed the anatomy and behavior of animals; Peter Peregrinus observed the phenomenon of magnetism; medieval astronomers looked for increasingly accurate observations of the movements of heavenly bodies; medieval physicians made careful clinical notes on their cases. Mathematics was also important for many medieval scientists. Scientists like Robert Grosseteste, Roger Bacon, and Theodoric of Freiberg developed a mathematical science of optics, while the Oxford Calculators and their successors, Buridan and Oresme, tried to devise ways to mathematically measure motion and other qualities of matter. Many writers on natural philosophy expressed an interest in the utility of natural products or using the power of nature to build labor-saving machinery, weapons, or other useful devices. A few, notably Bacon and the alchemists, explicitly articulated an ideal of future progress in these areas. By the fifteenth century, craft know-how began to be seen as transformable into theoretical, discursive knowledge. Least developed was a notion of controlled experiment, but even here we can find examples in the work of Grosseteste, Albertus Magnus, and others of simple experiments used to test a hypothesis. Moreover, there are indications that a model of the experimental method was developing at the University of Padua in the fifteenth century.

This is not to argue that early modern science was simply an outgrowth of medieval science. Medieval scientists as a group can be said to have failed to convert isolated, brilliant insights into a systematic overhaul of the Aristotelian system. As we saw in Chapter 3, modern science was built on very different metaphysical premises than was medieval science. At the same time, medieval natural philosophers consistently worked to refine, modify, and even challenge Aristotle on specific points. Even when they ultimately returned to the traditional viewpoint, as Buridan and Oresme did in their discussion of whether the earth rotated on its axis, they thoroughly discussed the evidence for the unconventional position. Moreover, medieval natural philosophers seem to have enjoyed asking new and difficult questions. In particular, it was the systematic hammering away at the Ptolemaic system and Aristotle's dynamics during the Middle Ages by both European and Arabic scientists that helped pave the way for the revolutionary work of Copernicus and Galileo.

Crucial to this endeavor was the "culture of poking around," as Edward Grant, historian of medieval science, puts it:

> What made it possible for Western civilization to develop science and the social sciences in a way that no other civilization had ever done before? The answer, I am convinced, lies in a pervasive and deep-seated spirit of inquiry that was a natural consequence of the emphasis on reason that began in the Middle Ages. . . . With the exception of revealed truths, reason was enthroned in medieval universities as the ultimate arbiter for most intellectual arguments and controversies. It was quite natural for scholars immersed in a university environment to employ reason to probe into their subject areas that had not been explored before, as well as to discuss possibilities that had not previously been entertained. . . .
>
> . . . [T]his spirit of inquiry can be aptly described as the spirit of "poking around," a spirit that manifests itself through an urge to apply reason to almost every kind of question and problem that confronts scholars of any particular period. . . . I regard the spirit of poking around as nothing less than the spirit of scientific inquiry.[3]

A word should be said about the institutional support for the practice of science in the Middle Ages. Science received a permanent, secure, and sympathetic home in the university. This seems to have been an important aspect in the continuing development of science in this period; it has been suggested that the lack of such a home in the Islamic world is one reason why science, after a brilliant start, failed to flourish there after the thirteenth century. That the universities were ecclesiastical organizations run by the Church does not seem to have had a detrimental effect on the pursuit of science; if necessary, natural philosophers seem to have had little difficulty in separating conclusions drawn from reason and scientific knowledge from those demanded by faith. Moreover, religious attitudes in many ways supported the investigation of nature, often called "the book of God," as part of human knowledge. The medieval Church, unlike early modern Protestants and Catholics, did not insist on a literal reading of scripture; rather, there was a well-developed tradition of reading the Bible for several layers of meaning, including the allegorical. As David Lindberg has pointed out, "in *technical* subjects such as mathematics, astronomy, optics, meteorology, medicine and natural history, there were virtually no constraints and no limitations" placed by theology or ecclesiastical authorities.[4] On the contrary, the idea of science as "handmaiden" to theology provided a powerful rationale for the "doing" of science.

At the same time, it must be acknowledged that modern science developed a scientific method very different from that found in the Middle Ages. Medieval science tended to leap from ordinary, commonsense observation and experience to logical, but highly abstract, a priori theory with very little reference to the "real world" in between. On the other hand, one of the great achievements of the Scientific Revolution was to bring together a commitment to empirically verifiable mathematical facts with a more abstract and mechanized view of nature, to enter into, in H. Floris Cohen's phrase, "the universe of precision."[5] The Middle Ages may, however, have indirectly contributed to this new method through its enthusiasm for technology.

Medieval technology had profound and far-reaching effects on the European world. Although the paucity of sources makes it difficult to assess precisely how technological innovation affected medieval life at any specific time and place, overall the expanded use of new and improved technologies helped transform Europe from a subsistence, almost entirely agricultural society in the early Middle Ages to an increasingly commercial and mechanized one by 1500. The use of water power and new inventions, such as the blast furnace and horizontal loom, changed iron-working and cloth-making from handicrafts to large-scale manufacturing operations. The invention and diffusion of the mechanical clock, together with the modern system of equal hour timekeeping, began the process, so much a part of modern life, of organizing human activities according to precise timetables rather than by lived experience. At the very end of the Middle Ages, the invention of the musket, pistol, and printing press contributed to the rising power and influence of the middle class and had a variety of other far-reaching effects on European society and culture. The European voyages of discovery, which forever changed the relationship of Europe and the rest of the world, depended on a century of previous improvements in ship design, navigational techniques, and firearms. Finally, the European habit of looking for technological solutions and pursuing them until they worked set western society and culture on the road to the domination of nature which has become the hallmark of the modern world.

Many of these inventions demonstrate a pervasive interest in doing things in a more exact and precise manner. While mechanization was not pursued by all groups at all times in all situations, the use of new, more efficient, and more impressive machines was of sufficient interest to enough people to have had a significant impact on late medieval society. The mechanical clock promoted an interest in more exact measurements of time; improved navigational tools allowed for the more exact placing of people on the earth's surface; printing made possible the more precise replication of images and words; advances in metallurgy encouraged the production of precision tools and instruments, such as the astronomical clock and pistol.

Historians have not yet reached a consensus on the origins of modern science or in what ways late medieval society may have contributed to new scientific thinking. The complex and tangled historical relationships between culture, science, technology, the nation state, and capitalism in the period between 1200 and 1700 are still being explored by historians and other scholars. The historical record, however, clearly shows that medieval technology and science bequeathed to the modern world at least some of the essential ingredients of modernity.

NOTES

    1. Edward Grant, *God and Reason in the Middle Ages* (Cambridge, England: Cambridge University Press, 2001), p. 327.

2. H. Floris Cohen, *The Scientific Revolution: A Historiographical Inquiry* (Chicago and London: University of Chicago Press, 1994).

3. Grant, *God and Reason*, p. 356.

4. David C. Lindberg, "Medieval Science and Its Religious Context," *Osiris*, 2nd Series, 10 (1995), p. 74.

5. Cohen, *Scientific Revolution*, p. 510.

BIOGRAPHIES

Adelard of Bath (c. 1080–c. 1152)

Adelard of Bath was one of the most important of the group of trans-lators who first brought Greek and Arabic natural philosophy to Europe in the twelfth century. Born in England, he traveled widely in France, Sicily, the Near East, and probably Spain. He may have had an asso-ciation with the court of the English king Henry I, and possibly Henry II. He remained a layman and probably worked as a tutor to the English nobility.

Among the most important of Adelard's works are his translations from Arabic into Latin of Euclid's *Elements* (in several versions) and the astronomical tables of the Arabic mathematician al-Khwarizmi. Adelard also translated several astrological works by Arabic writers. The most important of his original works is the *Questiones naturals* (Natural Ques-tions), in the form of a dialogue between Adelard and his nephew (c. 1116). This work expounds the "new" natural philosophy, that is, the natural philosophy of Aristotle and Arabic scientists, although Adelard never mentions an Arabic writer by name. Particularly noteworthy is Adelard's firm rejection of unquestioning reliance on written authorities, which he compares to being led around by a halter like a domestic animal. He also wrote the earliest known Latin treatise on falconry, a topic later taken up by Frederick II and Albertus Magnus. Among his other works are *De eodem et diverso*, an exhortation to study philosophy, and a work on mathematics.

Albertus Magnus (Albert the Great) (c. 1193–1280)

Albertus was one of the single most important scientists of the Middle Ages and he wrote on virtually every area of natural philosophy. His works in biology and zoology (*On Animals*), botany (*On Plants*), and mineralogy (*On Minerals and Stones*) represent the highest development of medieval science in these fields. Albertus was also the effective founder of the scientific study of geology in the Middle Ages. In addition, he wrote an original treatise on comets.

Albertus wrote over 100 distinct works, totaling over 20,000 pages. Albertus's twenty-four scientific books, some quite lengthy, were part of a grand project to explain the whole of human knowledge. Although most of his scientific works are framed as commentaries on the works of Aristotle, in many cases much of the work is drawn from Arabic and contemporary sources and Albertus' own researches.

Albertus' greatest contribution to medieval scientific method lay in his combination of thoughtful consideration of Aristotelian theory, his systematic review of the state of contemporary knowledge on the subject, and his emphasis on the empirical observation on nature. Although he was immensely learned in Greek and Arabic science, he did not hesitate to rule Aristotle or other authorities incorrect on specific points if necessary. Overall, his work shows a persistent effort to record concrete information based on his own and others' personal observations. He provides firsthand descriptions of many plants and animals, including the first known mentions of the weasel, the rat, the common dormouse, and spinach. He dissected a mole, cricket, and hen's eggs at different stages of development. He was equally interested in providing a coherent framework for scientific investigation—for example, developing an original classification of flowers and fruits and making a systematic study of embryology.

Albertus showed a distinctive interest in the practical uses of natural resources. His work on zoology includes lengthy accounts of contemporary practices in dog and horse training and care and references to local hunting, farming, and fishing techniques. He also describes contemporary mining practices.

Born in Bavaria, Albertus probably studied at the University of Padua before joining the Dominican Order in 1223. He taught in Dominican schools in Germany (1228–45; 1248–54) and in Paris (1245–48) and was the teacher of the future great scholastic philosopher Thomas Aquinas. He was also an exceptional administrator, being elected head of the Dominicans in Germany in 1254 and Bishop of Regensberg in 1260. Allowed to resign in 1262 to pursue his scholarship, he was nevertheless recruited to preach the crusade in Germany between 1262 and 1264. After 1264 he seems to have spent most of the remainder of his life writing, although he was frequently called upon to mediate various ecclesiastical disputes. He died in 1280, after a decline in physical and mental health beginning in 1279.

Albertus used his many travels by foot around Germany resulting from his administrative duties as opportunities to visit distant libraries, to observe local conditions, and even to interview the local population about the animals, plants, and technology in their area. One passage in his work on minerals, for example, records his own observation of veins of gold and silver ore ("I have learned by what I have seen by my own eyes") and what he has been told ("miners and smelters have told me").

Albertus was recognized as an exceptional scholar in his own lifetime, and was called "the Great" even before his death. During the fifteenth century, a variety of spurious works tinged with occultism were falsely attributed to him. The most important of these include the *Book of Secrets*, an alchemical work, and the *Secrets of Women*, a work on medicine and natural philosophy. In 1931 Albertus was canonized by Pope Pius XI and in 1941 he was made the patron saint of scientists by Pope Pius XII.

Alhazen (Ibn al-Haythan) (c. 965–c. 1039)

Alhazen was one of the most important Arabic scientists. He was chiefly known in Europe for his work in optics, but he also wrote on mathematics, astronomy, and medicine. He was born in Basra, in what is now Iraq. According to some accounts he moved to Egypt after being invited to design and build a system on the Nile to regulate the flow of water; this project, however, for reasons that remain unclear, was never started. He seems to have spent most of his life in Cairo, making his living as a copyist of mathematical texts and pursuing his studies.

Alhazen's contribution to optics was to formulate a new comprehensive theory which overcame significant difficulties in previous work on the subject. Earlier theories had postulated that vision occurred when some sort of image given off from seen objects entered or affected the eye. However, they failed to explain how the eye could sort out the multiple entering images or how objects could emit forms so that many different people in different locations could see the same object. Alhazen in his *Perspectiva* instead suggested that the eye registers only the single rays which enter the eye perpendicular to the points of the convex surface of the eye. This means that images from the visual field of the eye not only kept a fixed arrangement as they entered the eye, but that vision could be analyzed mathematically in terms of a "visual cone" with its point on the point at which the image enters the eye and its base on the object. Alhazen also formulated the idea of light as a physical ray and discussed the relationship of cognition and visual perception. In other works, he discusses the rainbow, burning mirrors, shadows, and a theory of the shape of the eclipse.

Alhazen's work in optics had a major influence on Roger Bacon (c. 1219–92) and other Latin writers on optics. The *Perspectiva* also seems to have been read by sixteenth- and seventeenth-century mathematicians.

Aristotle (384–24 B.C.E.)

Aristotle, one of the most important thinkers in the history of western civilization, almost single-handedly established the theory and content of western science before the Scientific Revolution. Born in northern Greece, he studied in Athens with the great philosopher Plato after the end of the Peloponnesian War. After Plato's death in 347 B.C.E., Aristotle left Athens and traveled in Asia Minor, returning to Macedonia in 342 to tutor King Philip's son, the future Alexander the Great. In 335, Aristotle established his own school, the Lyceum, in Athens. He left Athens again in 323, fearing that he would be tried on charges of impiety, and died the following year.

During his lifetime, Aristotle wrote definitive treatises on almost every known literary, philosophical, and scientific subject. (His works as we now have them are not finished texts designed for public consumption, but most probably are lecture notes.) His scientific works include works on biology (*On the Parts of Animals*, *On the Generation of Animals*), psychology (*On the Soul*, *Parva Naturalia*), cosmology (*On the Heavens*), natural philosophy (the *Physics*, *On Generation and Corruption*), and meteorology. He developed a scientific method based on empirical observation and careful analysis of both facts and principles, as well as a scientific vocabulary. Aristotle also established a tradition of systematic research at the Lyceum, which was carried on by his students. Especially important was Theophrastus, who wrote influential works on stones and botany.

The Aristotelian corpus became the foundation of science and natural philosophy in the West into the seventeenth century and, in biology, into the eighteenth. The extraordinarily long life of Aristotle's ideas is partly attributable to the fact that he provided a comprehensive and consistent account of the world which meshed with both a plausible metaphysics and with ordinary experience and common sense. Among his basic ideas are teleology (the idea that nature works toward "ends," rather than by random causes), that matter is found in the form of four elements (earth, water, air, fire) characterized by combinations of the four qualities (hot, cold, wet, dry), and that finding ways to logically analyze change is a fundamental task of science. Aristotle's discussion of dynamics and cosmology was heavily dependent on a priori assumptions, for example, that the heavenly bodies moved in uniform, circular motions because that is the most perfect form of motion. His zoological work, however, shows a systematic attempt to gather information on over 560 different species of animals largely based on careful observation of animal anatomy and behavior by himself, fishermen, farmers, and others. He performed some animal dissections. His view of human sexuality and gender posited that men, because they possessed more innate heat, supplied the form and spirit to the fetus, whereas women, who are colder, supply only the matter in the form of menstrual fluid; women, in Aristotle's view, were imperfect, immature men. (For a fuller discussion of Aristotle's natural philosophy, see Chapter 3.)

Aristotle's ideas passed from the Hellenistic world to Rome and then to the Islamic world. He was especially influential on Galen, the most important Hellenistic physician. During the early Middle Ages in the West, the only Aristotelian texts available in Latin were on logic. However, Arabic scholars translated most of the Aristotelian corpus during the ninth and tenth centuries. Their commentaries and expositions of Aristotle both transmitted Aristotle's original thought and modified it in the light of their own philosophical and scientific interests. In addition, sections of works by Plotinus and Proclus, two highly influential

Neoplatonic writers, circulated as works of Aristotle, leading to a tendency to blend Aristotelian and Platonic approaches.

The recovery of Aristotle in the Latin West was crucial not only for the breadth of Aristotle's philosophical framework and content, but also because it reinforced the status of philosophy and science as independent disciplines. During the translation movement of the twelfth and thirteenth centuries, gradually the whole body of Aristotle's work was translated into Latin, first from Arabic and then from the original Greek. By the thirteenth century, Aristotle was the foundation for the scientific curriculum at medieval universities and works by Aristotle were considered essential for study in the arts. Although an attempt was made to prohibit the teaching of some aspects of Aristotle's natural philosophy by the bishop of Paris and other ecclesiastical authorities in the early thirteenth century, culminating in the Condemnations of 1277, this attempt was short-lived and mainly attacked the more radical assertions of some Arabic scholars, rather than Aristotle himself.

Aristotle's authority was so great during the High and late Middle Ages that he was known simply as "the Philosopher" or, in the words of the poet Dante, "the master of those who know." One of the great achievements of medieval scholasticism was the synthesis of Aristotelianism and Christian faith by Thomas Aquinas (1225–74). Medieval natural philosophers, however, were not slavish imitators of Aristotle but frequently refined, modified, and even challenged his ideas. Their explicit and implicit criticism of Aristotle are part of the background to the Scientific Revolution.

Aristotelianism continued to be important through the Renaissance. In the fields of astronomy and dynamics, Aristotle's ideas were gradually discarded during the sixteenth and seventeenth centuries; in biology, his ideas, often in new guise, continued to be influential into the nineteenth century.

Avicenna (Ibn Sina) (980–1037)

Ibn Sina, known as Avicenna in the West, was one of the most influential and important Arabic thinkers, both in the Islamic world and in Europe. Although he was a prominent philosopher in Islam, he was mainly known as a physician in the West.

Avicenna was born in Afshana near Bukhara in what was then

northern Persia and is now Uzbekistan. He gravitated to philosophy and science at a very young age and was a practicing physician by age sixteen. At various times in his life he was a jurist, teacher, and civil servant. During his lifetime, he wrote almost 270 works, including books on logic, the division of the sciences, medicine, mathematics, metaphysics, and an autobiography.

Avicenna was influenced both by Neoplatonism and Aristotelianism. His most famous work in the West was his *Canon of Medicine*, an encyclopedic work of almost one million words. The *Canon* clarifies and organizes the material found in Galen, whose writings were often verbose; using Galen and other sources, Avicenna produced a rigorous, theoretically consistent account of contemporary medicine. As a side effect of its emphasis on clarity and logic, it decreased the clinical emphasis in Galen's original work. It was translated by Gerard of Cremona in the twelfth century and remained the chief medical textbook into the seventeenth century. It was also frequently translated into Hebrew.

Another work by Avicenna, known in the West as *The Book of the Healing*, covered metaphysics, physics, logic, and mathematics. It was influential in the thirteenth century before Aristotle's *Metaphysics* was widely studied. Avicenna also wrote a work titled *The Book of the Remedy*, sometimes mistakenly attributed to Aristotle, on stones, minerals, and related subjects. This work included an unusually cogent discussion of the formation of mountains and a detailed, precise refutation of the claims of alchemists to transmute metals.

Roger Bacon (c. 1219–92)

Roger Bacon was one of the most original medieval natural philosophers, and also one who has been most often misunderstood. Although many of his ideas were unusual in his own time, he does represent the synthesizing tendencies of thirteenth-century thought. He is chiefly recognized today for his theory of optics, his attempt to create a "universal science," and his enthusiasm for the technological advances he believed could result from the application of science to practical problems.

Bacon was born in England into a wealthy family. Almost nothing is known of his early life. He studied at the University of Paris from about 1237 to about 1247, when he returned to England to study the sciences at Oxford. About ten years later, when he was in his late thirties, he entered the Franciscan Order. Although he is known to have returned to Paris around 1260, it is not clear when, or whether, he left Paris again for Oxford. Bacon spent the rest of his life studying the sciences, primarily optics, mathematics, astrology, languages, and philosophy, and writing the books he is now best known for, the *Opus maius*, *Opus minus*, and *On the Multiplication of the Species* (*De multiplicatione specierum*).

Bacon is known to have come under suspicion by church authorities twice, once in about 1257 when he was transferred from Oxford to Paris, apparently so he could be supervised more closely, and after 1277 for "suspected novelties," when he may have been put under house arrest, perhaps until his death. Scholars today generally believe that these "novelties" were religious, rather than scientific, in nature and that Bacon may have been a supporter of the Spiritual Franciscans, a radical wing of the Franciscan order which resisted the increasingly conservative policies of the Franciscan leadership. The legend that Bacon was a magician seems to have been of Elizabethan origin.

Bacon made several important contributions to the history of medieval science. His writings on optics synthesized current views and established the view of the Arabic scientist Alhazen that rays emitted by objects were primarily responsible for vision. Bacon strongly emphasized that mathematics was an essential discipline in understanding the natural world and that the scientist should rely on a combination of reason and empirical experience. His "universal science" was an attempt to explain all natural causation through the generation of "species" (corporeal forms generated by some bodies which have a variety of effects), using optics as a model. Bacon shows an exceptional interest in applying theoretical science to technological problems and coined the term "experimental science." He explored calendar reform, the possibility of sailing from Spain to India, the possible practical applications of magnetism, and the use of medical knowledge and optics to make weapons. He may have been the first person in Europe to mention saltpeter, a key ingredient in gunpowder, and eyeglasses.

The intellectual influences on Bacon's thought were complex. On the one hand, Bacon was strongly influenced by Arabic and Latin astrological and alchemical writing, as well as by the *Secretum secretorum*, a work on natural magic falsely ascribed to Aristotle. On the other hand, Bacon was also very much a part of the Augustinian tradition which thought that all knowledge is ultimately dependent on the illumination of the mind by God. In addition, he may have been persuaded by contemporary apocalyptic beliefs in the imminent coming of a cosmic conflict between Christians and the Anti-Christ. These influences combined to persuade him that theoretical science could yield important practical benefits and that science, like all forms of knowledge, was ultimately subordinate to the higher purpose of the soul's progress toward God.

Bacon, therefore, was as much a publicist for what he felt was the proper use of scientific knowledge and proper scientific method as he was a scientist per se. His best known work, the *Opus maius* (c. 1266), is an impassioned plea for education in languages, mathematics, and the sciences so that human knowledge could more effectively be put in the service of Christian faith. The science of optics, for example, should be used to construct giant lenses which could focus the rays of the sun onto the armies of the Anti-Christ, burning them up. He also extols the virtues of "experimental science," which he believed could yield various practical benefits. In Bacon's view, however, the "experience" on which the scientist depends includes divine revelation as well as the observation and manipulation of nature. In the *Opus maius* and elsewhere, Bacon confidently refers to flying machines, cars that go by themselves, medicines to prolong life, and lenses that allow the viewer to see faraway things up close, although he himself does not claim to have made such things.

Bacon's work was not well known in his own lifetime. Few contemporary records refer to him. Around 1266 Bacon sent one or more of his works to Pope Clement IV, whose request for Bacon's writings probably originated in an earlier invitation by Bacon himself that the pope, then still a cardinal, read his work. There are no extant records showing that the pope, who died in 1268, ever actually read the books Bacon had so laboriously written.

Thomas Bradwardine (c. 1290–1349)

Bradwardine is known chiefly for his work as part of a group of exceptional mathematicians known as the Oxford Calculators. This group pioneered in the attempt to quantify qualities and were instrumental in elevating the role of mathematics in later medieval science.

Bradwardine was born in England. By 1323 he was a fellow at Merton College in Oxford and by 1348 seems to have received a degree in theology. In the early 1330s he held a variety of minor ecclesiastical appointments, but by 1338 he was chaplain and perhaps personal confessor to King Edward II. In 1349 he became archbishop of Canterbury, the most important Church position in England, but died shortly thereafter of the Plague.

Bradwardine's most important mathematical work was his *Treatise on Proportions* which attempted to mathematically relate changes in the speed of moving objects with changes in the resistance and forces impelling those objects. Bradwardine's work in this respect was the basis for the slightly later work of John Dumbleton, Richard Swineshead, and Nicole Oresme, who refined Bradwardine's formulations.

Bradwardine also wrote a number of logical works and a refutation of atomism based on mathematical principles.

Filippo Brunelleschi (1377–1446)

Brunelleschi was one of the earliest of a new type of engineer-artisan, one who combined practical experience, theoretical knowledge, and artistic talent, a combination that became increasingly common in the competitive commercial atmosphere of late medieval and Renaissance Italy. Brunelleschi was born and worked in Florence, where he won fame and renown by his design and construction of the new dome for the Cathedral of Florence, over 143 feet in diameter, which was in its time and until the nineteenth century the largest and highest dome in the world.

Brunelleschi was first trained as a goldsmith and clockmaker. After losing a competition in 1402 to design a second set of doors for the Baptistery of San Giovanni to Lorenzo Ghiberti, Brunelleschi went to Rome to study architecture accompanied by his friend, the sculptor Donatello. In 1413 he is known to have experimented with perspective by painting an image of what could be seen through the door of the cathedral so precisely that a viewer could not distinguish between the image of the painting reflected in a mirror and reality. Because of this painting he is often credited with inventing single-vanishing-point perspective. He may have studied geometry and perspective with the mathematician Paolo dal Pozzo Toscanelli.

In 1418 Brunelleschi entered and won a competition to design a method for completing the dome on the cathedral, a daunting prospect given the size of the structure demanded. Construction was begun in 1420 and continued until 1462, sixteen years after Brunelleschi's death.

Brunelleschi's solutions to the engineering problems involved in erecting the dome are noteworthy for their innovative design. In order to lift the hundreds of required sandstone beams, weighing as much as 1,700 pounds each, to the top of the existing octagonal cupola, over 170 feet in the air, Brunelleschi designed and built an ox-driven hoist capable of raising and lowering heavy loads exceptionally quickly and precisely through the use of five sets of gears. It has been calculated that with this hoist, one ox could lift a load of 1,000 pounds 200 feet in the air in thirteen minutes. He used other innovative techniques to strengthen and support the walls and control the curvature of the dome as it was being built. At its base, the shell of the dome was over twelve feet thick. Brunelleschi also invented a method of building without having to use scaffolding. The cupola was consecrated in 1436, even though the lantern (the final story) and spire were not yet built. To complete the lantern, Brunelleschi had to design a new hoist equipped with a braking system. Brunelleschi died in 1446, a month after the first stone of the lantern was consecrated. Toscanelli is thought to have used the lantern of the cathedral to make astronomical observations which he later incorporated into improved astronomical charts for navigational purposes.

As an architect, Brunelleschi was expected to help build fortifications for the defense of the city. Among his projects was an unsuccessful attempt to defeat the city of Lucca in 1430 by diverting flood waters into the city. He also in 1421 had designed and built a sort of large barge, possibly with paddle-wheels, to bring marble from the quarry near Pisa to Florence; the boat sank shortly into its maiden voyage. He also built a number of chapels and secular buildings.

John Buridan (c. 1300–c. 1358)

Buridan's importance lies in the fields of physics and philosophy. He was born in the diocese of Arras in France and studied at the University of Paris, where he later became a celebrated teacher. Documents dated 1328 and 1340 mention him as rector of the university. Buridan never took a degree in theology. His philosophical works, which include works on logic and commentaries on Aristotle, were still influential in the sixteenth century. Especially important was Buridan's view that science proceeded by empirical confirmation and that its premises need not be absolutely certain but need only be "observed to be true in many instances and to be false in none." Buridan thus reinforced the status of science as an independent discipline.

For the history of science Buridan is chiefly noted for his theory of impetus. Buridan rejected the Aristotelian principle that a projectile required an external cause continuously in contact with the moving object to keep it moving. Buridan argued instead that an object, once put in motion, acquires a tendency, or impetus, to continue in motion indefinitely if not diminished by the resistance of the medium or by a tendency to an opposing motion. A freely falling body acquires additional impetus as it falls, which explains why it accelerates.

Although Buridan's concept of impetus differs from the modern concept of inertia in several respects, Buridan's ideas do represent an important step in the rejection of Aristotelian dynamics. Buridan also discussed the possibility that the earth revolved on its axis and the heavens remained stationary, pointing out that it is impossible to tell visually which is the case.

Giovanni Dondi (1318–89)

Giovanni Dondi is most famous for his astronomical clock, or astrarium (planetarium), which he completed in 1364 and his detailed description of its workings, complete with diagrams. He was a physician and astrologer who also wrote works on diet and the Plague and on the medicinal uses of hot springs.

Dondi was born in Chioggia, Italy, the son of a physician, Jacopo Dondi, who was also a clockmaker. Giovanni Dondi became a professor of astronomy at the University of Padua around 1350 and also lectured on medicine. He worked for the governments of a number of Italian cities and at one time was the personal physician of the emperor Charles IV.

Dondi was not the inventor of the mechanical clock, which predates his astrarium probably by about fifty years. His importance lies partly in his invention of innovative gearing to demonstrate the motions of the planets and in how his life illustrates the increasing interest in mechanical "marvels" characteristic of the fourteenth century. His description of his clock is the earliest detailed description of any type of clock and is so precise that modern replicas have been built. One, now in the Smithsonian Museum in Washington, D.C., contains over 289 parts and is four feet, four inches high. In his own time, Dondi's clock was famous and continued to be a prized possession until 1529, even though it never worked properly after the death of its maker.

Dondi's achievements also appear to be representative of a growing interplay between engineering, medicine, and theoretical astronomy which was becoming increasingly common in the fourteenth century. This combination of craft experience and learned science was part of the essential background to the Scientific Revolution.

Leonardo Fibonacci (Leonardo of Pisa) (c. 1179–after 1240)

Leonardo was the most important mathematician of the European Middle Ages. His historical importance lies primarily in his introduction of Indian ("Arabic") numerals into Italy and his application of new calculating techniques to accounting problems in business. He is the author of five mathematical treatises. In addition to practical mathematics, he also made advances in number theory.

Leonardo was born into an old Pisan family. He was brought to a trading colony of Pisa, in what is now Algeria, by his father around 1192, in order to learn business math. On subsequent trips to Byzantium, Syria, Egypt, and Sicily, Leonardo continued to learn new algebraic and geometrical techniques which, upon his return to Pisa around 1200, he taught to his fellow Italians. He is also known to have corresponded with Frederick II and scholars connected to Frederick's court.

Galen of Pergamum (129 C.E.–199 or 200)

Galen's life is unusually well documented, in part because he wrote several autobiographies. He was born in Pergamum, a leading intellectual center in Asia Minor. His father, an architect, was an educated man who saw to it that his son received early training in philosophy, mathematics, and medicine. Some of Galen's works date from his teens. After his father's death in 149, Galen began studying, practicing, and traveling throughout the Hellenistic world, including at Corinth, Alexandria, and finally Rome, where he became a controversial public figure. At one point, he was a physician to gladiators. After several years in Rome, he returned to Pergamum but returned to Italy at the summons of the Roman emperor Marcus Aurelius. Galen also became a protégé of Aurelius' son, Commodus, and the emperor Septimius Severus.

Galen was a leading medical authority in his own time, and during the Middle Ages his influence was overriding. In part this was due to the volume of his works (twenty-two volumes in the modern edition), but it was mainly because of his grand conception of medicine as a discipline, his synthesis of Hippocratic, Aristotelian, and Stoic ideas, and his attention to both theory and clinical practice. Although Galen was not a Christian, he did incorporate the Stoic idea of a divine creator who ordered the world according to the best possible design, a conception which made his thought attractive in the Christian empire and later in the Middle Ages.

Galen emphasized the theory of the four humors, clinical observation, anatomy, the classification and causes of disease, and physiology. Although dissection of humans was impossible in his time, Galen did dissect monkeys and recommended examination of any human skeletons which might turn up. His most notorious mistake in anatomy, discovered during the Renaissance, was his belief that some of the blood passes through pores, so small that they were invisible to the naked eye, from the right ventricle of the heart to the left (the circulation of the blood through the capillaries of the arteries and veins was not recognized until the sixteenth century). Although this and some of his other conclusions were wrong, Galen's work remains the most systematic account of human anatomy until the Renaissance.

Galen also reinforced and developed the idea of the four humors (blood, yellow bile, phlegm, and black bile) which dominated medieval and early modern medicine. Health and illness were determined by the balance of the humors, each with its characteristic qualities, within the body; diet, medicines, and regimen (exercise, sleep habits, etc.) helped to keep each individual's constitution properly balanced. Galen made a special study of fevers. His ideas on physiology were complex: he believed in three distinct systems centering respectively on the brain, heart, and liver (see Chapter 5 for more detail).

Galen's work was widely translated into Arabic and Latin during the Middle Ages. The great Arabic physician Avicenna (980–1037) organized Galen's ideas in his vast medical encyclopedia, the *Canon*. These many works, as well as spurious ones attributed to Galen, contributed to medieval and Renaissance "Galenism," which was not always precisely congruent with Galen's original ideas. Galenism remained the basis for European medicine into the modern period, and echoes of his ideas persist into the nineteenth century.

Gerard of Cremona (c. 1114–87)

Gerard of Cremona was the most prolific and influential of the twelfth-century translators of Greek and Arabic natural philosophy from Arabic into Latin; seventy-one translations are listed in the bibliography possibly compiled by his students after his death. Of these, the most important include Ptolemy's *Almagest*; nine works by Galen from their Arabic translations; Avicenna's *Canon*; works by Aristotle (*Physics*, *On the Heavens*, and *On Generation and Corruption*) again from their Arabic versions; and Alkindi's *On Optics*. Gerard also translated numerous Arabic philosophical, astronomical, alchemical, and mathematical works. Gerard's extraordinary output has been credited with definitively shaping western science and philosophy from the twelfth to the fourteenth century, especially in the European dependence on Arabic scholarship. The translation of Avicenna's *Canon*, for example, transformed European medicine, as his translation of Alkindi's work on optics transformed that field.

Gerard was born in Cremona, Italy. He did almost all his work in Toledo in northern Spain. Toledo, reconquered by Christian armies from the Muslims in 1085, was a center of translation into the thirteenth century. Little is known about Gerard's life, beyond the fact that he probably studied in Italy or elsewhere before moving to Toledo by about 1144. The English scholar Daniel of Morley described hearing Gerard publicly lecture on the astrology of Abu Ma'shar in Toledo. He may have been the author of a few minor original works, although this is disputed.

Robert Grosseteste (c. 1168–1253)

Grosseteste wrote extensively on a wide range of topics, including commentaries on some of Aristotle's logical and scientific works, original works on astronomy and optics, and commentaries on the Bible. As an ecclesiastical administrator and bishop he was known for his rigorous support of the Church's independence from secular or political goals.

Grosseteste is best known in the history of science for his work in optics and for his investigations into scientific method. Grosseteste not only revived the study of optics in the West, but also attempted to construct a "metaphysics of light," according to which the universe was created through the expansion of an original point of concentrated power (*lux*), which had visible light (*lumen*) as its most obvious effect, into successively less dense cosmic spheres. It followed that all natural phenomena could be explained through the action of the species of light.

Grosseteste also initiated a much more effective study of the rainbow, which influenced Roger Bacon, Witelo, and finally Theodoric of Freiberg, who formulated the modern understanding of how light is refracted in a rainbow. Grosseteste used his observations of light passing through a glass flask filled with water as part of his research into the rainbow; this attempt to experiment, along with his emphasis on mathematics and the complementary uses of deductive and inductive reasoning, have led some historians of science to describe Grosseteste as one of the originators of modern scientific method. Grosseteste also initiated a plan for the reform of the calendar which influenced other writers on the calendar through the fourteenth century.

Little is known of Grosseteste's early life, although he probably studied at both Oxford and Paris. Between 1214 and 1231, he became one of the first chancellors of Oxford University and in 1235 he was elected bishop of Lincoln.

Hildegard of Bingen (1098–1179)

Hildegard of Bingen was abbess of Disibodenberg and later of Rupertsberg in north central Germany. Widely venerated in her own time and in the late Middle Ages as a preacher, composer, artist, and visionary, she was also the author of two works on natural philosophy and medicine. Hildegard's importance for the history of science lies in her originality and her special attention to female physiology. She is one of only two women writers on natural philosophy and medical topics known from the Middle Ages.

Born near Mainz, Hildegard was the tenth child of a noble family and was dedicated to the religious life by her parents at the age of seven. She took permanent vows sometime between the ages of fourteen and seventeen and was elected abbess of her small Benedictine community by her fellow nuns in 1136 at the age of thirty-eight. Around 1141, after receiving a divine command to write and recovering from a serious illness, she began the first of her three major prophetic works, the *Scivias*. In 1150 she again asserted her independence by moving her nuns to Rupertsberg over the initial protests of her male superiors. At Rupertsberg she continued to write and to perform extensive administrative duties, which after 1165 included governing a sister-house across the Rhine River at Eibingen. Between 1158 and 1170 or 1171, with the approval of Pope Eugenius III, she undertook four preaching tours around Germany pressing for spiritual reform within the Church. Throughout her life, she carried on an active correspondence with church leaders and political figures, including Bernard of Clairvaux, Pope Eugenius III, the Holy Roman emperor Frederick I, and the bishop of Jerusalem, as well as many ordinary people who wrote to her for advice and counseling. She died in 1179 at the age of eighty-two.

Hildegard's strong public presence and prolific writing were highly unusual for a woman in the twelfth century. In this, Hildegard represents one of the last of a series of learned and powerful female abbesses known from the early Middle Ages. Her success can be attributed to her political astuteness and intelligence, her own sense of divine inspiration, and perhaps the fact that she came from an influential family.

Hildegard's scientific works, the *Liber simplicis medicinae*, later called the *Physica* (Natural History), and *Causae et curae* (Causes and Cures) were written between 1150 and 1160. They demonstrate both an understanding of Galenic medical theory on the humors and an original perspective. *Causae et curae* places cosmology and medical theory in the context of Christian history and salvation. It begins with an account of the creation and the effects of the sun, moon, planets, and winds on the earth and human bodies. Hildegard then discusses the four elements, the four humors, reproduction and human sexuality, and the effects of the Fall on human health and well-being. Because of the Fall, humans developed the unhealthy humors of phlegm and black bile, which cause infirmities, anger, and sadness, and the "poison" of semen entered the blood of men and women. This is followed by a detailed discussion of the physiological basis for personality through the predominance of one of the four humors. In the remainder of the work she covers various disorders and diseases, as well as detailed recommendations for a healthy diet and regimen, herbal and other remedies, and useful diagnostic signs. A person with toothache, for example, should use wormwood and verbena cooked in wine as a poultice and also lance the flesh around the tooth "so that the pus can come out." Sleep disorders and dreams are discussed at some length. Moderation in food and drink is recommended to maintain health. Bloodletting is useful but must be performed with caution. Attention should be paid to the condition of the pulse, urine, skin, and eyes in assessing the health of the patient.

The *Physica* treats the elements, animals, stones, fish, birds, metals, and especially plants primarily from the point of view of their humoral character and usefulness in supplying medical remedies. Chamomile is recommended for the intestines, for example, as is cooked nettle. A bath in cooked wild lettuce is suggested for extinguishing lust in both men and women. Placing a diamond in the mouth helps a malicious person and repels the devil. While some of the more strictly medicinal material may reflect Hildegard's direct experience, much of her discussion reflects the mixture of humoral theory, moral fables, and practical folk medicine characteristic of contemporary bestiaries, lapidaries, and herbals.

Hildegard's special attention to sexuality, reproduction, and female physiology are part of what make Hildegard's work unique. Rather than taking the male as the sole model for human biology and psychology, for example, she is the only Latin medieval writer to outline four distinct female, as well as male, temperaments. She provides an extended and, in some respects, original account of the male and female roles in conception. Her vivid descriptions of sexual intercourse and female pleasure are also noteworthy. She also focuses on Adam's transgression in the Fall, rather than Eve's, as was more common.

Hildegard's scientific ideas are also reflected in her visionary writing. The *Scivias*, for example, depicts an egg-shaped cosmos. Hildegard also uses many metaphors drawn from the natural world, including the notion of *viriditas* ("greenness"), the force of life generated by God. Medical ideas also appear throughout her visionary work, the *Book of Divine Works*.

Until recently, Hildegard's reputation as a visionary, which lasted into the Reformation, eclipsed her scientific work. Lately, however, scholars have paid more attention to her unusual blending of physiological and religious ideas. She is also widely appreciated as a composer today and recordings of her liturgical works have been best-sellers in Europe and the United States.

Isidore of Seville (c. 570–636)

Isidore of Seville, archbishop of Seville in Spain from around 600 until his death in 636, is chiefly known for two works, *De natura rerum* (On the Nature of Things) and, most famously, the *Etymologiae* (Etymologies). These two works were encyclopedias, covering a wide range of topics with material compiled from Christian and Latin sources, as well as from Isidore's sometimes fertile imagination. They remained important textbooks throughout the Middle Ages.

Isidore's primary interests were literary rather than scientific, and many of his comments show a faulty understanding of scientific concepts well known in the ancient world. At the same time, Isidore did provide a usefully packaged compendium of basic scientific learning as it existed in the late Roman Empire. He included sections on astronomy, arithmetic, geometry, medicine, geography, botany, and mineralogy, as well as six books relating to technological subjects which included the names and descriptions of tools used in farming and building, the types and parts of ships, weapons, and clothing.

In the seventh century, when education and scientific inquiry had been profoundly disrupted by the Germanic invasions and the dissolution of the Roman Empire, Isidore stands out as unusually accomplished. He was a valued administrator and presided over church councils in Seville (619) and Toledo (633). He was recognized in his own time as an exceptionally learned man and several of his works were commissioned by the Visigothic rulers of Spain. His inclusion of scientific subjects in his encyclopedias, even on a very simple level, helped ensure that science would remain a normal part of monastic education. His works were also widely read by scholars involved in the later Carolingian Renaissance. The *Etymologiae* exists today in over 1,000 manuscripts, an indication of its continuing popularity.

Nicole Oresme (c. 1325–82)

Nicole Oresme is best known for his work in dynamics, monetary policy, and mathematics. He was born in Normandy in France and probably studied theology at Paris in the 1340s and 1350s. He held various teaching and ecclesiastical posts before being appointed Bishop of Lisieux in 1377. From 1369 at the request of the French king, Charles V, he translated Aristotle's works on ethics, politics, and cosmology for the first time into French and wrote commentaries on them.

Much of Oresme's writing was strikingly original in his own time. His treatise on money and monetary policy, probably written between 1355 and 1360, was the first such work written in Europe and remained influential into the sixteenth century. In it Oresme introduced a more strictly rational way of looking at economic behavior which placed less emphasis on ethical considerations. Oresme also developed a new approach to the problem of "incommensurability," that is, mathematical operations which yield an irrational number, such as finding the square root of two. Oresme, who preferred to express mathematical problems in geometrical terms, attempted to show that the ratio of any two unknown distances, times, or velocities was more likely to be incommensurable than commensurable, which, he argued, demonstrated the diversity and therefore the beauty of the universe. He also in a famous metaphor compared the workings of the universe to those of a mechanical clock. Finally, Oresme marshaled a series of carefully thought out and persuasive arguments for the diurnal rotation of the earth, only to retract them at the last minute on grounds of "faith."

Oresme was influenced by the work of the Oxford Calculators and by John Buridan, who may have been his teacher. Like the Oxford Calculators, Oresme developed ways of representing changes in the intensity of qualities, including velocity, geometrically, leading to a more precise definition and understanding of acceleration. Oresme also argued strongly against astrology and magic, which he found "foolish, wicked, and dangerous" to pursue. As a philosopher, Oresme was a part of the deeply skeptical mood of the fourteenth century and the breakdown of the thirteenth-century synthesis. He separated the world of science from that of faith, according certainty only to the latter; while he preferred naturalistic explanations for physical phenomena, he gave the final word to faith. He attributed visions of demons, for example, primarily to poor mental health, while also pointing out that faith shows that demons do in fact exist.

Peter Peregrinus (Peter of Maricourt) (fl. c. 1269)

Almost nothing is known about Peter Peregrinus beyond the fact that he was the author of the first systematic treatise on the magnet, upon which his importance for the history of science rests. His name as given as the author of *De Magnete* (On the Magnet), written in the form of a letter, indicates that he was a soldier originally from Picardy; the honorific "Peregrinus" ("Pilgrim") indicates that he may have participated in a crusade. Peter also indicates that he completed his work while serving as an engineer under Charles Anjou during the siege of Lucera, a town in southern Italy. Roger Bacon refers in glowing terms to a "Master Peter" as a "master of experiment," knowledgeable in natural history, physics, alchemy, military matters, and agriculture. It is possible, although uncertain, that Bacon was referring to Peter of Maricourt.

The "Letter on the Magnet" first describes the properties and effects of the lodestone. Peter includes a method for locating the poles of the magnet, how to construct a simple compass, a description of how the north pole of one lodestone attracts the south pole of another and vice versa, and an argument that the power of the magnet to attract iron derives from the poles of the heavens. (Although Peter was incorrect on this last point, he was among the first to recognize that the magnet points to the celestial pole and not to Polaris, the pole star, which revolves around the true celestial pole.) In the last part of the treatise, Peter describes three instruments that can be built using a magnet. The first two of these are improved compasses, one of which is a "dry compass," which does not require the magnet and pointer to float in water but uses a needle as a pivot. (Although the compass was first invented in China, the Chinese did not know of the dry compass until the sixteenth century when it was introduced by European trading ships. Peter's account appears to be the first of this improvement.)

Finally, Peter describes how to use a magnet to make a "wheel of perpetual motion." In this construction a revolving wheel with iron teeth is placed next to a magnet so that each tooth is first attracted toward the magnet and then, as it passes, is repelled. Properly built, Peter claims, the device will keep the wheel spinning continuously.

The "Letter on the Magnet" is distinguished by its combination of precise and careful description with a thoughtful and original attempt to determine causation in a scientific manner. It also aptly illustrates an instance of medieval interest in the mechanization of power and the improvement of technological devices. The "Letter on the Magnet" was popular during the Middle Ages and influenced sixteenth- and seventeenth-century writers on the magnet, including William Gilbert, who cites it in his *De magnete* (1600).

Plato (427–348 B.C.E.)

Although Plato was not himself an empiricist, he had an immense direct and indirect influence on the history of science in the West. Plato lived and taught in the city of Athens during and after the Peloponnesian War. A student of the famous teacher Socrates, he was disenchanted by democracy after Socrates' trial and execution for impiety. In 388 B.C.E., Plato founded the Academy, a school for training men in philosophy. Plato was the teacher of Aristotle, the great Greek philosopher, who disagreed with him on many fundamental points.

Plato's influence on medieval thought was less direct than Aristotle's. With one exception, Plato's works were not known in Europe until the Renaissance. The fundamentals of Plato's thought, however, were absorbed into Christianity through the medium of Neoplatonism ("new Platonism"), a revived and spiritualized form of Platonism founded by the Greek philosophers Plotinus and Porphyry in the third century C.E. and developed by Proclus and others in the fifth and sixth centuries. Neoplatonism was a major influence on St. Augustine (354–430 C.E.) and also had an important impact on many Arabic philosophers and scientists.

Plato's interests lay not in science but in ethics, politics, and metaphysics. Plato himself said that the study of the material world was at best a "likely story." True reality existed only at the level of completely abstract and eternal forms; physical objects were merely shadowy and imperfect copies of these forms and could never be genuinely known or understood (for example, the concept of a circle in our mind or as expressed in a mathematical formula is a more accurate rendering of a circle than any physical circle one could draw or create). Many medieval thinkers indirectly influenced by the Platonic tradition, therefore, thought the study of nature to be an unworthy and even dangerous distraction from religion; others accepted science only in a subordinate position as the "handmaiden" of theology.

Despite this denigration of the physical world, Plato provided a kind of natural philosophy in the *Timaeus*, the only Platonic work known in the Middle Ages. Here Plato described the construction of the universe as the work of a divine craftsman, or "Demiurge," who fashioned the world out of the five regular geometrical solids. Mathematics was thus built into the very framework of the physical world. Plato also described the world as living creature, animated by a "world soul."

Plato's ideas as developed by later traditions had positive as well as negative effects on science and technology. On the one hand, as suggested above, some Christian writers in the Platonic tradition so subordinated the study of nature to the needs of faith that science lost all its autonomy and interest. On the other hand, the position of "handmaiden" could give science a valued and essential role as an adjunct to faith. Moreover, other aspects of Platonism and Neoplatonism actively fostered creative approaches to understanding the natural world. Plato's view that numbers were the basic building blocks of the universe, developed from the earlier ideas of the Pythagoreans, encouraged the application of mathematics to scientific problems. Neoplatonism developed the idea that emanations from the One (God) constituted and sustained a Great Chain of Being from the most spiritual to the most material entities. As adapted by medieval Arabic and Latin scientists, these ideas lent philosophical backing to the sciences of astrology and alchemy and contributed to the development of the ideal of the discovery of a "universal science." Robert Grosseteste (c. 1168–1253) and Roger Bacon (c. 1219–92) are two examples of important medieval scientists whose thought was influenced by Neoplatonism.

Finally, Platonic ideas as they appeared in the Augustinian tradition fostered the idea that all knowledge should be used in the service of God and human salvation. As explained by Hugh of St. Victor and his followers, just as science was the "handmaiden" of theology, so could technology or "the mechanical arts" serve God's purpose for humans. Even if this attitude ultimately subordinated science and technology to faith, it also provided a powerful rationale for their practice.

Claudius Ptolemy (fl. Second Century C.E.)

Ptolemy was the most influential writer on astronomy before Copernicus in the sixteenth century. Although Ptolemy made no fundamental changes in the field of astronomy as it had developed in the ancient world, he systematized and developed current models into a comprehensive, mathematically sophisticated, and highly accurate method of predicting the movements of the planets, sun, and moon. Ptolemy's *Almagest* was the essential astronomical text until the publication of Copernicus' *De revolutionibus* (1543). Other astronomical works dealt with the physical structure of the universe. Ptolemy also wrote on geography, optics, and music.

Despite Ptolemy's enormous influence, we know almost nothing about his life. He performed observations at Alexandria, one of the great scientific centers of the ancient world, between 127 and 145. His name suggests that he was a Roman citizen, and his family were Greeks who were long-time residents of Alexandria.

The basic model of the universe inherited by Ptolemy posited a stationary earth at the center of the world. The heavenly bodies (sun, moon, Mercury, Venus, Mars, Jupiter, Saturn) moved in uniform, circular motions around the earth. The outermost sphere, that of the fixed stars, was concentric with the earth. (For the philosophical and scientific reasons for the plausibility of this system, see Chapters 3 and 4.) Ptolemy made this system much more mathematically precise by inventing new geometrical mechanisms which reconciled the observations of planetary movements with the principle of uniform, circular motion. These mechanisms were the eccentric, the epicycle, and the deferent (see Figure 2). He also significantly refined the model for the moon. His catalogue of 1,022 stars was derived from that of the earlier Hellenistic astronomer Hipparchus (fl. c. 150–127 B.C.E.).

The *Almagest* was known by the year 800 to Arabic astronomers, who further refined Ptolemy's system. It was translated from Arabic by Gerard of Cremona around 1175. The *Almagest* and digests based on it were the standard astronomical textbooks throughout the Middle Ages. Some significant challenges to the Ptolemaic system were made before Copernicus, chiefly John Buridan's and Nicole Oresme's arguments for the daily rotation of the earth and the lunar model of the Arabic astronomer Ibn al-Shatir (fl. 1350), but these had little influence in the West.

The *Almagest* was a work of mathematical analysis. Ptolemy addressed the question of the physical structure of the universe in a work called the *Planetary Hypotheses*, which posited that the planetary spheres, here assumed to be material, were contiguous. This work was unknown in Latin translation during the Middle Ages, although its main ideas seem to have influenced European astronomy indirectly through Arabic sources. Ptolemy also wrote an astrological work, the *Tetrabiblos*, or *Quadrapartitum* as it was known in Latin translation. This work described the visible and invisible properties of the planets and discussed how power emanating from the heavenly bodies affects the earth. One aspect of its astrological theory which would have a long life in European culture was the idea that peoples living in different parts and climates have different temperaments due to different planetary influences and that people move through seven stages of life as influenced by the five planets, sun, and moon.

Ptolemy wrote several other astronomical works, only parts of which survive. His *Geography* attempted to map the known world using latitudes and longitudes. His work in optics, which is extant only in its Arabic translation, was the most successful mathematical analysis of reflection and refraction to date. Ptolemy also wrote on musical theory and on mechanics. A widely read astrological work, the *Centiloquium*, was falsely attributed to him in the Middle Ages.

Trotula (Eleventh Century)

"Trotula" was the name given to the assumed female author of several important medical works on gynecology and the diseases of women written in the eleventh century and associated with the medical community of Salerno in southern Italy. In fact, "Trotula" was originally the overall title given to these anonymous works. *Conditions of Women* and *Women's Cosmetics* were probably written by men, but *Treatments of Women* was likely written by a practicing female physician, possibly named Trota. Other evidence indicates that it was not uncommon for women to practice medicine in eleventh- and twelfth-century Salerno.

The three texts later attributed to Trotula are *Treatise on the Diseases of Women* (revised as *Conditions of Women*), *Treatments of Women*, and *Women's Cosmetics*. The first of these shows the influence of Galenic and Arabic medicine. It emphasizes the importance of regular menstruation for women's health and discusses such peculiarly female complaints as "uterine suffocation" when the uterus moves up from its usual place in the body to the respiratory organs. Therapy included holding foul-smelling substances to the nose in order to drive the womb back to its normal position. The work also covers contraception, pregnancy, miscarriage, infertility on the part of both the man and the woman, and childbirth.

Treatments of Women is a more original work. It is interesting in its unusual view that sexual intercourse can cause medical problems for women in some cases and in its attention to how women can artificially restore the physical appearance of virginity. It also provides remedies for skin blemishes and a few remedies for male problems such as swelling of the penis or testicles. *Women's Cosmetics* provides recipes for care of the skin, hair, and teeth and recommends washing of the vagina.

The *Trotula*, in several different versions, was extremely popular in the Middle Ages and continued to be copied and translated (from Latin into English, Dutch, German, and French) into the fifteenth century. Overall, it was one of the most important gynecological texts of the medieval period.

PRIMARY DOCUMENTS

DOCUMENT 1
Aristotle On Final Causes in Nature; from the *Physics*

Fundamental to Aristotelian philosophy was the view that order and purpose pervaded the natural world. Natural processes and living organisms were not the chance results of random events but instead were carefully designed parts of a unified whole which always tended toward "the best." This view of nature fit well with the idea of a divine Creator and was almost universally accepted during antiquity and the Middle Ages. Today, Aristotle's view has largely been replaced by the mechanistic philosophies of Isaac Newton and Charles Darwin.

In this passage, Aristotle makes his argument that nature works toward ultimate goals, or what he calls "final causes." To put this another way, he argues that nature works according to a design or plan, in the same way that a craftsman makes an object with its final design and function in mind.

In the second paragraph Aristotle asks whether nature might work "by necessity," that is, by coincidence or contingency. For example, could humans have sharp front teeth and broad molars by chance and not because the sharpness of the front teeth is useful for tearing food and the broadness of the molars useful for grinding food? Aristotle answers in the third paragraph that this is not possible, because "all things by nature come to be either always or for the most part," that is, natural things occur with great regularity, which would not be possible if they were produced by chance or luck or for random reasons. Finally, he suggests *that nature, like an artist or craftsman, works in stages in which each part of the process moves toward completion of the whole and each part has a function which contributes to the overall functioning of the organism. Occasionally, mistakes occur, resulting in "monstrosities," but, on the whole, nature is like a "doctor who heals himself."*

We must discuss first (a) why nature is a cause for the sake of something; then (b) how necessity exists in physical things, for all thinkers make reference to this cause by saying, for example, that since the hot and the cold and each of such things are by nature of such-and-such a kind, certain other things must exist or come to be (for even if they mention some other cause—one of them mentions Friendship and Strife, another mentions Intelligence—they just touch upon it and let it go at that).

The following question arises: What prevents nature from acting, not for the sake of something or for what is better, but by necessity, as in the case of rain, which does not fall in order that wheat may grow. For, one may say, what goes up must be cooled, and the resulting cold water must come down, and when this takes place, the growth of corn just happens; similarly, if a man's wheat is spoiled on the threshing floor, rain did not fall for the sake of spoiling the wheat, but this just happened. So what should prevent the parts in nature, too, from coming to be of necessity in this manner, for example, the front teeth of necessity coming out sharp and so fit for tearing but the molars broad and useful for grinding food, not however for the sake of this but by coincidence? A similar question arises with the other parts in which final cause seems to exist . . .

. . . This is the argument, then, or any other such, that might cause a *difficulty*. Yet it is impossible for things to come to be in this manner; for the examples cited and all things by nature come to be either always or for the most part, but none of those by luck or *chance* do so likewise. It is not during the winter that frequent rain is thought to occur by luck or by coincidence, but during the summer, nor frequent heat during the summer, but during the winter. So if these be thought to occur either by coincidence or for the sake of something and if they cannot occur by coincidence or by chance, then they occur for the sake of something. Besides, those who use the preceding arguments, too, would admit that all such things exist by nature. There is, then, final cause in things which come to be or exist by nature.

Moreover, in that which has an end, a prior stage and the stages that follow are done for the sake of that end. Accordingly, these are done in the manner in which the nature of the thing disposes them to be done; and the nature of the thing disposes them to be done in the manner in which they are done at each stage, if nothing obstructs. But they are done for the sake of something; so they are by nature disposed to be done for the sake of something. For example, if a house were a thing generated by nature, it would have been generated in a way similar to that in which it is now generated by art. So if things by nature were to be generated not only by nature but also by art, they would have been generated just as they are by nature disposed to be generated. So one stage is for the sake of the next . . .

This is most evident in those of the other animals which make things neither by art nor by having inquired or deliberated about them; and from this latter fact arise discussions by some thinkers about the problem of whether spiders and ants and other such animals work by intellect or by some other power. If we go a little further in this direction, we observe that in plants, too, parts appear to be generated which contribute to an end, for example, leaves for the sake of protecting the fruit. So if it is both by nature and for the sake of something that the swallow makes its nest and the spider its web and that plants grow leaves for the sake of fruit and send their roots not up but down for the sake of food, it is evident that there exists such a cause in things which come to be or exist by nature. And since nature may be either matter or *form*, and it is the latter that may be an end while all the rest are for the sake of an end, it is *form* that would be a cause in the sense of a final cause.

Now error occurs even with respect to things produced according to art, for example, a grammarian did not write correctly and a doctor did not give the right medicine; so clearly this may occur also in things that come to be according to nature. If then there are (a) things produced according to art in which there is a right final cause and (b) also things done erroneously when the final cause has been aimed at but failed, a similar situation would exist also in natural things, and monstrosities in these would be failures of final causes . . .

. . . For what exists by nature is a thing which, having started from some principle in itself, finally arrives by a continuous motion at a certain end. . . . But if it takes place always or for the most part, it is not an accident nor does it come to be by luck; and in natural things it takes place always, if nothing obstructs.

It is absurd to think that nothing comes to be for the sake of something if the moving cause is not observed deliberating (and we may add, even art does not deliberate) and if the ship-building art were in the wood, it would have produced results similar to those produced by nature. So if there is a final cause in art, so also in nature. This is most clearly seen in a doctor who heals himself; nature is like that.

It is evident, then, that nature is a cause and that it is a cause also in this manner, namely, for the sake of something. (Excerpts from: Bk. B. 8 198b10–28; 198b33–199a16; 199a20–199b5;199b16–199b18; 199b25–199b33.)

Source: *Aristotle's* Physics, trans. Hippocrates G. Apostle (Bloomington: Indiana University Press, 1969), pp. 37–40.

DOCUMENT 2
Galen (129–199 or 200) On Female Physiology and Inferiority

> In Aristotelian natural philosophy, nature was hierarchical. That is, some organisms were considered higher and more developed than others. For example, humans were more valued than animals, because they possessed a rational soul and other animals did not. This hierarchical view also applied to the sexes. In these passages, Galen, the great Hellenistic physician, reinforces Aristotle's view that men are "more perfect" than women because men possess more innate heat. One result of women's greater coldness was that their sexual organs are internal, rather than external, as is the case for men. Note how Galen uses the Aristotelian idea that nature always works "for the best."
>
> Galen was the foremost authority for medical theory in the Middle Ages. This rationale for female inferiority was a central tenet of medicine and natural philosophy into the eighteenth century.

Now just as mankind is the most perfect of all animals, so within mankind the man is more perfect than the woman, and the reason for his perfection is the excess of heat, for heat is Nature's primary instrument. Hence in those animals that have less of it, her workmanship is necessarily more imperfect, and so it is no wonder that the female is less perfect than the male by as much as she is colder than he. In fact, just as the mole has imperfect eyes, though certainly not so imperfect as they are in those animals that do not have any trace of them at all, so too the woman is less perfect than the man in respect to the generative parts. For the parts were formed within her when she is still a fetus, but could not because of the defect in the heat emerge and project on the outside, and this, though making the animal itself that was being formed less perfect than one that is complete in all respects, provided no small advantage for the race; for there needs must be a female. Indeed, you ought not to think that our Creator would purposely make half the whole race imperfect and, as it were, mutilated, unless there was to be so great advantage in such a mutilation.

Let me tell what this is. The fetus needs abundant material both when it is first constituted and for the entire period of growth that follows. Hence it is obliged to do one of two things: it must either snatch nutriment away from the mother herself or take nutriment that is left over. Snatching it away would be to injure the generant, and taking left over nutriment would be impossible if the female were perfectly warm; for if she were, she would easily dispense and evaporate it. Accordingly, it was better for the female to be made enough colder so that she cannot dispense all the nutriment which she concocts and elaborates.

Reprinted with permission from Galen, *Galen on the Usefulness of the Parts of the Body*. Translated by Margaret Tallmadge May. Copyright © 1968 by Cornell University Press, pp. 630–31.

DOCUMENT 3
Trotula On the Diseases of Women (Eleventh Century)

Three important and widely read gynecological works were ascribed to "Trotula," an anonymous woman physician associated with the medical school of Salerno in southern Italy, during the Middle Ages. In fact, probably only one, Treatments of Women, *was written by a woman doctor, while the other two,* Conditions of Women *and* Women's Cosmetics, *were probably written by men.*

The following selections illustrate common medical learning on women's diseases in the Middle Ages. As generally in Galenic medicine, health depended on the proper balance of the four humors (blood, yellow bile, black bile, and phlegm) in the body. In women, because their innate coldness prevented them from otherwise purging their bodies of bad and superfluous humors, regular menstruation was regarded as essential to health. Much attention, therefore, was given to medical remedies for absent or insufficient menses. (Lack of sexual intercourse was also thought to promote ill-health in women.) The remedies suggested for these and other difficulties are largely composed of herbs and other plants and, sometimes, animal parts. Some are magical in nature, as when a woman who wishes to avoid getting pregnant is told to wear the testicles of a male weasel against her breasts.

Attention was also given to promoting conception and for the preservation of the health of the woman in pregnancy and childbirth. It is noteworthy, however, that recipes are also given for contraceptives; even if these were almost certainly not effective, the desire of women to avoid pregnancy is treated with respect and understanding. Although the Conditions of Women *begins with an extended discussion of how women's coldness makes them the weaker sex, it is recognized that sterility can result from defects in the man as well as the woman.* Treatments of Women *recognizes the pragmatic needs of some women, namely, nuns and widows, to reduce sexual desire and also provides five methods (not included here) for constricting the vagina or making it bleed upon intercourse so that a woman may appear to be a virgin when she is not.*

Here Begins "The Book on the Diseases of Women According to Trotula" [*Conditions of Women*]

[1] When God the creator of the universe in the first establishment of the world differentiated the individual natures of things each according to its kind, He endowed human nature above all other things with a singular dignity, giving to it above the condition of all other animals freedom of reason and intellect. And wishing to sustain its generation in perpetuity, He created the male and the female with provident, dispensing deliberation, laying out in the separate sexes the foundation for the propagation of future offspring. And so that from them there might emerge fertile offspring, he endowed their complexions with a certain

pleasing commixtion, constituting the nature of the male hot and dry. But lest the male overflow with either one of these qualities, He wished by the opposing frigidity and humidity of the woman to rein him in from too much excess, so that the stronger qualities, that is the heat and the dryness, should rule the man, who is the stronger and more worthy person, while the weaker ones, that is to say the coldness and humidity, should rule the weaker [person], that is the woman. And [God did this] so that by his stronger quality the male might pour out his duty in the woman just as seed is sown in its designated field, and so that the woman by her weaker quality, as if made subject to the function of the man, might receive the seed poured forth in the lap of Nature.

[2] Therefore, because women are by nature weaker than men and because they are most frequently afflicted in childbirth, diseases very often abound in them especially around the organs devoted to the work of Nature. Moreover, women, from the condition of their fragility, out of shame and embarrassment do not dare reveal their anguish over their diseases (which happen in such a private place) to a physician. Therefore, their misfortune, which ought to be pitied, and especially the influence of a certain woman stirring my heart, have impelled me to give a clear explanation regarding their diseases in caring for their health. And so with God's help, I have labored assiduously to gather in excerpts the more worthy parts of the books of Hippocrates and Galen, so that I might explain and discuss the causes of their diseases, their symptoms and their cures.

[3] Because there is not enough heat in women to dry up the bad and superfluous humors which are in them, nor is their weakness able to tolerate sufficient labor so that Nature might expel [the excess] to the outside through sweat as [it does] in men, Nature established a certain purgation especially for women, that is, the menses, to temper their poverty of heat. The common people call the menses "the flowers," because just as trees do not bring forth fruit without flowers, so women without their flowers are cheated of the ability to conceive. This purgation occurs in women just as nocturnal emission happens to men. For Nature, if burdened by certain humors, either in men or in women, always tries to expel or set aside its yoke and reduce its labor.

[4] This purgation occurs in women around the thirteenth year, or a little earlier or a little later, depending on the degree to which they have an excess or dearth of heat or cold. It lasts until the fiftieth year

if she is thin, sometimes until the sixtieth or sixty-fifth year if she is moist. In the moderately fat, it lasts until the thirty-fifth year. If this purgation occurs at the appropriate time and with suitable regularity, Nature frees itself sufficiently of the excess humors. If, however, the menses flow out either more or less than they ought to, many sicknesses thus arise, for then the appetite for food as well as for drink is diminished; sometimes there is vomiting, and sometimes they crave earth, coals, chalk, and similar things.

[5] Sometimes from the same cause pain is felt in the neck, the back, and in the head. Sometimes there is acute fever, pangs of the heart, dropsy, or dysentery. These things happen either because for a long time the menses have been deficient or because the women do not have any at all. Whence not only dropsy or dysentery or heart pangs occur, but other very grave diseases.

[6] Sometimes there is diarrhea on account of excessive coldness of the womb, or because its veins are too slender, as in emaciated women, because then thick and superfluous humors do not have a free passage by which they might break free. Or [sometimes menstrual retention happens] because the humors are thick and viscous and on account of their being coagulated, their exit is blocked. Or [it is] because women eat rich foods, or because from some sort of labor they sweat too much, just as Ruphus and Galen attest: for in a woman who does not exercise very much, it is necessary that she have plentiful menses in order to remain healthy.

[7] Sometimes women lack the menses because the blood in their bodies is congealed or coagulated. Sometimes the blood is emitted from other places, such as through the mouth or the nostrils or in spit or hemorrhoids. Sometimes the menses are deficient on account of excessive pain or wrath or agitation or fear. If, however, they have ceased for a long time, they make one suspect grave illness in the future. For sometimes women's urine turns red or into the color of water in which fresh meat has been washed. For the same reason, sometimes their face changes into a green or livid color or into a color like that of grass.

On the Paucity of the Menses

[19] If women have scant menses and emit them with pain, take some betony or some of its powder, some pennyroyal, sea wormwood, mug-

wort, of each one handful. Let them be cooked in water or wine until two parts have been consumed. Then strain through a cloth and let her drink it with the juice of fumitory.

[20] If, however, the menses have been deficient for a long time, take two drams of rhubarb, one dram each of dry mugwort and pepper, and let there be made a powder and let her drink it morning and evening for three days, and let her cover herself so that she sweats.

[21] Likewise, take one handful each of mint, pennyroyal, and rue; three drams of rock salt, one plant of red cabbage, and three heads of leek. Let all these be cooked together in a plain pot, and let her drink it in the bath.

[Here follow five similar herbal prescriptions for provoking menstruation.]

[27] Scarification also works well for the same condition, and coitus likewise. Phlebotomy from the hand, however, is harmful.

[28] If she has no fever, let her eat leeks, onions, pepper, garlic, cumin, and fishes with scales. Let her drink strong wine if she has no pain in the head nor any nervous disorder nor any fever, because wine is harmful in any fever.

[Procedures for Becoming Pregnant]

[76] If she wishes to conceive a male, let her husband take the womb and the vagina of a hare and let him dry them, and let him mix the powder with wine and drink it. Similarly, let the woman do the same thing with the testicles of a hare, and at the end of her period let her lie with her husband and then she will conceive a male.

[82] If a woman wishes to become pregnant, take the testicles of an uncastrated male pig or a wild boar and dry them and let a powder be made, and let her drink this with wine after the purgation of the menses. Then let her cohabit with her husband and she will conceive.

[On Women Who Ought Not Have Sexual Relations with Men]

[83] Galen says that women who have narrow vaginas and constricted wombs ought not have sexual relations with men lest they conceive and die. But all such women are not able to abstain, and so they need our assistance.

On Those Who Do Not Wish to Conceive

[84] If a woman does not wish to conceive, let her carry against her nude flesh the womb of a goat which has never had offspring.

[85] Or there is found a certain stone, [called] "gagates," which if it is held by the woman or even tasted prohibits conception.

[86] In another fashion, take a male weasel and let its testicles be removed and let it be released alive. Let the woman carry these testicles with her in her bosom and let her tie them in goose skin or in another skin, and she will not conceive.

[87] If she has been badly torn in birth and afterward for fear of death does not wish to conceive any more, let her put into the afterbirth as many grains of caper spurge or barley as the number of years she wishes to remain barren. And if she wishes to remain barren forever, let her put in a handful.

On Impediment of Conception

[129] Conception is impeded as much by the fault of the man as by the fault of the woman. The fault of the woman is double: either excessive warmth or humidity of the womb. For the womb at times, because of its unnatural slipperiness, is unable to retain the seed injected into it. And sometimes from its excessive humidity it suffocates the seed. And sometimes she is unable to conceive because of the excessive heat of the womb burning the semen. If, therefore, excessive heat and dryness is the cause, the signs will be these: their lips are ulcerated and excoriated as if from the north wind, they have red spots, unremitting thirst, and loss of hair. When, therefore, you see this, and if the woman is thirty years old and has suffered this for a long time, you will judge it to be untreatable. If she is young and the disease is not chronic, you should aid her in this way: take marsh mallow and mugwort, and cook them in water, and with such a decoction you should fumigate the patient three or four times. Between these fumigations you will make suppositories and also pessaries for the vagina with musk oil and some musk itself, so that the womb might be strengthened. But on the seventh day after her purgation or after the fumigation has been made, take *trifera magna* [a compound remedy made up of twenty-eight ingredients in-

cluding "juice of opium poppy"] in the size of an acorn and similarly wrap it in cotton, and from this you will make a suppository for the vagina, so that from the many fumigations the womb receives some strength, smoothness, and softness, and from the benefit of this suppository and these fumigations it will be dried out, and from this medicine she should receive some strength. On the following day, you will make her have sex with her husband, and if necessary you will use the same treatment the following week, making the above-mentioned fumigations and applying the other remedies, as noted. You should do this until the above-mentioned symptoms have subsided, and you should make her have intercourse twice or three times a week, because thus more quickly will she be able to become pregnant.

[130] If, on the other hand, she is not able to conceive because of excessive humidity of the womb, these will be the signs: she will have teary eyes constantly. For because the womb is tied to the brain by nerves, it is necessary that the brain suffer with the womb. Whence, if the womb has within itself excessive humidity, from this the brain is filled, which [humidity], flowing to the eyes, forces them involuntarily to emit tears. And because the brain suffers together with the womb, the sign of this is mental distress of the woman [when she suffers] from retention of the menses. Therefore, first of all let her be purged with *Theodoricon euporiston* [another compound remedy including, among other things, pepper, rhubarb, and St.-John's-wort.] Afterward we prescribe that you make three or five pills of the same *Theodoricon* or of *Paulinum*, and also that you wrap them in cotton lest they dissolve, and insert however many you can via the genitals. If the womb has not been well purged, on the second day you will make a pessary in the same manner of *trifera* with some musk. You should do this for a long time until you see that she has been evacuated of the superfluous humidity, and afterward take a little bit of musk with oil or another odoriferous substance which again you insert into the vagina. And if she has been well purged, she will sense the odor [of the musk] in her mouth, and if anyone should kiss, he will think that she is holding musk in her mouth. Likewise, if she becomes thirsty on account of this purgation, you should know that she has been well purged. And thus purged, let her have intercourse frequently so that she might conceive.

On Sterility on the Part of the Man

[131] If conception is impeded because of the fault of the man, either this comes about from a defect of the spirit impelling the seed, or from a defect of spermatic humidity, or from a defect of heat. If from a defect of heat, he will not desire intercourse. Whence it is necessary in such men to anoint the loins with *arrogon* [a compound remedy], or take rocket seed and spurge and reduce them into a fine powder, and you should mix these with musk oil and pennyroyal oil and anoint the loins. If it happens from defect of the spirits, he will have no desire and he will not be able to have an erection. We aid him with an unguent generative of many spirits. If it is because of a defect of the seed, when they have intercourse they emit little or no semen. We help men such as this with substances which augment and generate seed, such as onions, parsnip, and similar things.

On Treatments for Women

On the Preservation of Celibate Women and Widows

[141] There are some women to whom carnal intercourse is not permitted, sometimes because they are bound by a vow, sometimes because they are bound by religion, sometimes because they are widows, because to some women it is not permitted to take fruitful vows. These women, when they have desire to copulate and do not do so, incur grave illness. For such women, therefore, let there be made this remedy. Take some cotton and musk or pennyroyal oil and anoint it and put it in the vagina. This both dissipates the desire and dulls the pain. Note that a pessary ought not be made lest the womb be damaged, for the mouth of the womb is joined to the vagina, like the lips to the mouth, unless, of course, conception occurs, for then the womb withdraws.

Source: *The* Trotula: *A Medieval Compendium of Women's Medicine*, ed. and trans. Monica H. Green (Philadelphia: University of Pennsylvania Press, 2001), pp. 71, 73, 79, 95, 113, 115, 121.

DOCUMENT 4
Adelard of Bath (c. 1080–1142) On the Important Scientific Questions in the Twelfth Century; from His *Questions on Natural Science*

> *Adelard of Bath is representative of the questioning and curious spirit of the Renaissance of the Twelfth Century. In this work, he uses the device of a dialogue with his "nephew" to explore the Aristotelian and Arabic scientific learning newly available in Europe in the early twelfth century. Adelard himself translated several mathematical works from Arabic, including the Arabic translation of Euclid's* Elements.
>
> *In the introduction, Adelard provides a (probably fictionalized) setting of his dialogue, in which he explains how, having recently returned from traveling abroad in order to study, he is asked by his nephew to "put forward some new item of the studies of the Arabs." Adelard aptly conveys the complex reaction of some Europeans to the new learning, a mixture of intense curiosity, fear, and resentment. Adelard himself vigorously upholds the importance of a disinterested and independent use of reason, later in the work complaining, "For what else can authority be called other than a halter? As brute animals are led wherever one pleases by a halter, but do not know where or why they are led, and only follow the rope by which they are held, so the authority of written words leads not a few of you into danger, since you are enthralled and bound by brutish credulity" (p. 103).*
>
> *After the introduction, Adelard lists the topics he will discuss in the course of the book. It provides a summary of current scientific questions.*

When I recently returned to England during the reign over the English of Henry, son of William, since I had absented myself from my native land for a long time for the sake of study, meeting friends was both delightful and helpful for me. So when on our first meeting, as happens, the questions came thick and fast concerning our health and the health of friends, the fact impressed itself on my mind that I should get to know the character of our own people. Pursuing this plan, when I found the princes barbarous, the bishops bibulous, judges bribable, patrons unreliable, clients sycophants, promisers liars, friends envious, and almost everybody full of ambition, I said that nothing was further from my course than paying attention to this wretched situation. Then they said: "So what do you think should be done, when you neither wish to join, nor are able to ward off, this moral depravity?" At this point I said: "One should forget it. The only medicine of ills that cannot be rebuffed is forgetfulness. For whoever ponders what he hates, in some way suffers what he does not love." When these words had been exchanged, since a considerable part of the day remained, so that there was time for saying something, among the others who were paying their calls was a certain nephew of mine, who, in investigating the causes of things, was tying them in knots rather than unravelling them. He urged me to put forward some new item of the studies of the Arabs. As the others agreed with him, I undertook the following treatise, which I know will be useful to its auditors, but whether it is pleasant, I do not know. For the present generation suffers from this ingrained fault, that it thinks that nothing should be accepted which is discovered by the "moderns." Hence it happens that, whenever I wish to publish my own discovery, I attribute it to another person saying: "Someone else said it, not I!" Thus, lest I have no audience at all, some teacher came up with all my opinions, not I. So much for that! But now, since it is right for me to say something at the request of friends, I should like to be more confident, following your scrutiny, as to whether it is said correctly. For nothing is so well dealt with in the liberal arts that it cannot bloom more splendidly through your action. So, please lend me your attention. For I shall be succinct and start by giving the chapter-headings. Then I shall reply to my nephew's questions concerning the causes of things.

The prologue ends. The chapter headings begin.

1. The reason why plants grow without a seed being sown beforehand.
2. In what way some plants are to be called hot, when they are all more earthy than fiery.
3. How plants of contrary natures grow in the same spot.
4. Why, as they grow from earth, they do not grow in the same way from water, air or even fire.
5. Whether, as earthy natures grow in earth, and watery natures in water, so also, in air and fire, airy and fiery natures grow.
6. Why the fruit follows the graft, not the trunk.
7. Why some brute animals chew the cud, but others not.

8. Why all those that chew the cud lie down with their hindquarters first, and their forequarters afterwards.
9. Why the same animals do not stand up first from their forequarters.
10. Why not all those which drink urinate.
11. Why some animals have a stomach, others not.
12. Why some of them see more clearly by night.
13. Whether brute animals have souls.
14. Whether opinion is founded in an animate body.
15. Why men do not have innate horns or other armour.
16. By what observation the web of nerves and blood-vessels is detected.
17. Why men who have a fine intelligence are lacking in memory, and vice versa.
18. By what reasoning the seats of imagination, reason and memory in the brain were discovered.
19. Why the nose is placed above the mouth.
20. Why men go bald from the front part of their head. [Why men go grey in old age.]
21. By what nature voices are carried through the air and heard by us.
22. By what nature a voice, when it comes to the ears, can penetrate any obstacle.
23. What opinion should be held about sight.
24. Whether the visual spirit is a substance or an accident.
25. How that spirit goes to a star and returns in such a brief space of time.
26. How, when the eye is closed, the visual spirit is not left outside.
27. How the same spirit does not get in the way of itself if it returns at the same time as it goes out.
28. By what means the soul receives forms from that spirit.
29. Why that spirit is not reflected from the most transparent glass in the same way that it is reflected from a mirror, to shape again the face.
30. Why, when one can see from the dark into the light, one cannot similarly see from light into dark.
31. By what nature we smell, taste and touch.
32. By what nature joy is the cause of weeping.
33. By what nature we breathe out from the same mouth now hot air, now cold.
34. Why fanning generates coldness, if movement generates heat.
35. Why the fingers are created uneven.
36. Why the palm is hollow.
37. Why men do not walk as soon as they are born, when brute animals do this.

38. Why men have such soft limbs. Why they walk upright.
39. Why human beings are nourished rather by milk.
40. Why milk is not appropriate to the same human beings when they are youths or old.
41. Why, if you have intercourse with a woman after she has coupled with a man suffering from leprosy, you are affected with the disease, not the woman.
42. Why, if women are colder then men, they are more lustful.
43. Why all men die.
44. Why, when the human body has once been established in a balanced and appropriate way, it is deprived of this balance.
45. What the reason is for restoring the body with food, and why it is done so frequently.
46. Why we fear the bodies of the dead, when we are alive.
47. Why a live body, if it falls into a river, sinks to the bottom, while the same body, after a few days, now dead, "swims."
48. Why, or by what nature, the globe of the earth is held up in the middle of the air.
49. Where, if the globe of the earth were bored through, a rock thrown into the hole would end up.
50. From what cause an earthquake occurs.
51. Why sea water is salty.
52. Why the flows and ebbs of the tide occur.
53. How the Ocean is not increased by the flowing in of rivers.
54. Why some rivers are not salty.
55. How the flow of rivers can be perpetual.
56. From what cause waters arise on the tops of mountains.
57. Whether there are any true springs.
58. Why water does not flow out from a full vessel which is open at the bottom, unless a higher opening is uncovered.
59. Where winds arise from.
60. From where the first movement of the air proceeds, or whether, if everything that is moved is moved by another, there is no first movement.
61. Whether, when one atom is moved, all atoms move, since whatever is moved moves another, and thus movement, once it has begun, is infinite.
62. Why wind moves around the earth and not to the higher realms.
63. Why and from where it has such force.
64. Where thunder comes from.
65. Where lightning comes from.
66. Why lightning is not struck from every clap of thunder.

67. By what force lightning penetrates stone and bronze structures.
68. Why it is that when we see the flashes, we do not hear such crashes at the same time, and sometimes not at all.
69. Why the Moon is deprived of light.
70. Why perpetual shadow enshrouds it.
71. From what cause the planets—and the Sun above all—do not keep to a course through the middle of the aplanos [outermost sphere of the heavens] without winding about.
72. By what necessity or reason the planets run in the opposite direction to the aplanos.
73. Whether the stars fall when they seem to fall.
74. Whether the stars are animate.
75. What food the stars eat, if they are animate.
76. Whether one should say that the aplanos is an inanimate body, or an animate one, or a god.

Source: *Adelard of Bath, Conversations with His Nephew*: On the Same and the Different, Questions on Natural Science, *and* On Birds, ed. and trans. Charles Burnett, with the collaboration of Italo Ronca, Pedro Mantuas España, and Baudouin van den Abeele, Cambridge Medieval Classics, 9 (Cambridge, England: Cambridge University Press, 1998), pp. 83, 85, 87, 89. Reprinted with the permission of Cambridge University Press.

DOCUMENT 5
Albertus Magnus (c. 1193–1280) On Animals: The Rabbit and Spiders

Albertus Magnus, like Aristotle, by whom he was profoundly influenced, was a careful and thorough observer of animals and their behavior. His massive work on biology, On Animals, *from which these selections are drawn, represents the highest level of zoological science in the Middle Ages.*

Albertus' On Animals *was meant to be a compendium of current knowledge about animals. As such, it combines material drawn from Aristotle and Arabic writers, Albertus' own observations, information told to him by farmers, hunters, and others, medical information, and folklore. The selections below illustrate these characteristics. Several things stand out. First, Albertus is careful to identify his sources. When reporting on how spiders carry their eggs, he remarks, "I have personally seen all these ways"; on the other hand, stories such as how the weasel*

toys with a captured rabbit are prefaced with the caveat "they say."
Medical information on the uses of hare rennet is attributed to Avicenna.
Secondly, Albertus' descriptions are, for the most part, straightforward,
accurate and detailed. In the case of his account of spiders, there is no
trace of fable or fantasy. On the other hand, his description of the hare
combines close observation (for example, of the relationship between the
color of the hare's coat and climate) with material drawn from legends
and hearsay.

[60] LEPUS: The hare is a well-known animal, thriving in its speed-iness. It has rear legs that are longer than its front ones and it therefore climbs a mountain faster than it descends it. It has hairy feet and is a timid animal even though it has a large heart. But it has cold blood and a cold heart. This is why it goes out to feed only at night. It never grows very fat, and when it is fed in an enclosure and does not move around, sometimes its right kidney is covered with fat, whereupon it dies. Among animals having teeth in both jaws it alone has rennet, and this is better the older the little hare becomes. In very cold lands the hares are white, as they are in the Alps, but in other lands some of them grow white in the winter but revert to their natural color in the summer. They can hardly ever be ousted from places where they have customarily lived and this is due to their multiple impregnation. They say that there are no hares in Cytacha, just as no deer, boars, goats, or bears live in Africa.

It is a simple animal, with its only defense found in flight and in sleeping with its eyes open. They say that the weasel plays in a cunning manner with this animal and that when the weasel has tired of the game, it seizes the hare by the throat and, holding on tightly, holds it in place. The hare runs but cannot free itself, and the weasel finally kills the tired animal and eats it.

Hare flesh generates thick blood and causes black bile to multiply. However, it does dry and thin and it therefore is good against pain in the viscera and it stops diarrhea. If an enema is made of its flesh fried with oil, it stops diarrhea and ulcers of the intestines. If its flesh is eaten roasted in an oven or on a pan, it acts the same way. If very bad, shadowy black spots are anointed with its blood, they are removed. If the head of a hare, burned and ground with vinegar, is anointed on one with hair loss, the condition is cured. If the head is roasted and the brain eaten, it is good against trembling that is caused by illnesses. If hare liver is dried and if an epileptic takes an ounce of it, it helps. Hare droppings, liquefied with vinegar and smeared on coarse ulcerations or on impetigo from which yellow water is coming, cures them. If hare droppings are placed on a woman who has never given birth, she will never do so as long as she has it on her. And if a little bit of this is placed in the vulva, it dries out the menses and it dries the womb excessively. If a person has a toothache and places one of a hare's teeth in the area that hurts, it takes away the pain. The ashes of a hare burned whole are good against kidney stones. If, after her period, a woman drinks hare rennet for three straight days, some people say that it prevents conception and it sometimes helps in this regard, according to Avicenna. If, however, she puts this in her vulva after her period, it is always of help in conception. Hare bile, mixed with clear honey, is good against "white of the eye." Hare lung, placed on the eyes, helps them, but ground and used as an ointment, it heals feet.

We call every vermin a spider which is round, has long legs that number eight, and is given to hunt animals. The difference based on hunting is based on the fact that some hunt flies, some hunt creeping things [*reptilia*] like small lizards and caterpillars, some hunt fish, and some hunt insects by leaping at them.

They are differentiated by work since some spiders weave a web and others do not. One that weaves attends to five points in its weaving. The first is the material to weave with. This arises from a superfluity of the food-moisture [*humidum cibale*], and a spider therefore wastes away when it empties itself too greatly. Second, it pays attention to time, for all day long it reweaves a web broken in the morning; at dawn, however, it turns its attention to the movement of the animal it hunts.

Third is the placement of the web. Some hang the web in the air where the animals they hunt have their pathways. Some hang it in the angle between two walls so that animals coming from either direction fall into the netlike web. This happens because small animals readily follow the surface of a wall to its corner. Fourth, it pays attention to the shape of the web and does so in two ways: namely, in the shape of the web as a whole and in producing lines with the threads between which it weaves the web. For some make a totally round web and suspend themselves in the middle of it, whereas others make a triangular one. These make a weblike opening in one part of it in which they stay, waiting. Again, another type makes a reticulated web, stretching from thread to thread, as do almost all the larger spiders that make round nets. Some, however, weave a web like fine cloth with the workmanship of a weaver. Examples include those which stretch their nets in the angles of walls. Fifth is the manner of its work. Large ones attach the thread that is produced from the anus to their rear foot. Others, however, send the thread out from their mouth and weave with the front foot. These are the ones that make the dense web with the workmanship of a weaver.

Spiders are differentiated by size and by the shape of that size. Now, they are all made up of three parts, namely, a head, a chest, and the rearmost parts, which are the largest and which lie behind the point of intersection (that is, the waist [*succinctorium*]). But some are large and sort of round, others are oblong like a compressed column, and some are small and thin.

They differ in color as well since some are ash grey and some are totally green. Other are variously colored throughout their entire body, flecked with bright white and bright blue, both on its legs and on its body. They also have several very white lines on their back, behind the waist.

There are three types of those that do not work in our lands. One has long legs, is round, and runs in the grass. It sucks the moisture out of fruit and dead animals if it finds them. Others sit in holes in the ground, leap onto small animals that pass by, and suck them. These are black. Others run about on the water with uplifted legs and prey on mosquitos [*cinifes*] and tiny little fish and suck on them once they are caught.

Every spider, however, lays eggs and wraps its eggs in a web. Spiders sometimes carry the eggs with them at all times in a little pouch, as does the spider we said lies in wait in a hole in the ground. When it carries its eggs it looks as if it were made up of two globes, one white and one black, for the eggs are very white. Other spiders, however, sometimes keep the eggs in their mouth, sometimes under their chest, and sometimes separate from them. I have personally seen all these ways.

The spider copulates at the end of spring. When it wants to copulate it drags in the male on a thread. The male is much smaller than the female, makes no web, and lives off the female's hunting. The spider lays its eggs in the fall and the small spiders come forth at the beginning of spring. They are so small that a large number of them hang down on one thread when the nest is moved.

Let these things, then, along with what was said previously, suffice concerning spiders.

Source: Albertus Magnus, *On Animals: A Medieval* Summa Zoologica, trans. and annotated by Kenneth F. Kitchell Jr. and Irven Michael Resnick, vol. 2 (Baltimore: Johns Hopkins University Press, 1999), pp. 1515–16, 1743–44. Reprinted with permission of The Johns Hopkins University Press.

DOCUMENT 6
Guy de Chauliac (c. 1290–c. 1367–70), Medieval Surgeon, On What Makes a Good Doctor

> *Born in France into a peasant family, Guy de Chauliac was one of the most influential and well-known surgeons and physicians of the Middle Ages. Unlike many surgeons in the Middle Ages, he was well educated in theoretical medicine, anatomy, and the liberal arts, as well as trained in the techniques of performing operations. His major work, the* Chirurgia, *from which this excerpt is taken, includes a history of medicine and basic information on anatomy, wounds and fractures, some diseases, diet, surgical instruments, and operations. Guy de Chauliac's account of the Plague, from which he himself suffered and recovered, is one of the best descriptions of the Black Death from the Middle Ages.*
>
> *In this excerpt, Guy lays out what is required of a good physician in terms of knowledge, skill, character, and bedside manner. The patient, also, is admonished to be obedient and faithful and to have patience. The* Chirurgia *was the standard work on surgery from the fourteenth into the seventeenth century.*

Let us return to our theme, and put down the conditions which are requisite to every surgeon, who wishes by art to exercise on the human body the aforesaid manner and form of operating, which conditions Hippocrates, who guides us well in everything, concludes with a certain subtle implication, in the first of the *Aphorisms*: life is short, and art prolix, time and chance sharp or sudden, experience fallacious and dangerous, judgment difficult. But not only the doctor must busy himself in doing his duty but also the sick person and the attendants, and he must also put in order external things.

There are then four conditions which are valued here, according to Arnald, a very eloquent Latinist. Some are required of the surgeon, others of the sick, others of those present, others in those things which come in from outside.

The conditions required of a surgeon are four: the first is that he be educated; the second, that he be well behaved. It is then required in the first place that the surgeon be educated, not only in the principles of surgery, but also of medicine, both in theory and practice.

In theory he must know things natural, non-natural and unnatural. And first, he must understand natural things, principally anatomy, for without it nothing can be done in surgery, as will appear below. He must also understand temperament, for according to the diversity of the nature of bodies it is necessary to diversify the medicament (Galen against Thessales, in all the *Therapeutics*). This is shown by the virtue and strength of the patient. He must also know the things which are not natural, such as air, meat, drink, etc., for these are the causes of all sickness and health. He must also know the things which are contrary to nature, that is sickness, for from this rightly comes the curative purpose. Let him not be ignorant in any way of the cause; for if he cures without the knowledge of that, the cure will not be by his abilities but by chance. Let him not forget or scorn accidents; for sometimes they override their cause, and deceive or divert and pervert the whole cure, as is said in the first to Gisuconius.

In practice, he must know how to put in order the way of living and the medicaments; for without this surgery, which is the third instrument of medicine, is not perfect. Of which Galen speaks in the *Introduction*: as pharmacy has need of regimen and of surgery, so surgery has need of regimen and pharmacy.

Thus it appears that the surgeon working in his art should know the principles of medicine. And with this, it is very fitting that he know something of the other arts. That is what Galen says in the first of his *Therapeutics* against Thessales, that if the doctors have nothing to do with geometry, or astronomy, or dialectics, or any other good discipline, soon the leather workers, carpenters, smiths, and others, leaving their own occupations, will run to medicine and make themselves into doctors.

In the second place, I have said he must be skilled and have seen others operate; I add the maxim of the sage Avenzoar [twelfth century], that every doctor must have knowledge first of all, and after that he must have practice and experience. To the same testify Rhazes, in the fourth *Book for Almansor*, and Haly Abbas on the testimony of Hippocrates, in the first of his *Theory*.

Thirdly, he must be ingenious, and of good judgment and good memory. That is what Haly Rodan [eleventh century] says in the third of his *Techni*; the doctor must have good memory, good judgment, good motives, good presence, and sound understanding, and that he be well formed, for example, that he have slender fingers, hands steady and not trembling, clear eyes, etc.

Fourth, I have said, he should be well mannered. Let him be bold in safe things, fearful in dangers, let him flee false cures or practices. Let him be gracious to the sick, benevolent to his companions, wise in his predictions. Let him be chaste, sober, compassionate, and merciful; not covetous, or extortionate, so that he may reasonably receive a salary in proportion to his work, the ability of his patient to pay, the nature of the outcome, and his own dignity.

The conditions required of the sick man are three: that he be obedient to the doctor, as the servant is to the master, in the first of the *Therapeutics*; that he have faith in the doctor, in the first of the *Prognostics*; that he be patient, for patience conquers malice, as it is said in other writing.

The conditions for the attendants are four, that they be peaceable, polite or agreeable, faithful, and discreet.

The conditions for things coming from outside are many, all of which ought to be arranged for the advantage of the sick, as Galen says, at the end of the commentary of the *Aphorisms* mentioned above.

Source: "The History of Surgery" by Guy de Chauliac, trans. James Bruce Ross, from *The Portable Medieval Reader* by James Bruce Ross and Mary Martin McLaughlin, copyright © 1949 by Viking Penguin, Inc. Copyright renewed © 1976 by James Bruce Ross and Mary Martin McLaughlin. Used by permission of Viking Penguin, a division of Penguin Group (USA) Inc. Originally translated from *La grand chirurgie de Guy de Chauliac*, E. Nicaise, ed. (Paris: F. Alcan, 1890).

DOCUMENT 7
A Medieval Herbal (Thirteenth Century)

Herbs were an essential part of medieval medicine and herbals were less works of scientific botany than practical handbooks on the medicinal effects of specific plants. In this herbal, the author, Rufinus (fl. 1287–1300), gives his own information, along with citations from the major authorities available to him. The main interest is how to use the plant in question for medical problems, along with a description that would presumably enable a reader to identify and gather the herb. (It is often difficult for the modern scholar to identify the plants involved due to the lack of illustrations, the sometimes vague descriptions, and confusion over names.)

Plants are labeled in terms of their humoral qualities; centaury, for example, is hot and dry "in the second degree," meaning the second "degree" of intensity in its effects. Although some later physicians tried to be more precise in assigning appropriate dosages, there is little attention to this issue in most herbals. Plants that produced obvious and immediate physiological changes, especially vomiting, sneezing, sweating, and elimination, were seen as particularly efficacious because of the belief that purging the body of bad humors was essential to health. Plants that smelled strongly were also favored.

The authorities cited by Rufinus include Dioscorides (fl. 50–70), the author of De materia medica, *the foremost herbal known from antiquity; the otherwise unknown "Copho"; and Alexander. He also cites "Circa instans," a twelfth-century work,* On Simple Medicines, *known by its opening words and associated with the medical school at Salerno, and the anonymous* Masters of Salerno, *also from the twelfth century. The detailed and informative notes made by Edward Grant, the translator, have been included.*

(ACRIMONIA OR AGRIMONIA)[31] AGRIMONY

Dioscorides. It is also called *sarutium.* It is an herb known in many places whose powers counteract poisons. Its root is called *eupatorium* by the Greeks and it is very diuretic. Moreover, agrimony that has been dried, pounded, sifted, and placed near the nostrils (*naribus*) causes one to sneeze a great deal. Again, when you see it pounded, it causes you to sneeze. Again Dioscorides:[32] *sarutium* is called *acrimonia.* By its roughness it provokes urine and menstruation and causes one to sneeze a great deal after it has been pounded and sifted and placed near the kidneys.[33]

Rufinus: Agrimony has hairy leaves that are cut between [or into] quite a bit (*multum intercisa*) and in July it produces pointed yellow flowers.[34] After softening in lye (*in lixivio macerta*) for several days, it produces golden hairs (*capillos aureos*); or boil it in oil until its substance [or matter] is consumed [and then] clean and oil the hairs.

(CENTAUREA) CENTAURY OR FEVERWORT[35]

Dioscorides: It is similar to *origanum*,[36] one greater, another smaller. It has relaxing powers with some roughness, and it purges the bowels and brings forth black bile and causes menstruation and expels the embryo [that is, causes abortion] (*partum expellit*) and makes for difficult breathing and coughing.

Circa instans: Centaury is hot and dry in the third degree; moreover, it is a very bitter herb, so that it is called "gall of the earth" (*fel terre*). Now, there is a "greater centaury" (*centaurea maior*), which is of a greater efficacy, and a "smaller centaury" of lesser efficacy. Constantine says that the root of the "greater" is hot and dry in the second degree and has a bitterness with some sweetness. It also has astringency (*ponticitatem*) and therefore has the power of joining by virtue of its astringency, and from bitterness it has a diuretic power. The greater centaury has efficacy in its leaves and in its flowers; therefore, when it begins to produce flowers, they ought to be gathered and suspended and dried in a dark place. Through a year it is preserved with its power largely intact. It has a diuretic, attractive, and consumptive power. Note that when centaury is mentioned simply [that is, by itself], the greater should be understood. . . . [37]

Alexander: Centaury is hot and dry. It has the power to dissolve and consume excess humors; it is diuretic. The centaury herb is bitter, in the manner of gall, and is called by another name, "gall of the earth" (*fel terre*). Moreover, there is a greater and a smaller. When "centaury" is found alone in a recipe, the greater should be assumed, namely the one which produces flowers in the manner of hypericum. After removal of the stems, the leaves and flowers should be used in medicine. When this herb produces flowers, it ought to be gathered and dried in a dark place. It retains much of its power throughout the year.

Master of Salerno (*Magister Salernus*): Greater centaury. The smaller is hot in the third degree. It is not called "smaller" or "greater" because of the smallness or greatness of its effect but [rather because of the size] of its leaves. The smaller purges yellow bile (*coleram*); the greater, black bile (*melancholiam*). The smaller can be given for centonic against stomach worms.

Synonyms: Greater centaury joins the leaves near the branch; smaller centaury, *Febrifuga*, or "gall of the earth" (*fel terre*) are the same, and we use the whole herb.

Copho:[38] Centaury is twofold: greater and smaller. Some say that it is hot and dry in the second degree. Galen says that the root of the greater centaury has diverse qualities according to taste and therefore has diverse actions. Indeed, it has a sharp and astringent (*ponticitatem*) taste with a considerable sweetness. And so it is that with its sharpness it provokes menstruation and expels the dead fetus; with its astringency it closes a wound and restricts the flow of blood. . . .

Rufinus: Greater centaury (*centaurea maior*) has a round stem, very bright and green, and leaves like *matersilve*, although small. And the stem passes through the middle of the leaf, and the distance between leaf and leaf is four fingers, and at the top of the stem it has many yellow flowers. The height of the stem is approximately a cubit, and its taste is very bitter, but in its flower there are eight very yellow leaves.

There is also a "middle centaury" (*centaurea media*) which is not mentioned by the philosophers cited above but about which all the herbalists (*herbolarii*) in Bologna and Naples were in agreement. Perhaps the above-mentioned philosophers associated the "middle" with the "smaller" [centaury] as a single type, since these two have a certain similarity in their leaves and flowers. Nevertheless, this "middle centaury" produces many stems on one root and has leaves similar to *maiorane*. Its leaves are separated by three fingers and are sharp and narrow; from two leaves two small branches come forth, and it produces many small purple flowers at the top.

The "smaller centaury" springs forth at the end of May and produces only one stem on one root. Its leaves are similar to middle centaury, and its flower is similar in form to middle centaury; but the smaller centaury has a white and purple flower, for the greater part just like middle centaury; and it is very small and acrid.[39]

(MANDRAGORA) MANDRAKE[40]

Dioscorides: This is an herb whose bark (*cortex*) when mixed with wine is drunk so that those may sleep and feel no pain whose bodies are about to be cut [surgically] for the purpose of effecting a cure. There are two species of it; a female [species] with leaves like lettuce (*lactuce*) and cheeks in the likeness of prunes; and a male species with leaves like those of a beet. The mandrake is an herb which some call *appolinaris* [that is, henbane].[41] It has cooling powers and can make one very faint, so that it is believed to be soporific. For it suppresses pain and sleeplessness in men.

Circa instans: The mandrake is of a cold and dry complexion. Its excess is not determined by authors [of this subject]. There are two species of it, male and female. The leaves of the female species are rough [or uneven], and some say that it is more suitable for use as a medicine; [however,] we use them indifferently. Some say that the female has been shaped in the form of a woman and the male in the form of a man, which is false. For nature never assigns the human form to an herb.[42] We have heard from farmers, however, that some [of these herbs] assume such forms.

As for use in medicine, the bark of the root is most suitable, secondly the fruit, and thirdly the leaves. The barks of the root that are gathered are preserved and are very efficacious over [a period of] four years. They have a power to constrict and cool, and a harmless power of causing a small bit of death, that is, causing sleep. For inducing sleep in fevers a powder of its bark is prepared with the milk of a woman and the white of an egg and is placed on the brow and temples. Against a headache from heat its ground leaves are placed on the temples (*tympora*). They [the temples] could also be smeared with mandrake-ish (*mandragoraceo*) oil, which is made in this way: After grinding the fruits of the mandrake, let them be softened for some time in common oil; afterward boil it a little and strain [or filter] it. This oil is called *Mandragoraceum* (mandrake-like or mandrake-ish) and would be powerful for producing sleep and for [reducing] a headache from heat if the brow and temples were smeared with oil. Indeed, if the pulse were smeared [with this oil], it would check [and repress] a hot fever. For use against a hot abscess one could spread this oil at the beginning, since it repels matter. . . . [43]

Alexander.[44] Mandrake is cold and dry in the fourth degree. It has a gross substance and can easily be resolved into a great deal of thick smoke. It has a constrictive and enotic (*emoticam*) power, that is, it induces sleep. Its root is medicinal. It should be gathered in summer and dried; it ought to be chosen for heaviness and should be continuous and unperforated. The leaves and fruits of it should be used in unguents, and the root in other medicines. Its powder sucked up with [that is, absorbed by] an egg could cure dysentery from above, and applied in a clyster with barley water, it could cure dysentery from below. Furthermore, a poultice made from its root with the proper juice [or sap], and applied to feverish temples, induces sleep quickly.

NOTES

31. Perhaps *Agrimonia Eupatoria*, or common agrimony, which "has an old reputation as a popular domestic medicinal herb, being a simple well known to all country-folk. It belongs to the Rose order of plants...." (M. Grieve, *A Modern Herbal* [New York: Hafner, 1959] I, 12). "The name Agrimony is from *Argemone*, a word given by the Greeks to plants which were healing to the eyes, the name *Eupatoria* refers to Mithridates Eupator, a king who was a renowned concoctor of herbal remedies" (I, 13).

Although in addition to his own description Rufinus here gives only a quotation he ascribes to Dioscorides, I have not located this herb in Goodyer's translation of the *De materia medica* [*The Greek Herbal of Dioscorides* ... Englished by John Goodyer A.D. 1655; edited and first printed A.D. 1933 by Robert T. Gunther (reprinted, New York: Hafner, 1959)]. However, in Book IV, chapter 41, of the latter treatise (pp. 434–435) we find *Eupatorium cannabinum* (common hemp agrimony), one of a number of plants which although "not actually related botanically to the Common Agrimony ... were given the same name by the older herbalists because of their similar properties" (p. 14). The description of Dioscorides' *Eupatorium cannabinum* bears no actual similarity to the agrimony described by Rufinus' Dioscorides. It should be noted that Pliny (*Natural History*, Bk. XXV, ch. 6, 29) speaks of *eupatoria*, which is also called *agrimonia*.

32. Thorndike [*The Herbal of Rufinus edited from the Unique Manuscript* by Lynn Thorndike, assisted by Francis J. Benjamin, Jr. (Chicago: University of Chicago Press, 1946] comments (p. 8, n. "d") that "this second excerpt from Dioscorides does little but repeat the first. It would seem either that two versions of Dioscorides are being cited or that two chapters from one version of *Acrimonia* and *Sarutium*, respectively, are here combined."

33. The effects described here are consequences of a histamine-like reaction. So powerful is agrimony that, if brought into contact with the mucous membranes, it could produce anaphylactic shock, and perhaps death. Hence the instruction to place it "near the nostrils." The urination and menstruation caused by placing agrimony on the skin near a kidney could also be produced by placing it on any other part of the body. In specifying the kidney, the author is probably reflecting a traditional medical belief that proximity of the medicinal agent to the bodily part or organ affected is partially responsible for producing the observed effect.

34. Grieve observes (I, 12) that "its slender spikes of yellow flowers, which are in bloom from June to early September, and the singularly beautiful form of its much-cut-into leaves, make it one of the most graceful of our smaller herbs."

35. Other names by which it was known are cited in note 22. For a full description, see Grieve, I, 182–184.

36. Wild marjoram (*origanum vulgare*), a perennial herb used by the Greeks for fomentations.

37. Rufinus' citation from *Macer Floridus* is omitted.

38. Probably not the Copho to whom has been ascribed the *Anatomy of the Pig (Anatomia porci)*, written sometime during the first half of the twelfth century. . . . Thorndike, who does not identify Copho, says (p. xxx) that the quotations for which Rufinus cites Copho "almost always correspond closely to passages in the *Liber graduum [Book of Degrees-Ed.]*, which is found among the works ascribed to Constantinus Africanus in the 1536 edition of his *Opera*.

39. Perhaps this is red centaury (*Erythraea centaurium*), which is described by Grieve (I, 182) as "an annual with a yellowish, fibrous, woody root, the stem stiff, square and erect, 3 to 12 inches in height, often branching considerably at the summit. The leaves are of a pale green colour, smooth and shiny, their margins undivided. The lowest leaves are broader than the others, oblong or wedge-shaped, narrowed at the base, blunt at the end and form a spreading tuft at the base of the plant, while the stalkless stem-leaves are pointed and lance-shaped, growing in pairs opposite to one another at somewhat distant intervals on the stalk, which is crowned by flat tufts (*corymbs*) of rose-coloured, star like flowers, with five-cleft corollas. . . . A variety is sometimes found with white corollas."

40. *Atropa mandragora.* "It has a large, brown root, somewhat like a parsnip, running 3 or 4 feet deep into the ground, sometimes single, sometimes divided into two or three branches. Immediately from the crown of the root arise several large, dark-green leaves, which at first stand erect, but when grown to full size— a foot or more in length and 4 or 5 inches in width—spread open and lie upon

the ground. They are sharp pointed at the apex and of a foetid odour . . ." (Grieve, I, 511).

The leaves have a cooling effect and were used in ointments and poultices; the roots were powerful emetics and purgatives. In large quantities it could produce delirium. When the root was chewed, it could serve as an anesthetic in surgical operations.

41. Probably *hyoscyamus niger*, which like the mandrake was used to induce sleep and to alleviate pain. Dioscorides (Bk. IV, ch. 69) distinguishes three varieties: *niger* (black), *albus* (white), and *aureaus* (golden or yellows) (see Goodyer, p. 464).

42. Although the author of *Circa instans* denied this belief, the Mandrake was the object of much superstition: "The roots of Mandrake were supposed to bear a resemblance to the human form, on account of their habit of forking into two and shooting on each side. In the old Herbals we find them frequently figured as a male with a long beard, and a female with a very bushy head of hair. Many weird superstitions collected round the Mandrake root. As an amulet, it was once placed on mantelpieces to avert misfortune and to bring prosperity and happiness to the house. Bryony roots were often cut into fancy shapes and passed off as Mandrake. . . . In Henry VIII's time quaint little images made from Bryony roots, cut into the figure of a man, with grains of millet inserted into the face as eyes, fetched high prices. These were known as *puppettes* or *mammettes*, and were credited with magical powers" (Grieve, II, 511–512).

43. Approximately three lines are omitted.

44. This is the second and final entry on the mandrake; Rufinus himself added nothing to his authorities.

Source: Reprinted by permission of the publisher from *A Sourcebook in Medieval Science*, ed. Edward Grant, pp. 783–85. Cambridge, MA: Harvard University Press, copyright © 1974 by the President and Fellows of Harvard College. The translation was done from the Latin text published in *The Herbal of Rufinus edited from the Unique Manuscript* by Lynn Thorndike, assisted by Francis J. Benjamin, Jr. (Chicago: University of Chicago Press, 1946).

DOCUMENT 8
Nicole Oresme (c. 1325–82) and Arguments for the Diurnal Rotation of the Earth

Nicole Oresme was one of the most innovative thinkers of the late Middle Ages. An able administrator, he was also a mathematician, the translator of Aristotle's Ethics, Politics *and* De caelo *into French, and the author of his own important work on money and finance.*

In this selection from Oresme's Le Livre du ciel et du monde *(1377), his translation and commentary on Aristotle's* De caelo, *Oresme discusses the arguments for the earth's daily rotation on its axis. These are noteworthy for their recognition that our perception of motion is relative: we cannot tell from our senses whether the heavens revolve around the earth or the earth itself is turning. Oresme also points out that if the air and everything in it turned with the earth, there would not be any wind resulting from the earth's motion nor would an arrow shot up in the air be left behind. In another part of the argument not reproduced here, Oresme discusses the biblical account of God stopping the sun so that Joshua could win the battle of Jericho. If read literally, as it often was in the early modern period, the wording of this story would support the view that the heavens, not the earth, revolve. Oresme, however, responds that the story describes merely how things appear to us and there are many expressions in the Bible "which are not to be taken literally" (p. 531).*

Oresme's abrupt retraction of his argument (in nine lines, compared to nine pages of argument for the motion of the earth) has been attributed to his belief that faith should be considered above and beyond reason and to his ultimate skepticism about reason's ability to decide fundamental problems.

*Oresme's arguments are similar to those of his teacher, John Buridan. In the sixteenth century, Nicholas Copernicus would persuasively argue for the first time that the earth both rotated on its axis and revolved around the sun (*De revolutionibus, *1543). Although there is no evidence that Copernicus read their work, Copernicus' arguments bear a strong resemblance to those of Buridan and Oresme.*

However, subject, of course, to correction, it seems to me that it is possible to embrace the argument [that the earth moves circularly and that the heavens remain at rest] and consider with favor the conclusions set forth in the above opinion that the earth rather than the heavens has a diurnal or daily rotation. At the outset, I wish to state that it is impossible to demonstrate from any experience at all that the contrary is true; second, that no argument is conclusive; and third, I shall demonstrate why this is so. As to the first point, let us examine one experience: we can see with our eyes the rising and setting of the sun, the moon, and several stars, while other stars turn around the arctic pole.

Such a thing is due only to the motion of the heavens, as was shown in Chapter Sixteen, and, therefore, the heavens move with daily motion. Another experience is this one: if the earth is so moved, it makes its complete course in a natural day with the result that we and the trees and the houses are moved very fast toward the east; thus, it should seem to us that the air and wind are always coming very strong from the east and that it should make a noise such as it makes against the arrow shot from a crossbow or an even louder one, but the contrary is evident from experience. The third argument is Ptolemy's—namely, that, if someone were in a boat moving rapidly toward the east and shot an arrow straight upward, it would not fall in the boat but far behind it toward the west. Likewise, if the earth moves so very fast turning from west to east and if someone threw a stone straight upward, it would not fall back to the place from which it was thrown, but far to the west; and the contrary appears to be the case.

. . . It is stated in Book Four of *The Perspective* by Witelo that we do not perceive motion unless we notice that one body is in the process of assuming a different position relative to another. I say, therefore, that, if the higher of the two parts of the world mentioned above were moved today in daily motion—as it is—and the lower part remained motionless and if tomorrow the contrary were to happen so that the lower part moved in daily motion and the higher—that is, the heavens, etc.— remained at rest, we should not be able to sense or perceive this change, and everything would appear exactly the same both today and tomorrow with respect to this mutation. We should keep right on assuming that the part where we are was at rest while the other part was moving continually, exactly as it seems to a man in a moving boat that the trees on shore move. In the same way, if a man in the heavens, moved and carried along by their daily motion, could see the earth distinctly and its mountains, valleys, rivers, cities, and castles, it would appear to him that the earth was moving in daily motion, just as to us on earth it seems as though the heavens are moving. Likewise, if the earth moved with daily motion and the heavens were motionless, it would seem to us that the earth was immobile and that the heavens appeared to move; and this can be easily imagined by anyone with clear understanding. This obviously answers the first experience, for we could say that the sun and stars appear to rise and set as they do and that the heavens seem to revolve on account of the motion of the earth in which we live together with the elements. To the second experience, the reply seems to be that, according to this opinion, not only the earth moves, but also with it the water and the air, as we stated above, although the water and air here below may be moved in addition by the winds or other forces. In a similar manner, if the air were closed in on a moving boat, it would seem to a person in that air that it was not moving. Concerning the third experience, which seems more complicated and which deals with the case of an arrow or stone thrown up into the air, etc., one might say that the arrow shot upward is moved toward the east very rapidly with the air through which it passes, along with all the lower portion of the world which we have already defined and which moves with daily motion; for this reason the arrow falls back to the place from which it was shot into the air.

. . . Thus, it is apparent that one cannot demonstrate by any experience whatever that the heavens move with diurnal motion; whatever the fact may be, assuming that the heavens move and the earth does not or that the earth moves and the heavens do not, to an eye in the heavens which could see the earth clearly, it would appear to move; if the eye were on the earth, the heavens would appear to move. Nor would the vision of this eye be deceived, for it can sense or see nothing but the process of the movement itself. But if the motion is relative to some particular body or object, this judgment is made by the senses from within that particular body, as Witelo explains in *The Perspective*; and the senses are often deceived in such cases, as was related above in the example of the man on the moving ship. Afterward, it was demonstrated how it cannot be proved conclusively by argument that the heavens move. In the third place, we offered arguments opposing their diurnal motion. However, everyone maintains, and I think myself, that the heavens do move and not the earth: For God hath established the world which shall not be moved, in spite of contrary reasons because they are clearly not conclusive persuasions. However, after considering all that has been said, one could then believe that the earth moves and not the heavens, for the opposite is not clearly evident. Nevertheless, at first sight, this seems as much against natural reason as, or more against natural reason than, all or many of the articles of our faith. What I have said by way of diversion or intellectual exercise can in this manner serve as a valuable means of refuting and checking those who would like to impugn our faith by argument.

Source: Nicole Oresme, *Le Livre du ciel et du monde*, ed. Albert D. Menut and Alexander J. Denomy, trans. Albert D. Menut (Madison: University of Wisconsin Press, 1968), pp. 521, 523, 525, 535, 537, 539. Reprinted by permission of The University of Wisconsin Press.

DOCUMENT 9
Hugh of St. Victor On the Mechanical Arts

Hugh of St. Victor, first a monk and then a teaching master at the abbey of St. Victor near Paris from the 1100s until his death in 1141, is one of the most important figures in the history of medieval attitudes toward technology. Nicknamed by his contemporaries "a new Augustine," Hugh was a mystic, as well as a theologian and educator. He is best known for his vision of technology as part of man's religious and philosophical quest to restore himself to his happier life in Paradise before the Fall of Adam and Eve.

Although Hugh did not coin the term mechanical arts *(artes mechanicae) for technology, he was the first to describe in detail how they were an essential part of human knowledge. Hugh paired the seven mechanical arts (fabric making, armament and architecture, commerce, agriculture, hunting and food preparation, medicine, and theatrics and games) with the seven liberal arts. He also argued that technology, like the liberal arts, demonstrated human intelligence and man's God-given ability to reason. This was an important statement because some traditions inherited from antiquity had denigrated crafts and craftsmanship as purely physical labor and, therefore, as not qualifying as "knowledge."*

Hugh's conception of the mechanical arts was widely copied during the Middle Ages. He and other medieval writers on the classifications of the arts and sciences ensured that medieval culture would recognize technology as having an established and positive role in human life.

The first selection here places the mechanical arts in a biblical, philosophical, and religious context. Note that although Hugh, following Aristotle, says that art merely imitates nature, he also suggests in the last line that the ingenuity of the "artificer" or craftsman seems to rival that of nature. The second selection is comprised of Hugh's descriptions of the individual mechanical arts. Hugh puts each in a strikingly positive light, describing even commerce, often criticized by the Church as immoral, as pursued for the "common benefit of all." Together, the descriptions give a sense of daily life in the twelfth century.

Chapter Nine: Concerning the Three Works

"Now there are three works—the work of God, the work of nature, and the work of the artificer, who imitates nature." The work of God is to create that which was not, whence we read, "In the beginning God created heaven and earth"; the work of nature is to bring forth into actuality that which lay hidden, whence we read, "Let the earth bring forth the green herb," etc.; the work of the artificer is to put together things disjoined or to disjoin those put together, whence we read, "They sewed themselves aprons." For the earth cannot create the heaven, nor can man, who is powerless to add a mere span to his stature, bring forth the green herb.

Among these works, the human work, because it is not nature but only imitative of nature, is fitly called mechanical, that is adulterate, just as a skeleton key is called a "mechanical" key. How the work of the artificer in each case imitates nature is a long and difficult matter to pursue in detail. For illustration, however, we can show the matter briefly as follows: The founder who casts a statue has gazed upon man as his model. The builder who has constructed a house has taken into consideration a mountain, for, as the Prophet declares, "Thou sendest forth springs in the vales; between the midst of the hills the waters shall pass"; as the ridges of mountains retain no water, even so does a house require to be framed into a high peak that it may safely discharge the weight of pouring rains. He who first invented the use of clothes had considered how each of the growing things one by one has its proper covering by which to protect its nature from offense. Bark encircles the tree, feathers cover the bird, scales encase the fish, fleece clothes the sheep, hair garbs cattle and wild beasts, a shell protects the tortoise, and ivory makes the elephant unafraid of spears. But it is not without reason that while each living thing is born equipped with its own natural armor, man alone is brought forth naked and unarmed. For it is fitting that nature should provide a plan for those beings which do not know how to care for themselves, but that from nature's example, a better chance for trying things should be provided to man when he comes to devise for himself by his own reasoning those things naturally given to all other animals. Indeed, man's reason shines forth much more brilliantly in inventing these very things than ever it would have had man naturally possessed them. Nor is it without cause that the proverb says: "Ingenious want hath mothered all the arts." Want it is which has devised all that you see most excellent in the occupations of men. From this the infinite varieties of painting, weaving, carving, and founding have arisen, so that we look with wonder not at nature alone but at the artificer as well.

Chapter Twenty: The Division of Mechanical Sciences into Seven

Mechanical science contains seven sciences: fabric making, armament, commerce, agriculture, hunting, medicine, and theatrics. Of these, three pertain to external cover for nature, by which she protects herself from harms, and four to internal, by which she feeds and nourishes herself. In this division we find a likeness to the *trivium* and *quadrivium*, for the *trivium* is concerned with words, which are external things, and the *quadrivium* with concepts, which are internally conceived. The mechanical sciences are the seven handmaids which Mercury received in dowry from Philology, for every human activity is servant to eloquence wed to wisdom. Thus Tully, in his book on rhetoricians, says concerning the study of eloquence:

> By it is life made safe, by it fit, by it noble, and by it pleasurable: for from it the commonwealth receives abundant benefits, provided that wisdom, which regulates all things, keeps it company. From eloquence, to those who have acquired it, flow praise, honor, dignity; from eloquence, to the friends of those skilled in it, comes most dependable and sure protection.

These sciences are called mechanical, that is, adulterate, because their concern is with the artificer's product, which borrows its form from nature. Similarly, the other seven are called liberal either because they require minds which are liberal, that is, liberated and practiced (for these sciences pursue subtle inquiries into the causes of things), or because in antiquity only free and noble men were accustomed to study them, while the populace and the sons of men not free sought operative skill in things mechanical. In all this appears the great diligence of the ancients, who would leave nothing untried, but brought all things under definite rules and precepts. And mechanics is that science to which they declare the manufacture of all articles to belong.

Chapter Twenty-one: First—Fabric Making

Fabric making includes all the kinds of weaving, sewing, and twisting which are accomplished by hand, needle, spindle, awl, skein winder, comb, loom, crisper, iron, or any other instruments whatever; out of any material made of flax or fleece, or any sort of hide, whether scraped or hairy, out of cane as well, or cork, or rushes, or hair, or tufts, or any material of this sort which can be used for the making of clothes, coverings, drapery, blankets, saddles, carpets, curtains, napkins, felts, strings, nets, ropes; out of straw too, from which men usually make their hats and baskets. All these pursuits belong to fabric making.

Chapter Twenty-two: Second—Armament

Armament comes second. Sometimes any tools whatever are called "arms," as when we speak of the arms of war, or the arms of a ship, meaning the implements used in war or on a ship. For the rest, the term "arms" belongs properly to those things under which we take cover— like the shield, the breastplate, and the helmet—or those by which we strike—like the sword, the twofaced axe, and the lance. "Missiles," however, are things we can fling, like the spear or arrow. Arms are so called from the arm, because they strengthen the arm which we customarily hold up against blows. Missiles (*tela*), however, are named from the Greek word *telon*, meaning "long," because the things so named are long; therefore, we use the word *protelare*, or "make long," to mean "protect." Armament, therefore, is called, in a sense, an instrumental science, not so much because it uses instruments in its activity as because, from some material lying shapeless at hand, it makes something into an instrument, if I may so name its product. To this science belong all such materials as stones, woods, metals, sands, and clays.

Armament is of two types, the constructional and the craftly. The constructional is divided into the building of walls, which is the business of the wood-worker and carpenter, and of other craftsmen of both these sorts, who work with mattocks and hatchets, the file and beam, the saw and auger, planes, vises, the trowel and the level, smoothing, hewing, cutting, filing, carving, joining, daubing in every sort of material—clay, stone, wood, bone, gravel, lime, gypsum, and other materials that may exist of this kind. Craftly armament is divided into the malleable branch, which forges material into shape by beating upon it, and the foundry branch, which reduces material into shape by casting it—so that "founders" is the name for those who know how to cast a shapeless mass into the form of an implement.

Chapter Twenty-three: Third—Commerce

Commerce contains every sort of dealing in the purchase, sale, and exchange of domestic or foreign goods. This art is beyond all doubt a peculiar sort of rhetoric—strictly of its own kind—for eloquence is in the highest degree necessary to it. Thus the man who excels others in fluency of speech is called a Mercurius, or Mercury, as being a *mercatorium kirrius* (=*kyrios*)—a very lord among merchants. Commerce penetrates the secret places of the world, approaches shores unseen, explores fearful wildernesses, and in tongues unknown and with barbaric peoples carries on the trade of mankind. The pursuit of commerce reconciles nations, calms wars, strengthens peace, and commutes the private good of individuals into the common benefit of all.

Chapter Twenty-four: Fourth—Agriculture

Agriculture deals with four kinds of land: arable, set aside for sowing; plantational, reserved for trees, like the vineyard, the orchard, and the grove; pastoral, like the meadow, the hillside pasture, and the heath; and floral, like the garden and rose-hedges.

Chapter Twenty-five: Fifth—Hunting

Hunting is divided into gaming, fowling, and fishing. Gaming is done in many ways—with nets, foot-traps, snares, pits, the bow, javelins, the spear, encircling the game, or smoking it out, or pursuing it with dogs or hawks. Fowling is done by snares, traps, nets, the bow, birdlime, the hook. Fishing is done by drag-nets, lines, hooks, and spears. To this discipline belongs the preparation of all foods, seasonings, and drinks. Its name, however, is taken from only one part of it because in antiquity men used to eat merely by hunting, as they still do in certain regions where the use of bread is extremely rare, where flesh is the only food and water or mead the drink.

Food is of two kinds—bread and side dishes. Bread (*panis*) takes its name either from the Latin word for one's laying a thing out (*ponis*), or from the Greek word for all (*pan*), because all meals need bread in order to be well provided. There are many kinds of bread—unleavened, leavened, that baked under ashes, brown bread, sponge-cake, cake, pan-baked, sweet, wheaten, bun-shaped, rye, and many other kinds. Side dishes consist of all that one eats with bread, and we can call them victuals. They are of many sorts—meats, stews, porridges, vegetables, fruits. Of meats, some are roasted, others fried, others boiled, some fresh, some salted. Some are called loins, flitches also or sides, haunches or hams, grease, lard, fat. The varieties of meat dishes are likewise numerous—Italian sausage, minced meat, patties, Galatian tarts, and all other such things that a very prince of cooks has been able to concoct. Porridges contain milk, colostrum, butter, cheese, whey. And who can enumerate the names of vegetables and fruits? Of seasonings some are hot, some cold, some bitter, some sweet, some dry, some moist. Of drink, some is merely that: it moistens without nourishing, like water; other is both drink and food, for it both moistens and nourishes, like wine. Of the nutritious drinks, furthermore, some are naturally so, like wine or any other liquor; others accidentally so, like beer and various kinds of mead.

Hunting, therefore, includes all the duties of bakers, butchers, cooks, and tavern keepers.

Chapter Twenty-six: Sixth—Medicine

"Medicine is divided into two parts"—"occasions" and operations. "The 'occasions' are six: air, motion and quiet, emptiness and satiety, food and drink, sleep and wakefulness, and the reactions of the soul. These are called 'occasions' because, when tempered, they occasion and preserve health," or, when untempered, ill-health. The reactions of the soul are called occasions of health or ill-health because now and again they either "raise one's temperature, whether violently as does wrath or gently as do pleasures; or they withdraw and lower the temperature, again whether violently as do terror and fear, or gently as does worry. And among them are some which, like grief, produce their natural effects both internally and externally."

Every medicinal operation is either interior or exterior. "The interior are those which are introduced through the mouth, nostrils, ears, or anus, such as potions, emetics, and powders, which are taken by drinking, chewing, or sucking in. The exterior are, for example, lotions, plasters, poultices, and surgery, which is twofold: that performed on the flesh, like cutting, sewing, burning, and that performed on the bone, like setting and joining."

Let no one be disturbed that among the means employed by medicine I count food and drink, which earlier I attributed to hunting. For these belong to both under different aspects. For instance, wine in the grape is the business of agriculture; in the barrel, of the cellarer, and in its consumption, of the doctor. Similarly, the preparing of food belongs to the mill, the slaughterhouse, and the kitchen, but the strength given by its consumption, to medicine.

Chapter Twenty-seven: Seventh—Theatrics

The science of entertainments is called "theatrics" from the theatre, to which the people once used to gather for the performance: not that a theatre was the only place in which entertainment took place, but it was a more popular place for entertainment than any other. Some entertainment took place in theatres, some in the entrance porches of buildings, some in gymnasia, some in amphitheatres, some in arenas, some at feasts, some at shrines. In the theatre, epics were presented either by recitals or by acting out dramatic roles or using masks or puppets; they held choral processions and dances in the porches. In the gymnasia they wrestled; in the amphitheatres they raced on foot or on horses or in chariots; in the arenas boxers performed; at banquets they made music with songs and instruments and chants, and they played at dice; in the temples at solemn seasons they sang the praises of the gods. Moreover, they numbered these entertainments among legitimate activities because by temperate motion natural heat is stimulated in the body and by enjoyment the mind is refreshed; or, as is more likely, seeing that people necessarily gathered together for occasional amusement, they desired that places for such amusement might be established to forestall the people's coming together at public houses, where they might commit lewd or criminal acts.

Source: *The* Didascalicon *of Hugh of St. Victor: A Medieval Guide to the Arts*, trans. Jerome Taylor (New York: Columbia University Press, 1961), pp. 55–56, 74–78. Reprinted with the permission of the publisher.

DOCUMENT 10
Roger Bacon (c. 1219–92) On Experimental Science; from the *Opus maius*

Roger Bacon stands out among medieval natural philosophers for his explicit and strongly worded plea that science be used for the practical benefit of humankind. Although many medieval scientists were interested in the utility of nature and natural products, few expressed in such forthright terms the view that one of the primary purposes of science was to produce dramatic inventions, such as the fearsome weapons he describes in these excerpts from his Opus maius *(Greater Work). His mention of the explosive powers of saltpeter, the primary ingredient in gunpowder, is the first known in European writing. In his section on optics (not reproduced here), he suggests that lenses could be made so that "from an incredible distance we might read the smallest letters and number grains of dust and sand" (p. 582). Even more imaginatively, he suggests a sort of biological mind-control, in which the will of the enemy could be controlled by changing the complexion of the air. In other writings, he also refers to the possibility of building flying machines and cars that went by themselves.*

Bacon also is unusual in his emphasis on "experience," as well as reason, in scientific method. On the one hand, by "experience" he clearly means that the scientist should personally test out his ideas in a concrete fashion whenever possible. On the other hand, he also believes that divine inspiration is a key element in scientific discovery.

The influences on Bacon's thought were complex. Like most thirteenth-century natural philosophers, he was strongly influenced by Aristotle and Arabic scientific writings. In addition, however, he absorbed the Augustinian notion of the divine illumination of the mind as a route to knowledge and, most probably, was influenced by the apocalyptic prophecies of Joachim of Fiore (d. 1202), whose late thirteenth-century followers predicted the imminent coming of the Anti-Christ. Finally, he had an interest in alchemy, which had a tradition of emphasizing the powers of human art over nature.

The Opus maius *(c. 1266) was written in an effort to persuade the pope to institute a massive reform of education emphasizing mathematics, languages, and experimental science. The following is from the sixth part of the* Opus maius, *"On Experimental Science."*

CHAPTER I

Having laid down fundamental principles of the wisdom of the Latins so far as they are found in language, mathematics, and optics, I now wish to unfold the principles of experimental science, since without experience nothing can be sufficiently known. For there are two modes of acquiring knowledge, namely, by reasoning and experience. Reasoning draws a conclusion and makes us grant the conclusion, but does not make the conclusion certain, nor does it remove doubt so that the mind may rest on the intuition of truth, unless the mind discovers it by the path of experience; since many have the arguments relating to what can be known, but because they lack experience they neglect the arguments, and neither avoid what is harmful nor follow what is good. For if a man who has never seen fire should prove by adequate reasoning that fire burns and injures things and destroys them, his mind would not be satisfied thereby, nor would he avoid fire, until he placed his hand or some combustible substance in the fire, so that he might prove by experience that which reasoning taught. But when he has had actual experience of combustion his mind is made certain and rests in the full light of truth. Therefore reasoning does not suffice, but experience does.

This is also evident in mathematics, where proof is most convincing. But the mind of one who has the most convincing proof in regard to the equilateral triangle will never cleave to the conclusion without experience, nor will he heed it, but will disregard it until experience is offered him by the intersection of two circles, from either intersection of which two lines may be drawn to the extremities of the given line; but then the man accepts the conclusion without any question. Aristotle's statement, then, that proof is reasoning that causes us to know is to be understood with the proviso that the proof is accompanied by its appropriate experience, and is not to be understood of the bare proof. His statement also in the first book of the *Metaphysics* that those who understand the reason and the cause are wiser than those who have empiric knowledge of a fact, is spoken of such as know only the bare truth without the cause. But I am here speaking of the man who knows the reason and the cause through experience. These men are perfect in their wisdom, as Aristotle maintains in the sixth book of the *Ethics*, whose simple statements must be accepted as if they offered proof, as he states in the same place.

He therefore who wishes to rejoice without doubt in regard to the truths underlying phenomena must know how to devote himself to experiment. For authors write many statements, and people believe them through reasoning which they formulate without experience. Their reasoning is wholly false. For it is generally believed that the diamond cannot be broken except by goat's blood, and philosophers and theologians misuse this idea. But fracture by means of blood of this kind has never been verified, although the effort has been made; and without that blood it can be broken easily. For I have seen this with my own eyes, and this is necessary, because gems cannot be carved except by fragments of this stone. Similarly it is generally believed that the castors employed by physicians are the testicles of the male animal. But this is not true, because the beaver has these under its breast, and both the male and female produce testicles of this kind. Besides these castors the male beaver has its testicles in their natural place; and therefore what is subjoined is a dreadful lie, namely, that when the hunters pursue the beaver, he himself knowing what they are seeking cuts out with his teeth these glands. Moreover, it is generally believed that hot water freezes more quickly than cold water in vessels, and the argument in support of this is advanced that contrary is excited by contrary, just like enemies meeting each other. But it is certain that cold water freezes more quickly for any one who makes the experiment. People attribute this to Aristotle in the second book of the Meteorologics; but he certainly does not make this statement, but he does make one like it, by which they have been deceived, namely, that if cold water and hot water are poured on a cold place, as upon ice, the hot water freezes more quickly, and this is true. But if hot water and cold are placed in two vessels, the cold will freeze more quickly. Therefore all things must be verified by experience.

But experience is of two kinds; one is gained through our external senses, and in this way we gain our experience of those things that are in the heavens by instruments made for this purpose, and of those things here below by means attested by our vision. Things that do not belong in our part of the world we know through other scientists who have had experience of them. As, for example, Aristotle on the authority of Alexander sent two thousand men through different parts of the world to gain experimental knowledge of all things that are on the surface of the earth, as Pliny bears witness in his Natural History. This experience is both human and philosophical, as far as man can act in accordance with the grace given him; but this experience does not suffice him, because it does not give full attestation in regard to things corporeal owing to its difficulty, and does not touch at all on things spiritual. It is necessary, therefore, that the intellect of man should be otherwise aided, and for this reason the holy patriarchs and prophets, who first gave sciences to the world, received illumination within and were not dependent on sense alone. The same is true of many believers since the time of Christ. For the grace of faith illuminates greatly, as also do divine inspirations, not only in things spiritual, but in things corporeal and in the sciences of philosophy; as Ptolemy states in the Centilogium, namely, that there are two roads by which we arrive at the knowledge of facts, one through the experience of philosophy, the other through divine inspiration, which is far the better way, as he says.

Moreover, there are seven stages of this internal knowledge, the first of which is reached through illuminations relating purely to the sciences. The second consists in the virtues. For the evil man is ignorant, as Aristotle says in the second book of the Ethics. Moreover, Algazel says in his Logic that the soul disfigured by sins is like a rusty mirror, in which the species of objects cannot be seen clearly; but the soul adorned with virtues is like a well-polished mirror, in which the forms of objects are clearly seen. For this reason true philosophers have labored more in morals for the honor of virtue, concluding in their own case that they cannot perceive the causes of things unless they have souls free from sins. . . .

Chapter on the Third Prerogative or the Dignity of the Experimental Art

. . . Moreover, certain bear witness that activities of this science which display philosophy consist in changing the character of a region, so that the habits of its people are changed. One of such witnesses was Aristotle himself, the most learned of philosophers. When Alexander asked him in regard to the nations which he had discovered, whether he should exterminate them because of the ferocity of their character, or should permit them to live, he replied in the book of Secrets, "If you can alter the air of those nations, permit them to live; if you cannot, then kill them." For he maintained that the air of these nations could be changed advantageously, so that the complexions of their bodies would be changed, and then their minds influenced by their complexions would choose good morals in accordance with the freedom of the will. This is one of the secrets.

Moreover, certain assert that change is effected by the sun. There is, as an illustration, the example of Aristotle when he said to Alexander, "Give a hot drink from the seed of a plant to whomsoever you wish, and he will obey you for the rest of your life." Some maintain that an army may be stupefied and put to flight. Of this number is Aristotle, who says to Alexander, "Take such a stone, and every army will flee from you." They bear witness that these statements and innumerable others of this kind are true, not meaning that violence is done to the freedom of the will, since Aristotle, who maintains this view, says in the Ethics that the will cannot be coerced. The body, moreover, can be changed by the influence of things, and the minds of people are then aroused and influenced to desire voluntarily that to which they are directed; just as we see in the book of Medicine that through potions and many medicines people can be changed in body and in the passions of the soul and in the inclination of the will.

There are, moreover, other inventions belonging more to nature which do not have as their object a marvelous change in the will, and they are diversified in character. Some of these possess an excellence of wisdom with other advantages, as, for example, perpetual baths most suitable for human use that do not require any artificial renewal; and ever-burning lamps. For we see many things that cannot be impaired by fire, nay, that are purified by fire, like the skin of the salamander and many other things of this kind, which also can be so prepared that they are externally luminous of themselves, and retain the power of fire, and give forth flame and light. Moreover, against foes of the state they have discovered important arts, so that without a sword or any weapon requiring physical contact they could destroy all who offer resistance. There are many kinds of these inventions. Some of these are perceived by no one of the senses, or by smell alone, and of these inventions Aristotle's book explains that of altering the air, but not those of which I spoke above. These last are of a different character, since they act by means of an infection. There are others also that change some one of the senses, and they are diversified in accordance with all the senses.

Certain of these work a change by contact only and thus destroy life. For malta, which is a kind of bitumen and is plentiful in this world, when cast upon an armed man burns him up. The Romans suffered severe loss of life from this in their conquests, as Pliny states in the second book of the Natural History, and as the histories attest. Similarly yellow petroleum, that is, oil springing from the rock, burns up whatever it meets if it is properly prepared. For a consuming fire is produced by this which can be extinguished with difficulty; for water cannot put it out. Certain inventions disturb the hearing to such a degree that, if they are set off suddenly at night with sufficient skill, neither city nor army can endure them. No clap of thunder could compare with such noises. Certain of these strike such terror to the sight that the coruscations of the clouds disturb it incomparably less. Gideon is thought to have employed inventions similar to these in the camp of the Midianites. We have an example of this in that toy of children which is made in many parts of the world, namely, an instrument as large as the human thumb. From the force of the salt called saltpeter so horrible a sound is produced at the bursting of so small a thing, namely, a small piece of parchment, that we perceive it exceeds the roar of sharp thunder, and the flash exceeds the greatest brilliancy of the lightning accompanying the thunder.

There are also very many things that slay every poisonous animal by the gentlest touch, and if a circle is made around these animals with things of this kind the animals cannot get out, but die, although they are not touched. But if a man is bitten by a poisonous animal, by the application of the powder of such things he can be healed, as Bede states in his Ecclesiastical History and as we know by experience. And thus there are innumerable things that have strange virtues, whose potencies we are ignorant of solely from our neglect of experiment.

But there are other inventions which do not possess such advantage for the state, but are to be looked upon as miracles of nature, such as experiments with the magnet, not only on iron, but on gold and other metals. Moreover, if the experiment on iron were not known, it would be viewed as a great miracle. And surely in respect to the action of the magnet on iron there are phenomena unknown to those who use the magnet which show in a wonderful way the dissolutions of nature. . . .

. . . We must consider, however, that although other sciences do many wonders, as in the case of practical geometry, which produces mirrors that burn up every opposing object, and so too in the other sciences, yet all things of such wonderful utility in the state belong chiefly to this science. For this science has the same relation to the other sciences as the science of navigation to the carpenter's art and the military art to that of the engineer. For this science teaches how wonderful instruments may be made, and uses them when made, and also considers all secret things owing to the advantages they may possess for the state and for individuals; and it directs other sciences as its handmaids, and therefore the whole power of speculative science is attributed especially to this science. And now the wonderful advantage derived from these three sciences in this world on behalf of the Church of God against the enemies of the faith is manifest, who should be destroyed rather by the discoveries of science than by the warlike arms of combatants. Antichrist will use these means freely and effectively, in order that he may crush and confound the power of this world; and by these means tyrants in times past brought the world under their sway. This has been shown by examples without end.

Source: *The Opus majus of Roger Bacon*, trans. Robert Belle, 2 vols. (New York: Russell and Russell, 1962), pp. 583–86, 627–30, 633.

DOCUMENT 11
A Cistercian Monk Praises the Mechanized Water System of Clairvaux Abbey

Many social groups made use of new and improved technologies during the Middle Ages. The monks of the Cistercian Order, however, seem to have been among the most aggressive in pursuing state-of-the-art technology. Founded in 1098 at Citeaux by Robert of Molesme (c. 1027–1110), the Cistercians established monastic houses in isolated areas so that they could practice the ideal of poverty and be independent of secular control and influence. Paradoxically, their program of economic self-sufficiency within a century led them to become among the most productive communities in Europe.

As the following document illustrates, Cistercians were in the forefront of hydraulic technology. Clairvaux was among the most important Cistercian houses due to the prestige of its abbot, St. Bernard of Clairvaux (1090–1153), and seems to have had a policy of sending professional builders to newly founded houses to help set up water systems. The Cistercians also cornered the market in exports of English wool, developed a wine industry, and became leading producers of iron through the skillful use of water power and the application of new techniques. Other monastic orders, despite their original intentions, also became efficient participants in the more commercialized economy of the twelfth and thirteenth centuries. St. Francis of Assisi, who had founded the Order of the Franciscans in 1215 on the ideals of apostolic poverty and kinship with nature, eventually became the patron saint of merchants!

The river enters the abbey as much as the wall acting as a check allows. It gushes first into the corn-mill where it is very actively employed in grinding the grain under the weight of the wheels and in shaking the fine sieve which separates flour from bran. Thence it flows into the next building, and fills the boiler in which it is heated to prepare beer for the monks' drinking, should the vine's fruitfulness not reward the vintner's labour. But the river has not yet finished its work, for it is now drawn into the fulling machines following the corn-mill. In the mill it has prepared the brothers' food and its duty is now to serve in making their clothing. This the river does not withhold, nor does it refuse any task asked of it. Thus it raises and lowers alternately the heavy hammers and mallets, or to be more exact, the wooden feet of the fulling-machines. When by swirling at great speed it has made all these wheels revolve swiftly it issues foaming and looking as if it had ground itself. Now the river enters the tannery where it devotes much care and labour to preparing the necessary materials for the monks' footwear; then it divides into many small branches and, in its busy course, passes through the various departments, seeking everywhere for those who require its services for any purpose whatsoever, whether for cooking, rotating, crushing, watering, washing, or grinding, always offering its help and never refusing. At last, to earn full thanks and to leave nothing undone, it carries away the refuse and leaves all clean [I].

Source: "Machines," Bertrand Gille in Charles Singer, E. J. Holmyard, A. R. Hall, and Trevor I. Williams, eds. *A History of Technology*, vol. 2, *The Mediterranean Civilizations and the Middle Ages c. 700 B.C. to c. A.D. 1500*, assisted by

E. Jaffé, Nan Clos, and R.H.G. Thomson (Oxford: Clarendon Press, 1956; reprint with corrections, Oxford: Clarendon Press, 1957), p. 650.

DOCUMENT 12
Medieval Alchemy

Of all the medieval sciences, alchemy most combined scientific theory with practical procedures. These extracts are from what Pearl Kibre, author of the introduction to the text, called a "pocket edition of alchemy" (p. xx), ascribed to Albertus Magnus but probably written in the fourteenth century, after Albertus' death. In the introduction the author first points out how he has had to depend on his own efforts to learn this art and the many pitfalls which have prevented others from becoming successful, including excessive drinking, running out of money, using porous vessels, lack of skill, or succumbing to the temptation to be deceitful. He continues by defending the basic premise of alchemy, that it can genuinely transmute metals and produce gold from "base" metals by applying the proper chemical procedures.

Most of the work is taken up with careful descriptions of these procedures and the required equipment. The first extract describes how to make a furnace for heating materials. In the text it is followed by directions on making other kinds of ovens and how to glaze clay vessels. Some of these describe the use of burying substances in dung pits, an effective method of keeping substances at a constant warm temperature of about 50–70 degrees (p. 42 n. 93). The second extract describes the preparation of sal alkali. The procedures described would produce several kinds of alkalis, including potassium carbonate or potash, sodium carbonate, and ammonia; the differences between potassium carbonate and sodium carbonate were not recognized until the eighteenth century. Potash was used for the manufacture of soap and glass in the late Middle Ages.

ON THE QUALITY AND QUANTITY OF FURNACES

Take common clay and to four parts add a fifth part of potter's clay and grind well, and add a little sand, grind again (some prudently add manure or salt water in which manure will have been dissolved); after doing this make a wall, as mentioned before, above the pit, two feet high or a little less, one span thick, and permit to dry. Then have a disc made of potter's clay, which can sustain strong fire, everywhere perforated with fifty or sixty holes, according to the size of the disc [with the perforations] made like a finger, the upper part narrow and the lower wider so that ashes can easily descend. Below, in the earth, make a canal through earth and wall before the disc has been put in place; this should be narrow at the pit end, while outside, at the wall, it should be wider, about one span in width, so that the wind may enter. This canal should be lined with clay; then the disc should be placed on top, in such a way that the wider openings of the perforations are on the underside. Next a wall is built upon the first wall and the disc, to the thickness of one span, but the wall should be above the disc to about the distance of one arm. The furnace should have a hole in the middle above the disc where the coals will be laid. At the top there should be a hole through which calcining vessels may be placed: this hole is to be covered over afterwards with a tight cover. The furnace may also have beneath four or five small holes about three digits wide.

This is the general plan of the furnace.

Note also that a clay tripod should be placed above the disc, upon which are to be placed the calcining vessels, and under which the coals.

What is the Use of Sal Alkali, and how is it Prepared?

Sal alkali is important in this art and, when it has been well prepared, frees all the calxes of bodies as a solid mass. By nature it is warm and moist. It is prepared in this manner: take a large quantity of putrid oaken ashes, or better clavellated ashes, which are used for washing garments, grind very finely, add a sixth part of quicklime, mix once and put a closely woven cloth over a tina and upon it as much of the ashes mixed with the calx as it will hold, and pour hot water over the whole from above. Then filter into the lye until all the bitterness has been extracted. Remove this solution and replace it by a fresh one, and repeat [the procedure] as before. Put all the filtrates into the same vessel until morning, and then distill through a filter. Heat in a small cauldron until the solution evaporates and does not fume. Allow to cool and a hard stone will remain which is called alkali, that is, dregs of bitterness. Half fill an earthen jar with this salt and set it uncovered in the furnace. Apply a slow fire at first, heating gently so that it does not boil over (or bump); afterwards increase the heat until the alkali reddens and liquefies as wax; then, using tongs, pour at once into another jar, for if you delay it quickly gets too hard to pour. Place this white alkali salt in a glass vessel in a warm, dry place, since it dissolves in a moist one.

ADDITION. Or this alkali salt can be made in another way. Take ashes of certain herbs, called Soda, crush well, [and] boil in a jar with water. Pass through a mesh, as with claret once or twice, [and] then distill through a filter. Afterwards place [the salt] in a new earthen pot and congeal with a slow fire at first, [then] increase the heat until the salt solidifies. Place the salt in a clean dry place.

Plant alum is called alkali alum, alkali salt, and clavellated ashes, or [it] is made from them.

Crush and dissolve alum of Yemen in three pounds of distilled urine water, distil through a new filter, then harden white, and, when this is done, crush on a marble slab. Sprinkle another marble slab with distilled vinegar, place the ground alum from the first slab upon it, raising the slab on one side so that the clear liquid may be drained into a glass vessel, while the residue remains on the slab as a white earth. This should be collected in a well-stoppered glass vessel. This liquid can be hardened in a slow, moist fire [water bath]. With this alum a spirit may be fixed, and with this liquid calcinated bodies may be washed.

Reprinted with kind permission of the publisher from Ps. Albertus Magnus, *Libellus de alchimia, ascribed to Albertus Magnus*, trans. Sister Virginia Heines, S.C.N., pp. 15–16, 29–31, Berkeley and Los Angeles: University of California Press, copyright © 1958, The Regents of the University of California.

GLOSSARY

A priori: Term from logic indicating that an argument or conclusion has been deduced from self-evident or already known premises without testing by experience.

Aristotelianism: The comprehensive understanding of the world based on the thought of the Greek philosopher Aristotle. Aristotelianism remained the fundamental framework of European thought in logic, metaphysics, natural philosophy, ethics, and political philosophy from the thirteenth to the seventeenth century.

Astrarium: An elaborate astronomical clock which represented the movements of the heavenly bodies through a series of gear works and dials.

Astrolabe: An astronomical instrument, consisting of a sighting rule and a set of circular metal plates, first invented in late antiquity and developed by Islamic and European medieval astronomers. The astrolabe was held in the hands and allowed the observer to calculate the altitude above the horizon of the star or planet under observation. The series of metal plates, engraved with projections of a star map and other astronomical information corrected for the latitude of the observer, then allowed the user to situate the star or planet in relationship to other heavenly bodies and perform various astronomical calculations.

Astrology: The science of how the stars and planets affected the climate, tides, the course of illness in humans, animal behavior, and other natural phenomena on earth. Scientific astrology attempted to explain the effects of the heavens on the earth through the physical effects of the ether and planetary qualities. Judicial astrology, which claimed to be able to predict specific events and human behavior on the basis of the positions of the heavenly bodies, was both widely practiced and widely criticized in the Middle Ages.

Bestiary: A collection of short accounts of the appearance and habits of animals for the purpose of moral instruction and entertainment or as a reference work for the writing of sermons. The animals ranged from the imaginary unicorn to exotic animals such as the lion to native species; the material about them drew heavily on folklore, fables, and moral symbolism.

Caravel: A highly maneuverable type of fishing vessel first developed by the Portuguese characterized by low sides, sharp ends, a combination of square and lateen sails, and no forecastle. Later modifications to the design made the ship larger and useful also as a cargo ship and warship. Columbus' *Nina* was a type of caravel.

Carrack: A large cargo ship developed in the fifteenth century.

Cathedral schools: Urban schools attached to a cathedral which became important centers of learning in the twelfth century. In the thirteenth century, cathedral schools were largely supplanted by universities.

Church Fathers: A collective term for the Christian writers of the second through the fifth centuries who helped formulate Christian theology, ethics, and social practices.

Complexion: A term in medieval medicine which referred to the balance of the four humors and Aristotelian qualities (hot, cold, dry, wet) in plants, animals, food, and individuals. Every being had its natural and appropriate complexion and ill health was attributed to an unbalanced complexion. The four complexions, or temperaments, were the sanguine (hot and wet, associated with a predominance of the humor blood), choleric (hot, dry, associated with a predominance of yellow bile), phlegmatic (cold, wet, associated with a predominance of phlegm), and melancholic (cold, dry, associated with a predominance of black bile).

Condemnations of 1277: A proclamation issued in 1277 by the bishop of Paris condemning 219 propositions associated with some aspects of Aristotelian and Arabic science and forbidding the reading of Aristotle's books on natural science. It is not certain how thoroughly the condemnations were ever enforced, and they were partially annulled in 1325.

Cosmology: The study of the structure of the universe.

Counter-weight trebuchet: An ancient weapon further developed in the Middle Ages. The trebuchet worked like a massive slingshot and by the fifteenth century used weights of up to three tons to propel 300-pound stones against defensive walls.

Eccentric model of planetary motion: In premodern astronomy, the idea that a planet is carried on a circle whose center is eccentric to the earth and the center of the universe. This geometrical model, elaborated by the Hellenistic astronomer Ptolemy, allowed astronomers to reconcile actual observations of planetary motions with the philosophical requirement that the heavenly bodies moved with a regular circular motion, defined as sweeping out equal angles in equal times measured from the center of the earth at rest at the center of the universe.

Ecliptic: The path of the sun's movement through the heavens over the course of a year as calculated by classical astronomers and adopted by medieval astronomers. The ecliptic is tilted about twenty-three degrees in relation to the celestial equator, intersecting with the equator at the fall and spring equinoxes. The moon and planets also follow the path of the ecliptic but at widely varying speeds.

Epicycle: In premodern astronomy, the idea that a planet is carried on a small rotating circle, the epicycle, mounted on a larger circle, the deferent, which also turns. The combination of the motions of the epicycle and the deferent allowed astronomers to reconcile actual observations of planetary motions, including their apparent retrograde motions (when the planet appeared to move backward over a period of days) with the philosophical requirement that the heavenly bodies moved with a regular circular motion, defined as sweeping out equal angles in equal times measured from the center of the earth at rest at the center of the universe.

Equant model of planetary motion: In premodern astronomy, an additional geometrical mechanism designed to reconcile observations of the movements of the planets with the philosophical requirement that the heavenly bodies moved with a regular circular motion. The equant model allowed motion to be measured from a secondary point, the equant, at a distance from the earth's center at rest at the center of the universe.

Equinox: The two points at which the sun intersects the celestial equator, marking either the beginning of fall (about September 21) or the beginning of spring (about March 21); at the equinoxes the lengths of the day and night are equal.

Ether: The fifth element which made up the celestial region including the stars and planets according to Aristotelian cosmology. The celestial ether was believed to be changeless and incorruptible, to be more noble than the four elements which made up the earthly region, and to naturally move in continuous circular motion.

Faculties: In Galenic medicine, the three fundamental functions of the body. The three faculties were the vital faculty (respiration, pulse), the natural (nutrition, growth, reproduction), and the animal (movement, sensation, mental activity).

Final cause: The term in Aristotelian philosophy for the ultimate purpose of any being, living or nonliving, also referred to as "the for sake of which" or, sometimes, the "final end." Aristotle himself used the example of a cup, whose final cause is to hold liquids. In the case of natural, as opposed to artificial, objects or beings, the final cause was usually to fulfill the potential of the thing by actualizing its natural capacities.

Fixed stars: Those heavenly bodies which appeared to never change their positions relative to each other. The fixed stars were thought to exist at or near the farthest regions of the heavens from the earth.

Flying buttress: An external structure in the shape of an arch attached to the outside walls of a cathedral as a brace in order to counteract the stresses tending to push the walls outward.

Fulling: The process by which woolen cloth is made more compact and thickened by soaking the cloth in an alkaline solution and then pummeling it, either by stamping on it or through the use of mechanized hammers.

Herbal: A medieval compilation of information on individual kinds of plants, primarily to identify plants for medicinal purposes.

Humors: In Galenic medicine, the four basic fluids which are produced by the ingestion of food and influenced by other environmental influences. The four humors are blood, phlegm, yellow or red bile, and black bile.

Impetus: A term developed by the mathematician John Buridan (c. 1295–c. 1358) for a quality impressed onto moving objects which caused the body to continue its motion. In the seventeenth century, the idea of inertia, which stipulated that no force is necessary for a body to continue moving if the motion is not resisted, and momentum replaced the idea of impetus.

Kinematics: The study of the movement of objects.

Liberal arts: The seven fundamental branches of knowledge at the introductory level, divided into the *trivium* (rhetoric, logic, and dialectic) comprising the arts of speech, writing, and argument, and the *quadrivium* (arithmetic, geometry, astronomy, and music) comprising the mathematical and scientific arts. The seven liberal arts were the basis of the university curriculum at the bachelor level in the Middle Ages.

Mean-speed theorem: A mathematical formula developed by the fourteenth-century mathematician William Heytesbury which stipulated that a body moving at a uniformly accelerated speed will travel the same distance in a given time as a body moving at a uniform speed equal to the average speed of the accelerating body.

Mechanical arts: The term developed in the Middle Ages equivalent to the modern term "technology." Most often, the mechanical arts were listed as comprising seven arts, armament (which included architecture), fabric making, agriculture, medicine, commerce, hunting and food preparation, and theater, paralleling the seven liberal arts.

Natural philosophy: The ancient and medieval term for the systematic study of the natural world. Natural philosophy, sometimes called "physics," was usually regarded as a division of philosophy as a whole, and usually grouped with other types of theoretical knowledge, including theology, ethics, mathematics, and logic.

Neoplatonism: "New Platonism," a revived and spiritualized form of Plato's thought developed by a number of thinkers, including Plotinus (205–70) and Dionysius the Areopagite (sixth century), which had a profound impact on medieval philosophy and scientific thought.

Oxford Calculators: A group of mathematicians associated with Oxford University in the fourteenth century who attempted to measure motion and qualitative changes in new and innovative ways.

Pre-Socratics: A group of ancient Greek philosophers who first developed fundamental questions and theories about the ultimate nature of physical reality. They have been dubbed the "Pre-Socratics" by historians because they lived before the time of the Athenian philosopher Socrates (469–399 B.C.E.).

Ptolemaic system: The astronomical system developed in the ancient world and systematized by the Hellenistic astronomer, Ptolemy. The system was based on the idea that a variety of mathematical devices, including the eccentric, epicycle, and equant, could reconcile observations of the movements of the heavenly bodies with the philosophical requirement that these bodies move with a continuous, regular circular motion, defined as sweeping out equal angles in equal times measured from the earth which is at rest at the center of the universe.

Renaissance of the Twelfth Century: Term applied by some historians to the general intellectual and economic revival beginning at the end of the eleventh century and continuing in the twelfth century.

Scholasticism: A method of organizing knowledge and argument developed in the twelfth and thirteenth centuries which came to dominate medieval thought. Scholasticism organized theological and philosophical issues into a series of closely linked questions designed in a "yes" or "no" format. For each question a series of arguments were supplied for a negative answer, followed by arguments for a positive response and a final resolution of the issue.

Scientific Revolution: The term used by historians to describe the overthrow of Aristotelian natural philosophy and its replacement by the premises of modern science in the sixteenth and seventeenth centuries.

Solstice: The two points at which the sun is most distant from the celestial equator. At the summer solstice (approximately June 21) the period of daylight is the longest of the year; at the winter solstice (about December 21) the period of daylight is the shortest of the year.

Sublunary sphere: In premodern cosmology, the region beneath the moon and including the earth, believed to be undergoing a constant process of change and corruption, in contrast to the heavenly sphere above the moon, believed to be changeless and incorruptible.

Three-field system: An innovative method of agricultural management which appeared in the early Middle Ages. The area to be cultivated was divided into three parts and alternately planted with a winter crop such as wheat, planted with a spring crop such as oats, or left fallow. Together with other agricultural innovations, the three-field system significantly raised agricultural productivity by the eleventh century.

Unmoved mover: The term, originating with Aristotle, for the first cause of all things, identified by medieval theologians with God.

Verge-and-foliot escapement: A device which allowed for the development of the first mechanical clocks. The verge regulated the motion of a weight-driven axle so that it turned at a predetermined uniform speed. The axle in turn moved a balance, the foliot, back and forth in an oscillating motion, whose duration could be regulated by weights set at the ends of the balance.

ANNOTATED BIBLIOGRAPHY

Books

Adelard of Bath. *Adelard of Bath, Conversations with His Nephew*: On the Same and the Different, Questions on Natural Science, *and* On Birds. Edited and translated by Charles Burnett, with the collaboration of Italo Ronca, Pedro Mantuas España, and Baudouin van den Abeele. Cambridge Medieval Classics. Vol. 9. Cambridge, England: Cambridge University Press, 1998.

Albertus Magnus. *On Animals: A Medieval* Summa Zoologica. Translated and annotated by Kenneth F. Kitchell Jr. and Irven Michael Resnick. 2 vols. Baltimore: Johns Hopkins University Press, 1999.

———. *Book of Minerals*. Translated by Dorothy Wyckoff. Oxford: Clarendon Press, 1967. Translation of this important work, the only effort at a scientific study of minerals from the Middle Ages. Useful introduction.

Ps.-Albertus Magnus. *Libellus de alchimia ascribed to Albertus Magnus*. Translated by Sister Virginia Heines, S.C.N. Berkeley and Los Angeles: University of California Press, 1958.

———. *Women's Secrets: A Translation of Pseudo-Albertus Magnus'* De Secretis Mulierum *with Commentaries*. Translated by Helen Rodnite Lemay. Albany: State University of New York Press, 1992. Translation of a late thirteenth- or early fourteenth-century work on human reproduction ascribed to Albertus Magnus and parts of two contemporary commentaries. These texts are especially interesting for their misogynistic interpretations of contemporary medical knowledge. Informative introduction by the translator.

Aristotle. *The Basic Works of Aristotle*. Edited by Richard McKeon. New York: Random House, 1941. There are many translations of Aristotle's works, both individually and collected. This is a useful one-volume version but other translations are also excellent. Especially recommended is the Penguin series of translations of Aristotle's works.

Bacon, Roger. *The Opus majus of Roger Bacon*. Translated by Robert Belle Burke. 2 vols. New York: Russell and Russell, 1962. English translation of one of Bacon's most important books, which includes his discussion of "experimental science."

Baxter, Ron. *Bestiaries and Their Users in the Middle Ages*. London: Sutton Publishing, in association with the Courtauld Institute, 1998. Scholarly study of the literary form of the bestiary; shows how and why English monks read bestiaries. Many interesting illustrations.

Bennett, Judith M. et al., eds. *Sisters and Workers in the Middle Ages*. Chicago and London: University of Chicago Press, 1976. Has an excellent article by Monica Green on women's medical practice and health care.

Bernard Silvester. *The Cosmographia of Bernardus Silvestris*. Translated by Winthrop Wetherbee. New York: Columbia University Press, 1973. Translation of an important literary and scientific work, reflecting the new intellectual curiosity about nature in the twelfth century.

The Bestiary: A Book of Beasts, being a Translation from a Latin Bestiary of the Twelfth Century. Edited and translated by T. H. White. New York: G. P. Putnam's Sons, 1960. A translation, with illustrations and notes, of a popular medieval bestiary, or collection of descriptions and stories about actual and legendary animals.

Boyer, Nice Marjorie. *Medieval French Bridges: A History*. Cambridge, MA: The Mediaeval Academy of America, 1976. Readable and thoroughly researched study of the construction, financing, and cultural meaning of bridges in medieval France.

Butterfield, Herbert. *The Origins of Modern Science 1300–1800* (New York: The Free Press, 1965). Lucid and important historical study.

Cadden, Joan. *Meanings of Sex Differences in the Middle Ages: Medicine, Science, and Culture*. Cambridge, England: Cambridge University Press, 1993. An important, impeccably researched study of how discussions of reproduction and sexuality in medieval medical, scientific, and philosophical texts reveal attitudes about gender and the social roles of men and women.

Chenu, M.-D. *Nature, Man, and Society in the Twelfth Century: Essays on New Theological Perspectives in the Latin West.* Selected, edited, and translated by Jerome Taylor and Lester K. Little. Chicago and London: University of Chicago Press, 1968. Has several chapters that show the interrelationship between theology, science, and technology in the twelfth century. Beautifully written and translated.

Clagett, Marshall. *The Science of Mechanics in the Middle Ages.* Madison: University of Wisconsin Press, 1959. Survey, with primary documents, by an authority in the field.

Cohen, H. Floris. *The Scientific Revolution: A Historiographical Inquiry.* Chicago and London: University of Chicago Press, 1994. An exhaustive and lucid account of the many interpretations of the Scientific Revolution over the past 200 years. Although its focus is on what encouraged the emergence of modern science in the sixteenth and seventeenth centuries, it contains several sections on possible relationships between medieval and modern science.

Cohen, Morris R., and I. E. Drabkin, eds. *A Source Book in Greek Science.* New York: McGraw-Hill Book Company, 1948. Excerpts from the important works of ancient science.

Courteney, Lynn T., ed. *The Engineering of Medieval Cathedrals.* Studies in the History of Civil Engineering, 1. Aldershot, Brookfield, Singapore, and Sydney: Ashgate, 1997. A very useful collection of previously published journal articles.

Crombie, A. C. *Medieval and Early Modern Science.* 2 vols. Garden City, NY: Doubleday and Company, 1959. A readable, lively, and still-valuable account by one of the foremost proponents of the "continuity" thesis that medieval science fed directly into the Scientific Revolution.

Crowe, Michael J. *Theories of the World from Antiquity to the Copernican Revolution.* New York: Dover Publications, 1990. Excellent on the mathematical aspects of Greek, Ptolemaic, and sixteenth- and seventeenth-century astronomical systems, with many useful diagrams. Very little specifically on the Middle Ages.

Dales, Richard C. *Medieval Discussions of the Eternity of the World.* Leiden: Brill, 1990. Examination of medieval responses to Aristotle's assertion of the eternity of the world, which was in conflict with Christian theology and Scripture.

DeVries, Kelly. *Medieval Military Technology*. Peterborough, Ontario: Broadview Press, 1992. Excellent survey.

Dohrn-van Rossum, Gerhard. *The History of the Hour: Clocks and Modern Temporal Orders*. Translated by Thomas Dunlap. Chicago and London: University of Chicago Press, 1996. An excellent account, beautifully researched and fascinating to read.

Dols, Michael W. *Majn- un: The Madman in Medieval Islamic Society*. Oxford and New York: Oxford University Press, 1992. Explores the social and intellectual context of mental illness in Arabic Galenic medicine.

Easton, Stewart C. *Roger Bacon and His Search for a Universal Science: A Reconsideration of the Life and Work of Roger Bacon in the Light of His Own Stated Purposes*. New York: Columbia University Press, 1952. Reprint, Westport, CT: Greenwood Press, 1970. The only biography in English of a fascinating figure in medieval science.

Eastwood, Bruce S. *Astronomy and Optics from Pliny to Descartes*. London: Variorum, 1989. Scholarly survey.

Esposito, John L., ed. *The Oxford History of Islam*. Oxford: Oxford University Press, 1999. Has an excellent chapter on science, medicine, and technology, as well as a chapter on philosophy and one on art and architecture.

Ferngren, Gary B., Edward J. Larson, Darrel W. Amundsen, and Anne-Marie E. Hakhla, eds. *The History of Science and Religion in the Western Tradition: An Encyclopedia*. New York and London: Garland Publishing, 2000. A collection of 103 short, authoritative, and readable articles on aspects of science and religion; almost half are relevant to the history of science and technology in the Middle Ages.

Fitchen, John. *The Construction of Gothic Cathedrals: A Study of Medieval Vault Erection*. Oxford: Clarendon Press, 1961. Good introduction.

Flanagan, Sabina. *Hildegard of Bingen 1098–1179: A Visionary Life*. 2nd ed. London and New York: Routledge, 1998. The only biography of Hildegard in English. Thoughtful and engaging.

Flint, Valerie I. J. *The Rise of Magic in Early Medieval Europe*. Princeton, NJ: Princeton University Press, 1991. A detailed study of Christian and non-Christian magic in the early Middle Ages. Includes material on astrology and medical magic.

Frugoni, Chiara. *Books, Banks, Buttons and Other Inventions from the Middle Ages.* Translated by William McCuaig. New York: Columbia University Press, 2003. Beautifully illustrated with color reproductions of 100 manuscript illuminations. The text is full of interesting anecdotes but is far from providing a comprehensive history.

Funkenstein, Amos. *Theology and the Scientific Imagination from the Middle Ages to the Seventeenth Century.* Princeton, NJ: Princeton University Press, 1986.

Galen. *On Respiration and the Arteries.* Edited and translated by David J. Furley and J. S. Wilkie. Princeton, NJ: Princeton University Press, 1984. Translation of one of Galen's many works.

———. *On the Natural Faculties.* Translated by A. J. Brock. London: Heinemann, 1963. Translation of one of Galen's most important works; explains his ideas on physiology.

———. *On the Usefulness of the Parts of the Body.* Translated by Margaret Tallmadge May. 2 vols. Ithaca, NY: Cornell University Press, 1968. Translation of one of Galen's greatest works; reveals his ideas on how human anatomy has been constructed to perfectly conform to the function of each organ and the workings of the human body overall. Very useful introduction and notes.

Gies, Francis, and Joseph Gies. *Cathedral, Forge, and Waterwheel: Technology and Invention in the Middle Ages.* New York: HarperPerennial, 1994. A popularized but well-researched account.

Gillispie, Charles Coulston, ed. *Dictionary of Scientific Biography.* 15 vols. New York: Charles Scribner's Sons, 1970–1980. In-depth biographies covering both the life and the work for all individuals relevant to the history of science. Also has detailed bibliographies for each listing.

Gimpel, Jean. *The Medieval Machine: The Industrial Revolution of the Middle Ages.* New York: Penguin Books, 1976. Entertaining, fact-filled, and readable account of technology and its economic and social effects in the Middle Ages, despite an unconvincing and outdated epilogue.

Glacken, Clarence J. *Traces on the Rhodian Shore: Nature and Culture in Western Thought from Ancient Times to the End of the Eighteenth Century.* Berkeley, Los Angeles, London: University of California Press, 1967. Reprint, 1973. Explores the idea of a "designed earth" from its beginnings in Greek thought through the Middle Ages to the early modern period. Beautifully integrates ideas about geography, man's control of nature, and religion in an interdisciplinary framework. Long but exceptionally readable.

Grant, Edward. *The Foundations of Modern Science in the Middle Ages: Their Religious, Institutional, and Intellectual Contexts.* Cambridge, England: Cambridge University Press, 1996. Excellent review of the history of natural philosophy in the Middle Ages, especially astronomy and cosmology, from the point of view of the arguments for continuity between medieval and modern science.

———. *God and Reason in the Middle Ages.* Cambridge, England: Cambridge University Press, 2001. An accessible and lucid account of how reason and "the spirit of inquiry" pervaded medieval thought. Beautifully written, and the fruit of a lifetime of remarkable scholarship.

———. *Much Ado about Nothing: Theories of Space and Vacuum from the Middle Ages to the Scientific Revolution.* Cambridge, England: Cambridge University Press, 1981. Demonstrates that late medieval astronomers developed the idea that an infinite space existed beyond the finite world, providing the framework for later ideas of an infinite universe.

———. *Physical Science in the Middle Ages.* John Wiley and Sons, 1971. Reprint, Cambridge, England: Cambridge University Press, 1977. Exceptional clear and brief summary of medieval astronomy and physics.

———. *Planets, Stars, and Orbs: The Medieval Cosmos, 1200–1687.* Cambridge, England: Cambridge University Press, 1994. An essential guide to medieval cosmology and astronomy which surveys and analyzes hundreds of medieval and early modern texts. Detailed but worth the effort.

———, ed. *A Source Book in Medieval Science.* Cambridge, MA: Harvard University Press, 1974. Over 800 pages of excerpts from the most important scientific texts of the Middle Ages. Excellent notes and introductions to each text. It also has brief biographies of each of the writers whose works are included. An indispensable reference work.

Grant, Edward, and John E. Murdoch, eds. *Mathematics and Its Applications to Science and Natural Philosophy in the Middle Ages: Essays in Honor of Marshall Clagett.* Cambridge, England: Cambridge University Press, 1987. Collection of specialized articles.

Haskins, Charles Homer. *Studies in the History of Mediaeval Science.* New York: Frederick Ungar Publishing Co., 1924. Collection of scholarly articles by one of the most important early historians of medieval science.

Hildegard of Bingen. *On Natural Philosophy and Medicine: Selections from* Cause et cure. Translated by Margret Berger. Cambridge, England: D. S. Brewer, 1999. Translation of parts of Hildegard's most important work in natural philosophy with a very useful introduction and commentary. Includes Hildegard's cosmology and medical ideas.

———. *Hildegard von Bingen's* Physica: *The Complete English Translation of Her Classic Work on Health and Healing.* Translated by Priscilla Throop. Rochester, VT: Healing Arts Press, 1998. The only English translation of Hildegard's handbook of herbal and other remedies.

Hugh of St. Victor. *The* Didascalicon *of Hugh of St. Victor: A Medieval Guide to the Arts.* Translated by Jerome Taylor. New York: Columbia University Press, 1961. Important work in the history of medieval attitudes toward technology.

Kaye, Joel. *Economy and Nature in the Fourteenth Century: Money, Market Exchange, and the Emergence of Scientific Thought.* Cambridge, England: Cambridge University Press, 1998. An innovative study which argues that the rapid development of a money economy in the late Middle Ages had an important effect on natural philosophy. Specifically, it suggests that the new emphasis on quantification, relativity, probability, and a mechanistic view of the world had its roots in the monetized marketplace of the fourteenth century. It addresses in depth the work of the Oxford Calculators, John Buridan, Nicole Oresme, and others and shows how many of these men were administrators used to financial dealings, as well as scientists.

Kieckhefer, Richard. *Magic in the Middle Ages.* Cambridge, England: Cambridge University Press, 1989. The best and most convenient overall account of medieval magic available. Has sections on medical magic, astrology, and alchemy, explaining both the theory and social context of these disciplines.

King, Ross. *Brunelleschi's Dome: How a Renaissance Genius Reinvented Architecture.* New York: Penguin, 2000. A lively, informative account of the life and career of Filippo Brunelleschi, the great architect and engineer of the dome of the Cathedral of Florence. Some of the author's claims about the degree of Brunelleschi's originality are somewhat overstated.

Kline, Naomi Reed. *Maps of Medieval Thought: The Hereford Paradigm.* Woodbridge, England: Boydell Press, 2001. Literary and philosophical study of the symbolism and meaning in the only surviving complete large-scale medieval "map of the world," in Hereford Cathedral, England, c. 1300. Many interesting photographs and reproductions.

Knowles, David. *The Evolution of Medieval Thought.* New York: Random House, 1962. Excellent study of medieval philosophy which synthesizes an enormous scholarly literature in a clear and understandable fashion.

Kren, Claudia. *Alchemy in Europe: A Guide to Research.* New York: Garland, 1990. Useful.

———. *Medieval Science and Technology: A Selected, Annotated Bibliography.* New York: Garland, 1985. Excellent research tool.

Landes, David S. *Revolution in Time: Clocks and the Making of the Modern World.* Cambridge, MA and London: Belknap Press of Harvard University Press, 1983. Explores the history of the invention of the mechanical clock and its implications for modern society.

Langdon, J. *Horses, Oxen and Technological Innovation: The Use of Draught Animals in English Farming from 1066 to 1500.* Cambridge, England: Cambridge University Press, 1986. Demonstrates that the replacement of oxen by horses took place very slowly over the course of the Middle Ages, not relatively quickly as Lynn White had argued.

Le Goff, Jacques. *Time, Work, and Culture in the Middle Ages.* Translated by Arthur Goldhammer. Chicago and London: University of Chicago Press, 1980. A collection of highly readable essays by one of France's foremost medievalists. This collection is especially interesting for the connections Le Goff makes between how different professions were viewed in the Middle Ages and the development of a more commercial economy.

Lewis, Archibald R., and Timothy J. Runyon. *European Naval and Maritime History, 300–1500.* Bloomington: Indiana University Press, 1985. An authoritative but accessible synthesis of literature on seafaring, military tactics, and naval technology by two top experts in the field.

Lindberg, David C. *The Beginnings of Western Science: The European Scientific Tradition in Philosophical, Religious, and Institutional Context, 600 B.C. to A.D. 1450.* Chicago and London: University of Chicago Press, 1992. The only one-volume survey of premodern science. Balanced and clearly written by an expert in the field. Has an excellent bibliography for further reading.

———. *Theories of Vision from al-Kindi to Kepler.* Chicago: University of Chicago Press, 1976. Scholarly and comprehensive.

Lindberg, David C., ed. *Science in the Middle Ages*. Chicago and London: University of Chicago Press, 1978. An indispensable collection of essays on all the medieval sciences by experts in their fields. Some of the discussion is fairly technical and difficult.

Lloyd, G.E.R. *Aristotle: The Growth and Structure of His Thought*. Cambridge, England: Cambridge University Press, 1968. A remarkably clear but still subtle analysis of Aristotle's thought.

———. *Greek Science After Aristotle*. New York: W. W. Norton and Company, 1973. Covers the Hellenistic period and Rome, with chapters on astronomy, mathematics, biology, medicine, and technology. Exceptionally clear without oversimplification.

Loeb Classical Library. Cambridge, MA: Harvard University Press, 1912–present. Collection of over 200 classical texts in two series, translated from Greek and Latin respectively, with the original text and the translation on facing pages. Extremely useful.

Long, Pamela O. *Openness, Secrecy, Authorship: Technical Arts and the Culture of Knowledge from Antiquity to the Renaissance*. Baltimore and London: Johns Hopkins University Press, 2001. Excellent study of the intellectual and social context of ancient, medieval, and Renaissance writing about technological apparatus and alchemical and other techniques. Illuminates the interaction of traditions supporting openness and those supporting the keeping of trade secrets.

———, ed. *Science and Technology in Medieval Society*. New York: New York Academy of Sciences, 1985. Collection of useful articles on aspects of medieval architecture, medicine, mechanical devices in medieval Islamic society, and other topics.

Magnusson, Roberta J. *Water Technology in the Middle Ages: Cities, Monasteries, and Waterworks after the Roman Empire*. Baltimore and London: Johns Hopkins University Press, 2001. An engaging discussion of water technology, including water systems for drinking, laundry, sanitation, and fountains. This book is especially interesting in the way it connects archeological and archival sources, allowing the reader to see both the technical and human aspects of medieval water technology. Bibliographical references are an excellent guide to further reading about building and construction in the Middle Ages.

Mark, Robert. *Light, Wind, and Structure: The Mystery of the Master Builders.* Cambridge, MA and London: MIT Press, 1990. Excellent chapter on structural experimentation in High Gothic architecture.

————, ed. *Architectural Technology up to the Scientific Revolution: The Art and Structure of Large-Scale Buildings.* Cambridge, MA: MIT Press, 1993. Contains much material on the Middle Ages by a number of experts. Many interesting and useful illustrations.

McCluskey, Stephen C. *Astronomies and Cultures in Early Medieval Europe.* Cambridge, England: Cambridge University Press, 1998. Demonstrates the importance of both theoretical and practical astronomy in the early Middle Ages.

McNeil, Ian, ed. *An Encyclopedia of the History of Technology.* London and New York: Routledge, 1990. Reprint, 1996. Although this volume deals mostly with the technology of the modern world, it also has some exceptionally clear and useful accounts of medieval technology.

McNeill, William H. *The Pursuit of Power: Technology, Armed Force, and Society since A.D. 1000.* Chicago: University of Chicago Press, 1982. A history of the "arms race" which has existed in western society since around 1000 C.E.; argues that military activity in the West has been a result of a "military-commercial complex." Several chapters on the medieval period.

Multhauf, Robert P. *The Origins of Chemistry.* New York: Franklin Watts, 1967. Detailed survey of chemistry and alchemy from antiquity through the eighteenth century, with several chapters on the Middle Ages.

Mumford, Lewis. *Technics and Civilization.* New York: Harcourt Brace, 1939. Important early study of the relationship of technology to human labor and culture.

Noble, David F. *The Religion of Technology: The Divinity of Man and the Spirit of Invention.* New York: Alfred A. Knopf, 1998. Argues that western enthusiasm for technology has its origins in the Christian quest for redemption. Has three chapters with material on the Middle Ages.

————. *A World Without Women: The Christian Clerical Culture of Western Science.* New York and Oxford: Oxford University Press, 1992. Shows how the deliberate exclusion of women from universities and the culture of learning from the twelfth century onward has had a negative effect on the practice and content of western science which continues into the present.

North, John. *The Norton History of Astronomy and Cosmology*. New York and London: W. W. Norton, 1995. Survey covering from prehistory through contemporary astronomy. Especially useful for its chapters on Islamic astronomy.

Oresme, Nicole. *Le Livre du ciel et du monde*. Edited by Albert D. Menut and Alexander J. Denomy. Translated by Albert D. Menut. Madison: University of Wisconsin Press, 1968. Oresme's translation of Aristotle's *De caelo* (On the Heavens) and his commentary. Contains Oresme's discussion of the possibility that the earth rotates daily on its axis.

Ovitt, George, Jr. *The Restoration of Perfection: Labor and Technology in Medieval Culture*. New Brunswick and London: Rutgers University Press, 1986. The best and most readable account of attitudes toward work in medieval monasteries and religious literature.

Panofsky, Erwin. *Gothic Architecture and Scholasticism*. New York: Meridian Books, 1957. By an important art historian. Outdated in many respects but still interesting for the parallel Panofsky draws between medieval philosophy and the architectural style of medieval cathedrals.

Ptolemy, Claudius. *Ptolemy's* Almagest. Edited and translated by G. J. Toomer. New York: Springer, 1984. Translation of the most important premodern work in astronomy.

Ridder-Symoens, Hilde, ed. *A History of the University in Europe*. Vol. 1, *Universities in the Middle Ages*. Cambridge, England: Cambridge University Press, 1992. Thorough, with separate chapters on organization, teachers, students, and programs of study, including astronomy, mathematics, and medicine.

Russell, Jeffrey Burton. *Inventing the Flat Earth: Columbus and Modern Historians*. New York, Westport, CT, and London: Praeger Publishers, 1991. Shows how the idea that medieval people thought the world was flat was invented in the late nineteenth century and exploited in the twentieth century in order to contrast "medieval superstition" with modern rationalism. A fascinating study of the ideological uses of history.

Sambursky, S. *The Physical World of Late Antiquity*. London: Routledge and Kegan Paul, 1962. Illuminating study with an emphasis on Stoic cosmology.

Shank, Michael H., ed. *The Scientific Enterprise in Antiquity and the Middle Ages: Readings from* Isis. Chicago and London: University of Chicago Press, 2000. Collection of important articles about ancient and medieval science from the scholarly journal *Isis*, the most important American journal for the history of science. Includes articles on astronomy, astrology, medicine, mathematics, and optics.

Shelby, Lon R., ed. *Gothic Design Techniques: The Fifteenth-Century Design Booklets of Mathes Roriczer and Hanns Schmuttermayter*. Translated by Lon R. Shelby. Carbondale: Southern Illinois University Press, 1977. Two important late fifteenth-century works on how to design pinnacles for Gothic cathedrals.

Simek, Rudolf. *Heaven and Earth in the Middle Ages: The Physical World before Columbus*. Translated by Angela Hall. Woodbridge, England: Boydell Press, 1996. Examines medieval geography, cosmology, and meteorology. Highly readable.

Singer, Charles, E. J. Holmyard, A. R. Hall, and Trevor I. Williams, eds. *A History of Technology*. Vol. 2, *The Mediterranean Civilizations and the Middle Ages c. 700 B.C. to c. A.D. 1500*. Assisted by E. Jaffé, Nan Clos, and R.H.G. Thomson. Oxford: Clarendon Press, 1956. Reprint with corrections, Oxford: Clarendon Press, 1957. Still authoritative, although some of the material on the Middle Ages may be becoming outdated. Excellent on the "nuts and bolts" of medieval technology, far less useful on the social and cultural context.

Siorvanes, Lucas. *Proclus: Neo-Platonic Philosophy and Science*. New Haven and London: Yale University Press, 1996. Provides an overview of Platonic and Neoplatonic ideas and their relevance to science. Unusually lucid and readable on a difficult topic.

Siraisi, Nancy G. *Medieval and Early Renaissance Medicine: An Introduction to Knowledge and Practice*. Chicago and London: University of Chicago Press, 1990. A very useful synthesis by the foremost historian of medieval and Renaissance medicine writing today in English. Especially interesting for its coverage of the social and cultural context of medieval medicine.

———. *Taddeo Alderotti and his Pupils: Two Generations of Italian Medical Learning*. Princeton, NJ: Princeton University Press, 1981. Specialized and scholarly, but still enlightening for the serious reader. Explores the intellectual, institutional, and social context of the practice of medicine in Italy from the late thirteenth century to the early fourteenth century.

Skelton, R. A., and P.D.A. Harvey. *Local Maps and Plans from Medieval England*. Oxford: Clarendon Press, 1986.

Smith, A. Mark. *Necessity, Cause, and Blame: Perspectives on Aristotle's Theory.* Ithaca, NY: Cornell University Press, 1980.

Smith, Elizabeth Bradford, and Michael Wolfe, eds. *Technology and Resource Use in Medieval Europe: Cathedrals, Mills and Mines.* Aldershot, Brookfield, Singapore, and Sydney: Ashgate, 1997. A collection of recent essays on the use of technology in the Middle Ages. Several of these pieces challenge the prevailing view of the Middle Ages as uniformly enthusiastic about technology and suggest that economic, technical, and social factors interacted in ways which often made new technologies unattractive or unworkable.

Steneck, Nicholas H. *Science and Creation in the Middle Ages: Henry of Langenstein (d. 1397) on Genesis.* Notre Dame, IN: University of Notre Dame Press, 1976.

Stock, Brian. *Myth and Science in the Twelfth Century: A Study of Bernard Silvester.* Princeton, NJ: Princeton University Press, 1972. Scholarly study of an important figure in the twelfth century.

Swanson, Heather. *Medieval Artisans: An Urban Class in Late Medieval England.* Oxford: Basil Blackwell, 1989. Examines the textile, food, leather, metalworking, and building industries in York, England, including the roles of women and social relations among the guilds and between artisans and merchants.

Sweeney, Del, ed. *Agriculture in the Middle Ages: Technology, Practice, and Representation.* Philadelphia: University of Pennsylvania Press, 1995. A collection of fifteen articles on various economic and cultural aspects of medieval agriculture. Topics include stockbreeding, tools, farming techniques, diet and clothing of medieval peasants, and images of peasants and farmers in art and literature.

Theophilus. *The Various Arts: De Diversis Artibus.* Edited and translated by C. R. Dodwell. Oxford: Clarendon Press, 1961. Reprint, Oxford: Clarendon Press, 1986.

Thorndike, Lynn. *History of Magic and Experimental Science.* 8 vols. New York: Columbia University Press, 1923–58. An indispensable reference work for medieval and early modern ideas on magic, technology, and scientific experimentation. Full of fascinating material.

The Trotula: *A Medieval Compendium of Women's Medicine.* Edited and translated by Monica H. Green. Philadelphia: University of Pennsylvania

Press, 2001. Translation of one of the most important gynecological works of the Middle Ages, with a lengthy and very informative introduction.

Turner, Howard R. *Science in Medieval Islam: An Illustrated Introduction.* Austin: University of Texas Press, 1997. Useful and very readable, with good pictures.

Unger, Richard W. *The Ship in the Medieval Economy 600–1600.* London: Croom Helm, 1980; Montreal: McGill-Queen's University Press, 1980. An excellent and thorough account of both the technology and economics of shipping in the Middle Ages.

Villard de Honnecourt. *The Sketchbook of Villard de Honnecourt.* Edited by Theodore Bowie. Bloomington: Indiana University Press, 1959. Drawings and brief descriptions of mechanical devices, cathedral towers, architectural plans, animals, and human figures by a thirteenth-century craftsman.

Weisheipl, James A., ed. *Albertus Magnus and the Sciences: Commemorative Essays 1980.* Toronto: Pontifical Institute of Mediaeval Studies, 1980. Collection of essays on Albertus Magnus' thought and writings on the sciences, including alchemy, chemical technology, and biology. Although these are quite specialized, they are an invaluable source on the work of one of the greatest medieval scientists.

White, Lynn, jr. *Medieval Religion and Technology: Collected Essays.* Berkeley, Los Angeles, and London: University of California Press, 1978. Nineteen collected articles by the founder of the study of medieval technology in the United States. Provocative and fascinating.

———. *Medieval Technology and Social Change.* London, Oxford, and New York: Oxford University Press, 1962. White's first and groundbreaking book in which he argues that the introduction of the stirrup created feudalism and new agricultural technologies produced the population explosion of the tenth and eleventh centuries. Although it has recently been much criticized for espousing "technological determinism," this book helped create the new field of medieval technology.

Whitney, Elspeth. *Paradise Restored: The Mechanical Arts from Antiquity through the Thirteenth Century.* Philadelphia: American Philosophical Society, 1990. Traces the history of how technology came to be included as a category of knowledge during the Middle Ages.

Web Sites

http://www.spartacus.schoolnet.co.uk/Medieval.htm. Under medieval warfare has illustrations of fifteen weapons with commentary.

http://members.aol.com/mcnelis/medsci_index.html. This page is intended to provide a convenient and comprehensive set of links to all Internet resources worldwide that deal with aspects of medieval science, in both western and other cultures. Some are subscriber only.

http://www.fordham.edu/halsall/sbook1r.html#Science%20and%20Technology. Has some texts relevant to medieval science, including excerpts from works by Roger Bacon, a medical treatise, Chaucer's work on the astrolabe, and works by Buridan and Oresme.

http://www.netserf.org/. Has sections on architecture (abbeys and monasteries, castles, cathedrals, cities) and science and technology (astronomy and timekeeping, botany, mathematics, medicine, military technology) which also provide links to other sites on these topics.

http://www.pitt.edu/~medart/. Pictures of cathedrals.

http://www.georgetown.edu/labyrinth/. Links to texts, databases, archives of images. Good materials but most useful if you know specifically what you are looking for.

http://www.avista.org. Web site for AVISTA, a scholarly organization dedicated to the interdisciplinary study of the art, technology, and science of the Middle Ages, with a special emphasis on architecture. Has links to online resources, recent articles on relevant topics, and college-level courses on medieval technology and science.

http://shot.jhu.edu. Web site for the Society for the History of Technology, devoted to the study of the development of the history of technology and its relations with society and culture. Although largely focused on modern technology, medieval and Renaissance technology is not ignored. Publishes the scholarly journal *Technology and Culture* and a series of pamphlets on the history of technology which can be ordered through the Web site. The pamphlets, designed to introduce students to the history of technology, include "Technology and Society in the Medieval Centuries: Byzantium, Islam, and the West, 500–1300" and "Technology, Society, and Culture in Late Medieval and Renaissance Europe, 1300–1600," both by Pamela O. Long.

www.msu.edu/~georgem1/history/medieval.htm. A site that organizes sites on medieval history. Although science and technology do not appear as categories, there are listings for sites on castles, cathedrals, military, and towns, as well as texts and bibliographies. Very useful guide to Internet resources.

CD-ROMs, Film, and Video Works

Gothic Cathedrals of Europe. CD-ROM. Has over 2,000 images.

The Mystery of the Master Builders. Coronet Film & Video. A 58-minute video showing how the interaction of structural and aesthetic considerations has influenced styles of architecture in ancient and medieval buildings. Originally broadcast as an episode of the television program Nova. Written, produced, and directed by Robin Bates; edited by Mavis Smull, presented by Robert Mark, and narrated by Sam Waterston.

Riddle of the Dome: Florence Cathedral and Filippo Brunelleschi. A 29-minute film about the construction of the dome of the cathedral in Florence in the fifteenth century.

A Wheel of Memory: The Hereford Mappamundi. Naomi Reed Kline. CD-ROM 0-472-00274-0. 2001. University of Michigan Press. Contains over a thousand images from the only extant thirteenth-century large-scale English "map of the world," a five-foot pictorial representation of monastic perspectives on geography, secular and religious history, natural history, and biblical interpretation, mounted on the wall of Hereford Cathedral. The CD-ROM also provides textual and artistic sources relevant to the Hereford map.

When the World Spoke Arabic. A 52-minute film in two parts (each 26 minutes) covering Arabic medicine and science. Other parts of the 12-part series cover Arabic philosophy and the European assimilation of Arab knowledge.

INDEX

About the Author

ELSPETH WHITNEY is Associate Professor of History at the University of Nevada, Las Vegas. She is the author of *Paradise Restored: The Mechanical Arts from Antiquity through the 13th Century* (1990), and she has published articles in *Annals of Scholarship, Medieval Latin Studies, Journal of Women's History,* and *Women in Medieval Culture.*

THE BRYANT LIBRARY

3 1490 00429 6600

WITHDRAWN
FROM THE COLLECTION OF
THE BRYANT LIBRARY

For Reference

Not to be taken from this room